Business Valuation Body of Knowledge

Exam Review and Professional Reference

SECOND EDITION

Shannon P. Pratt, CFA, FASA, MCBA

JOHN WILEY & SONS, INC.

To the business valuation profession,
its professional organizations, its leaders, and its participants

To the maturing of the profession,
and its developing cohesion of theory and practice

About the Author

Dr. Shannon P. Pratt is a founder and a managing director of Willamette Management Associates. Founded in 1969, Willamette is one of the oldest and largest independent valuation consulting, economic analysis, and financial advisory services firms, with offices in principal cities across the United States. He is also a member of the board of directors of Paulson Capital Corp., an investment banking firm.

Over the last 35 years, Dr. Pratt has performed valuation engagements for mergers and acquisitions, employee stock ownership plans (ESOPs), fairness opinions, gift and estate taxes, incentive stock options, buy-sell agreements, corporate and partnership dissolutions, dissenting stockholder actions, damages, marital dissolutions, and many other business valuation purposes. He has testified in a wide variety of federal and state courts across the country and frequently participates in arbitration and mediation proceedings.

He holds an undergraduate degree in business administration from the University of Washington and a doctorate in business administration, majoring in finance, from Indiana University. He is a Fellow of the American Society of Appraisers, a Master Certified Business Appraiser, a Chartered Financial Analyst, a Certified Business Counselor, and a Certified Mergers and Acquisitions Advisor.

Dr. Pratt's professional recognitions include being designated a life member of the Business Valuation Committee of the American Society of Appraisers, past chairman and a life member of the ESOP Association Advisory Committee on Valuation, a life member of the Institute of Business Appraisers, the recipient of the magna cum laude in business appraisal award from the National Association of Certified Valuation Analysts, and the recipient of the Distinguished Achievement Award from the Portland Society of Financial Analysts. He served two three-year terms (the maximum) as a trustee-at-large of The Appraisal Foundation.

Dr. Pratt is author of *Business Valuation Discounts and Premiums, Business Valuation Body of Knowledge*, 2nd edition, *Cost of Capital: Estimation and Applications*, 2nd edition, *Cost of Capital Workbook, Business Valuation Body of Knowledge Workbook*, and *The Market Approach to Valuing Businesses* (all published by John Wiley & Sons, Inc.), and *The Lawyer's Business Valuation Handbook* (published by the American Bar Association). He is coauthor of *Valuing a Business: The Analysis and Appraisal of Closely Held Companies*, 4th edition, and *Valuing Small Businesses and Professional Practices*, 3rd edition (both published by McGraw-Hill). He is also coauthor of *Guide to Business Valuations*, 12th edition (published by Practitioners Publishing Company).

He is the editor-in-chief of the monthly newsletter *Shannon Pratt's Business Valuation Update®*. He oversees *BVLibrary.com^sm*, which includes full texts of court cases, conference presentations and unpublished papers, IRS materials, restricted stock study papers, and pre-IPO study papers and data. He also oversees *Pratt's Stats™*, which is the official completed transaction database of the International Business Brokers Association, and *BVMarketData.com^sm*, which includes the online version *of Pratt's Stats™*, as well as *BIZCOMPS®*, *Mergerstat/Shannon Pratt's Control Premium Study™*, *The FMV Restricted Stock Study™*, and the *Valuation Advisors' Lack of Marketability Discount Study™*.

Dr. Pratt develops and teaches business valuation courses for the American Society of Appraisers and the American Institute of Certified Public Accountants, and frequently speaks on business valuation at national legal, professional, and trade association meetings. He has also developed a seminar on business valuation for judges and lawyers.

Contents

Preface

PURPOSE

The purpose of this book is to bring together the essentials of the core of knowledge as taught by the various business valuation professional associations today. It is both a study guide for those seeking any of the various business valuation professional accreditations and a reference guide for day-to-day use by practitioners. Its orientation is wide rather than deep; it outlines the basic topics and provides extensive references to more detailed source materials on each topic. Emphasis is primarily on valuation of closely held businesses and interests in them, but much of the material is also applicable to publicly traded companies.

The book represents a distillation of the major points covered in over 30 courses and books on business valuation in wide use today. It is not a substitute for basic study but a compendium of the essential materials in the field, most of which should be familiar to practitioners. It is intended to provide the reader with a comprehensive outline of the major topics involved in business valuation today, with references to detailed discussions of each topic in courses and books currently most widely used in professional education in closely held business valuation.

AUDIENCE AND NEEDS ADDRESSED

This text is designed to serve a variety of audiences and needs, including those described in the following sections.

The Practitioner Seeking Accreditation

- Outlines the topics generally covered in accreditation exams, providing a review of the basics.
- The accompanying workbook provides sample exam questions so that the candidate can evaluate topical strengths and weaknesses.
- Locates topics in each organization's materials and reference books.

In-House Review Guide for an Office or Firm

- Outlines topics that organizations may want to consider for in-house training.
- Provides references to source materials for each topic.

Review and Reference Guide for the Experienced Practitioner

- Reviews the current rulings and professional positions on basic business valuation topics.
- Provides a time-saving source of references for various views on basic topics.
- In case of litigation, serves as a guide to help ensure that some basic consideration has not been overlooked and includes sources for positions on controversial issues.

A Reference for Attorneys and Other Nonpractitioners

- Outlines the considerations that should be addressed within all broad, major business valuation topics.
- Directs the reader to additional material if needed.

ACCEPTED, REJECTED, AND CONTROVERSIAL POSITIONS

The business valuation profession has evolved to the point that some theories, methods, and bodies of information are universally or very widely accepted while others are universally or very widely rejected or subject to legitimate controversy. I make every attempt to objectively identify where the various theories, methods, and bodies of information fall within that spectrum of acceptance today.

ORGANIZATION AND USE OF THIS BOOK

The progression of the book is from the general to the specific, but a reader can pick up and understand any chapter without having read previous chapters.

Early Parts Present Core of Business Valuation

Part I describes the legal and professional environment within which business valuation is conducted. Part II presents a glossary of terms as used in business valuation (the meanings of such terms often differ from definitions of the same terms in accounting and other contexts) and the mathematical notation most commonly used in business valuation.

Parts III and IV, the real core of the book, present valuation approaches and methods, followed by company, industry, and economic analysis to provide the inputs to the valuation approaches and methods. Part V directs the reader to essential supporting data.

Sample Case and Exercises in Workbook Style

Part VI is a somewhat extensive sample case. It includes workbooklike exercises so that readers who so desire can practice working out their own solutions, followed by the solutions.

Valuations for Specific Purposes

Part VII discusses how valuation methods may differ for different purposes, including tax matters, employee stock ownership plans (ESOPs), shareholder buyouts and disputes, and marital dissolutions.

Appendixes and CPE Quiz

The appendixes include a useful bibliography of core reference sources, with ordering information, and key sections of the Federal Rules of Civil Procedure for readers' convenient reference. These are followed by a self-study CPE quiz, which readers can send in for eight hours of CPE credit.

References for Detailed Study Included Throughout

Throughout the book, references are included to Internal Revenue Service (IRS) publications and professional standards, texts, and courses where each topic is discussed. Some references are included at the end of topical sections, others at the end of chapters. Finally, the book concludes with a comprehensive index.

The book is presented largely in outline form, with some material in sentences or paragraphs and other material listed in bulleted points. My objective has been to create a working tool that is at once as comprehensive and as concise as possible.

COOPERATIVE EFFORT OF THE PROFESSION

All major professional associations and countless leaders and teachers within those associations have contributed greatly to this effort to solidify the existing core of the professional body of knowledge. Some are specifically recognized in the acknowledgments, but I am grateful to all.

This text is a living document, subject to frequent revision. If you have any suggestions for future editions or would like a complimentary current issue of the monthly newsletter *Shannon Pratt's Business Valuation Update®*, please contact me at the phone, e-mail, or address listed below.

Shannon Pratt
7412 S.W. Beaverton-Hillsdale Hwy, Suite 106
Portland, OR 97225
Phone: (503) 291-7963
Fax: (503) 291-7955
e-mail: *shannonp@bvresources.com*

Acknowledgments

I first wish to thank all of the North American professional business valuation organizations for sharing their courses, standards, and publications for this effort to update the common body of knowledge for the business valuation profession:

American Institute of Certified Public Accountants
American Society of Appraisers
Canadian Institute of Chartered Business Valuators
Institute of Business Appraisers
National Association of Certified Valuation Analysts
The Appraisal Foundation

Nine business valuation professionals reviewed the manuscript and made numerous corrections, suggestions, and additions as well as updated the course references that are incorporated herein. These dedicated reviewers include the following:

Pamela Bailey
National Association of Certified Valuation Analysts
Salt Lake City, Utah

Paul Baumann
Baumann, Raymondo & Company, PA
Tampa, Fla.

Brenda M. Clarke
Seigneur & Company, P.C. CPAs
Lakewood, Colo.

Nancy Fannon
Baker Newman & Noyes
Portland, Me.

Michele Miles
Institute of Business Appraisers
Plantation, Fla.

Alina Niculita
Business Valuation Resources, LLC
Portland, Ore.

Deborah Patry
Baker Newman & Noyes
Portland, Me.

Ronald L. Seigneur
Seigneur & Company, P.C. CPAs
Lakewood, Colo.

Heidi Walker
Baker, Newman & Noyes
Portland, Me.

For the sample case, which was not materially changed from the first edition, the historical and projected financial statements and the discounted cash flow valuation were prepared by Jeanie Spickelmier, the publicly traded guideline company valuation method by Jeff Dworniki, and the merger and acquisition guideline company method by Ethan Miller, all former interns at Business Valuation Resources. Terry Whitehead of Willamette Management Associates provided review and quality control for the sample case. Cary Carruthers, formerly of Business Valuation Resources, also provided final review of the sample case.

Richard Vander Ploeg, Mark Kangas, and Kevin Hsieh, all of the San Francisco office of Deloitte & Touche LLP, were very helpful in identifying guideline public companies and discussing restaurant chain economics for the sample case. In addition to generous telephone time, they provided a very useful D&T publication, the 1997 *Restaurant Industry Operating Report*, and also prepared a D&T *Peer View Corporate Analytics* custom report for the guideline public companies that we chose to use in the sample report.

Thanks are due to Michael Mard, The Financial Valuation Group, for writing Chapter 4 on litigation services engagements.

I also thank the professionals at John Wiley & Sons, Inc., for their work to help compress the schedule: John DeRemigis, executive editor; Judy Howarth, associate editor; and Louise Jacob, associate managing editor.

Last but not least, several individuals at Business Valuation Resources, LLC, contributed significantly to the second edition. Janet Marcley obtained permission to reprint material, Laurie Morrisey typed numerous additions, and associate editor Tanya Hanson coordinated the entire project, with substantial help from Linda Kruschke, Publications Department Manager.

Shannon Pratt
Portland, Oregon
November 2002

Listing of References and Reference Abbreviations

IRS Authority
Professional Association Publications (other than courses)
American Society of Appraisers
The Appraisal Foundation
Books
Professional Association Courses
American Institute of Certified Public Accountants (AICPA)
American Society of Appraisers (ASA)
Institute of Business Appraisers (IBA)
National Association of Certified Valuation Analysts (NACVA)

Throughout this book, following various topical discussions, references to source materials on the respective topics are provided. These references are grouped as follows:

- Internal Revenue Service (IRS) authority
- Professional association publications (other than courses)
- Books
- Professional association courses

Depending on the scope of the reference, an entire book, course, chapter, section, subsection, or page may be referenced. More complete bibliographical references are located in Appendix A. References are noted as follows:

Source	Example

IRS AUTHORITY

- Revenue Rulings

  RR59-60 Introduction
  RR59-60 Sect. 3.01

- *IRS Valuation Training for Appeals Officers Coursebook* (references are to the 1997 edition, available for reading or downloading at *BVLibrary.com*[sm]); the 1997 edition is also available in print from CCH, Incorporated

  VT (Valuation Training Online: use the key word search to find specific references)

- *IRS Business Valuation Guidelines*

  IRS BV 2.2

PROFESSIONAL ASSOCIATION PUBLICATIONS (OTHER THAN COURSES)

American Society of Appraisers

- *Principles of Appraisal Practice and Code of Ethics*

  ASA Ethics (p. 10)

- *Business Valuation Standards*

  ASA BVS II

The Appraisal Foundation

- *Uniform Standards of Professional Appraisal Practice*

  USPAP std. 9 (standards)

  USPAP smt. 2 (statements on standards)

  USPAP AO 16 (advisory opinions)

BOOKS

- *Business Valuation Discounts and Premiums*

  D&P App. A

- *Cost of Capital: Estimation and Applications* (2d ed.)

  CoC2 Ch. 14

- *Guide to Business Valuations* (12th ed.)

  Guide 1115 (reference to section numbers)

- *The Lawyer's Business Valuation Handbook*

  Lawyer pp. 35–47

- *The Market Approach to Valuing Businesses*

  Market Ch. 3

Source	Example
• *Quantifying Marketability Discounts*	QMD Ch. 1
• *Valuing a Business: Analysis and Appraisal of Closely Held Companies* (4th ed.)	VAB4 Ch. 11
• *Valuing Small Businesses and Professional Practices* (3d ed.)	VSB3 Ch. 10

PROFESSIONAL ASSOCIATION COURSES

American Institute of Certified Public Accountants (AICPA)

(The following are each three-day courses.)

- FBV I: Fundamentals of Business Valuation I FBVI
- FBV II: Fundamentals of Business Valuation II FBVII

American Society of Appraisers (ASA)

(The following are each three-day courses.)

- BV201: Introduction to Business Valuation, pt. 1 BV201 III (pp. 16–19)
- BV202: Introduction to Business Valuation, pt. 2
- BV203: Business Valuation Case Study
- BV204: Business Valuation Selected Advanced Topics

Institute of Business Appraisers (IBA)

(The following courses vary from two to eight days each.)

- IBA1: Workshop on Valuing Closely Held Businesses IBA1 A.6 (refers to section number in the course)
- IBA2: Valuation of the Closely Held Business—Advanced Theory and Applications
- IBA3: Seminars on How to Value Mid-Size and Smaller Businesses and Using Transaction Data to Value Closely Held Businesses
- IBA4: Seminar on Discount and Capitalization Rates

Source	Example

- IBA5: Seminar on Fractional Interest Premia and Discounts
- IBA6: Seminar on the Guideline Public Company Method/the Multi-Period Discounting Method
- IBA7: Seminar on Litigation Support; Workshop on Expert Testimony Skills
- IBA8: Seminar on Analyzing Financial Statements

National Association of Certified Valuation Analysts (NACVA)

(The following courses together constitute a five-day series.)

Source	Example
• NACVA-BV: Business Valuations—Fundamental Techniques and Theory	NACVA-BV Ch. 1
• NACVA: Being Effective in Litigation Support and Testimony and Development of Capitalization/ Discount Rates and Valuation Discounts and Premiums	NACVA Sect. 3
• NACVA-CA: Case Analysis 1 and Report Writing	NACVA-CA Sect. 6

Note: The preceding references constitute the core materials of the business valuation body of knowledge. All of the mentioned professional associations also have advanced courses on special topics not indexed herein. Other books, periodicals, and seminars on business valuation topics are available for the practitioner's continuing education.

PART I

Business Valuation Engagement Environment

Chapter 1

Business Valuation Legal and Regulatory Environment

Ownership of a business or an interest in a business or intangible asset consists of a combination of rights and obligations. Rights and constraints exist whether the interest is direct or through a partnership, stock, or other form of ownership.

The actual or inferred characteristics of the interest and the pertinent rights and obligations may vary from one legal context to another. For example, in most tax contexts, a minority stock position would be valued at something less than a pro rata portion of the value of the whole (reflecting a minority interest discount and, in most cases, a discount for lack of marketability). However, in the context of a minority oppression or dissenting stockholder appraisal, at least in some situations, the same shares may be determined by law to be worth a pro rata portion of the value of the whole.

Virtually every professional business valuation engagement is subject to attack by one or more parties, so it is important for the valuation professional to have some familiarity with the laws and regulatory environment pertinent to each engagement.

SOURCES OF ATTACK

Legal and Regulatory Authorities

- Internal Revenue Service (IRS)
- Department of Justice (DOJ)
- Department of Labor (DOL)
- Securities and Exchange Commission (SEC)
- State taxing authorities
- State eminent domain authorities
- State attorney general offices

Parties Related to a Transaction

- Direct parties to a transaction
- Spouses of parties to a transaction
- Beneficiaries
- Trustees
- Lenders
- Parties who in some way may be damaged

VALUE DEPENDS ON PURPOSE OF VALUATION

Often, the same share of stock may have different values depending on the purpose for which it is being valued. The value of the interest depends on the rights and obligations pertinent to that interest. Even for the same ownership interest, those rights (or legally assumed or ignored rights) can differ from one legal context to another.

For example, the same share of stock may have different values for various purposes:

- Gift and estate taxes
- Employee stock ownership plans (ESOPs)

- Dissenting stockholder or shareholder oppression actions
- Marital dissolutions
- Partnership or corporate dissolution
- Bankruptcy reorganization
- Liquidation
- Buy-sell agreement pricing

The valuation professional should be aware of the legal, regulatory, and contractual authorities that affect the acceptable methodology and, thus, often affect the ultimate value for the particular engagement. Appraisers are not lawyers, but the applicable law frequently is inextricably intertwined with the valuation.

LEGAL AUTHORITY

Legal authority can be promulgated at the federal, state, or local level, depending on jurisdiction over a particular transaction.

Federal versus State Jurisdiction

Federal Law

Federal law governs:

- Federal estate, gift, and income taxes
- ESOPs (under Employee Retirement Income Security Act [ERISA])
- Bankruptcy
- Public securities transactions
- Antitrust law
- Patent, trademark, and copyright violations

State Law

State law governs:

- State inheritance and income taxes
- Ad valorem (property) taxes
- Eminent domain proceedings
- Marital dissolution
- Corporate and partnership withdrawals and dissolutions
- Dissenting stockholder suits, shareholder oppression cases, buy-sell agreement disputes, and other shareholder matters

There are many other types of legal actions in which the appraiser may be involved (e.g., contract claims, fraud claims, etc.) that can be brought in either federal or state court at the choice of the suing party, depending on the circumstances of the case.

Types of Legal Authority

Whether under federal or state jurisdiction, most legal authority is promulgated in one of three forms:

1. Statutory law
2. Legally binding rules and regulations
3. Precedential court decisions

Statutory Law

Federal Statutes

Examples of federal statutes include:

- The Internal Revenue Code (IRC), especially section 2031 on estate taxes, section 2512 for gift taxes, and sections 2701 to 2704 on intrafamily transfers
- ERISA
- The Bankruptcy Code
- The Securities and Exchange Act

State Statutes

Examples of state statutes include:

- State revenue codes
- State commercial codes
- State securities codes
- State corporation codes (usually a variation of the Model Business Corporation Act), usually addressing dissenting stockholder valuations
- Statutes granting oppressed minority shareholder relief, including an appraisal option (in a growing number of states)
- Marital dissolution statutes, which generally do *not* address valuation matters

Legally Binding Rules and Regulations

Many legislative bills authorize rules and regulations that have the force of law, with implementation of the rules and regulations delegated to an administrative authority. Examples include:

- U.S. Treasury regulations
- Federal Rules of Evidence and Federal Rules of Civil Procedure (see Chapter 4)
- Various state revenue regulations
- DOL proposed regulation 29 CFR Part 2510 on Definition of Adequate Consideration (for ESOP stock)
  - Proposed regulation was issued in 1988 but never finalized.
  - Despite lack of finalization, it provides guidance, and most ESOP appraisers consider compliance with it important.

(See also Chapter 24.)

Precedential Case Law

The details of resolving most valuation issues are not specified in statutes, and the appraiser should consider the case law of the relevant jurisdiction to determine how the controlling courts treat various issues. The appraiser should discuss any legal issues with the attorney. As a practical matter, however, attorneys often look to the appraiser to be knowledgeable about case law affecting valuation issues.

Federal Case Law

Exhibit 1.1 summarizes the U.S. federal court system, including the relevant reporting services for each.

State Court Systems

- State court systems vary considerably from one state to another, but most have trial, appellate, and supreme court levels, in addition to specialized courts.
- If a state does not have a precedential case on point for a particular valuation issue, lawyers' briefs often will cite precedent from court decisions of other states with similar statutes, and the court's decision usually will cite cases from other states. In divorce cases and dissenting shareholder cases, decisions vary greatly from state to state, leading to much confusion in the courts for those states without clear precedent in their own case law.

IRS AUTHORITY

The IRS publishes its positions on many valuation issues. Although these pronouncements do *not* have the force of law, they are widely looked to for guidance on IRS positions.

Exhibit 1.1   Structure of the U.S. Court System

SPECIAL REPORT
Structure of the U.S. Court System
by Mozette Jefferson

I've got to admit that I have been testifying on valuation issues in Federal Courts for over 25 years without ever really understanding an overview of the total structure of the Federal Court system. I've always wanted to have a better understanding of it, and I thought that many of our readers would have a similar interest. So I asked Mozette to research and summarize it for us, and here is the result. I learned a few interesting things I didn't know, and I hope that you will, too! —SP

When reviewing legal issues and court cases for the newsletter, we often need to learn more about the federal judiciary system in order to bring timely and accurate information to our readers. We put a lot of time and effort into gaining a general working knowledge of the federal judicial system, and thought this information would be valuable as you review federal court decisions in your practice. Here's what we found.

Overview of the federal court system

"Cases heard in federal courts include those involving protections of the Bill of Rights, criminal and civil charges of antitrust violations, alleged stock fraud, federal laws, Social Security benefits, disputes between states, and bankruptcy matters." (The Office of the Ninth Circuit)

Although the Supreme Court is the only court specifically established by the Constitution, Article III provided for other inferior courts as Congress "may from time to time ordain and establish." As a result of the Constitution and various acts of Congress, our federal court system consists of the US Supreme Court, 13 US Courts of Appeals, 92 US district courts, and several specialized federal courts.

Most routine federal cases, including antitrust and those involving the Employee Retirement Income Securities Act (ERISA) under which valuing Employee Stock Ownership Plans (ESOPs) fall, begin in the district courts—the federal courts of original jurisdiction. These cases are usually appealed to one of the US Courts of Appeal in whichever particular circuit the district court lies. Those seeking further appeals may file a Supreme Court writ of certiorari, which is a discretionary device that the court uses to choose the cases it will hear. Most writs are denied.

Mandatory arbitration and mediation

Mediation requires an independent third party who listens to both sides and attempts to get the parties to arrive at a mutually acceptable agreement. Arbitration, on the other hand, requires a third-party arbiter who listens to each side and renders a decision. While some pilot programs requiring mandatory arbitration and mediation have been implemented in the federal court system in the past, at the present time no federal court has the authority to order mandatory arbitration.

Exhibit 1.1 (Continued)

Justices, judges, magistrates and rent-a-judges

Some federal courts employ both regular, full-time judges and magistrate judges, the latter being assistant judges who can handle civil cases upon consent of the parties involved.

In disputes settled by arbitration, the private parties can hire rent-a-judges, retired judges and attorneys to hear disputes and/or render decisions. Decisions made by rent-a-judges are considered contracts and are defensible as such.

The title "justice" is soley reserved for justices of the US Supreme Court.

Income, gift and estate tax matters

After the IRS examines and audits a domestic taxpayer's documentation, if the taxpayer is not in agreement with the agency's findings, the IRS issues a Statutory Notice of Deficiency which is more commonly known as a 90-day letter.

A taxpayer who does not wish to pay the tax has the option of complying with the terms stated on the *90-day* letter and filing a petition with the US Tax court disputing the IRS decision. In the US Tax Court the taxpayer sues the Commissioner of Internal Revenue which is counseled by the IRS District Counsel.

While in Tax Court the IRS may not attempt to assess or collect the proposed tax until the Court resolves the issue. Because this is the only "pre-tax" forum in existence, almost 90% of the contested disputes end up here.

There are two basic types of Tax Court cases: small tax cases and regular tax cases. If the proposed tax deficiency is $10,000 or less per year, the taxpayer can elect to have the case tried as a small tax case. Although the specific rules of small tax cases are not published, with this election the taxpayer gives up the right to an appeal in exchange for more relaxed rules. Because small tax cases are not published, the Tax Court judges tend to be more lenient and render unprecedential decisions which might not accurately represent the overall consistent views of the Tax Court.

All regular Tax Court case decisions are published as either Tax Court Memorandums (TCM) or Tax Court opinions (TC). A TCM is an opinion written by one Tax Court judge and not reviewed by a formal panel. A TC is written by one Tax Court judge and reviewed by a panel of Tax Court judges who debate and comment on the decision. A formal panel may consist of as few as two Tax Court judges; however, the usual number of participants is three.

The court's 19 regular full-time judges, appointed by the President for 15-year terms, are not assigned to any particular city, but travel to one of approximately 80 cities when they are assigned a "calendar," which usually lasts one or two weeks at a time.

Seldom do all of the Tax Court judges sit together to hear and decide on one particular case. This process, called *en banc*, only occurs when the chief judge of the Tax Court decides that the particular case has an important or novel issue. In addition to the court being able to decide to hear a case *en banc*, all petitioners to the Tax Court have the option to request that the judges sit *en banc*; however, these requests are usually denied.

If the taxpayer does not file a petition within 90 days, then the government has the right to assess and collect the tax. At this

(*continued*)

Exhibit 1.1 (Continued)

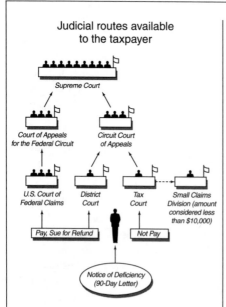

Judicial routes available
to the taxpayer

Source: Sommerfield's *Concepts of Taxation*, 1995 edition.

juncture, the only way a taxpayer can get to court is to pay the tax and go to either district court or the US Court of Federal Claims seeking a refund. In both of these judicial forums, the United States Court of Federal Claims and the district courts, the defendant is the United States of America instead of the Commissioner of Internal Revenue, and the United States of America is being counseled by the Department of Justice Tax Division rather than the IRS District Counsel.

Taxpayers seeking a refund have the option of deciding which of the two previously mentioned forums their case will be heard in. Some of the possible considerations taxpayers make when choosing a forum are:

- Court of Federal Claims does not necessarily interpret tax laws the same as the district courts
- Court of Federal Claims is not subject to

the same review as the district courts because Claims Court decisions can only be appealed to the US Court of Appeals for the Federal Circuit, whereas district court decisions are appealed to the particular Court of Appeals for the circuit in which the courts are located
- Either taxpayer or the United States of America may request a jury in district court. A jury cannot be requested in the US Court of Federal Claims
- US Court of Federal Claims hears cases at locations convenient to the parties involved (hearings are held at federal court facilities, including district and US Tax Court rooms).

Bankruptcy

A federal bankruptcy district court has jurisdiction over all civil proceedings arising in or related to bankruptcy cases. However, infrequently a federal bankruptcy judge will decline jurisdiction after which time the debtor must rely on state or other federal courts.

Federal bankruptcy cases are first heard in the district bankruptcy courts, which have their own judges, and may be either voluntary or involuntary, the latter being filed by a creditor seeking liquidation or reorganization of a debtor's estate.

Two levels of appeal exist for federal bankruptcy proceedings. At the first level, the petition can choose to be heard in front of the district court under which the bankruptcy is situated. Another option in some districts is to be heard by a Bankruptcy Appellate Panel, which is made up of three bankruptcy judges from districts outside of the one in which the case originated.

Bankruptcy Appellate Panels are made

Exhibit 1.1 (Continued)

up of three bankruptcy judges from districts outside of the district in which the case originated. For those districts not having a Bankruptcy Appellate Panel, the appeal will be heard in the district court. District court bankruptcy decisions may be published or unpublished. Bankruptcy Appellate Panels publish many decisions for precedential reasons.

Some of the factors petitioners consider when choosing either the Bankruptcy Appellate Panel or the district court forum on the first level of an appeal are:

- Precedential decisions of the forum
- Likelihood of the appeal being assigned to a particular judge
- Reversal rate of the appellate forum
- Whether the case is being filed primarily to set precedent.

Petitioners choose to be heard in front of the panel for the following reasons:

- District court decisions are not necessarily binding outside of the district
- Many bankruptcy judges view Bankruptcy Appellate Panel decisions as either binding or, more simply, to be followed circuit-wide
- District courts and their clerks' offices have less experience dealing with bankruptcy because appeals are a small part of their work as compared to the Bankruptcy Appellate Panels.

Furthermore, a Federal Judicial Center survey found that attorneys believed Bankruptcy Appellate Panels gave more in-depth consideration on very complex issues in appeals than district courts and were more likely to correctly decide cases.

If the petitioner disputes the first level appellate decision, the next step is to file a second appeal, which will be heard in the Court of Appeals for the appropriate circuit. If taxpayers dispute the second appeal they can file a Supreme Court writ of certiorari. Of the approximate 150 appeals the Supreme Court grants each year, on average only about two or three of those appeals are bankruptcy cases.

So, there you have it—a very generalized introduction to areas of the federal court system that valuation experts want to know about. Beware! This article is intended to provide you with a general understanding of the federal court system's tax and bankruptcy forums. Exceptions to the rules do exist. When reviewing prior cases, realize that, because our judicial process is dynamic and evolving, the process used today may not be the process used in the past.

When you are reviewing court case decisions, in the future, this article should give you an understanding of the judicial process involved.

US Supreme Court

1 First Street NE, Washington, DC 20534; (202) 479-3000

- Highest court in the Federal Court system
  - final arbiter of law
- Nine judgeships, each holding title of "justice"
  - only the Court itself or Congressional legislation can reverse its decisions
- Justices appointed by the president for life
  - follows Rules of the Supreme Court of the United States (last revised 10/2/95)
- Official Reporter: *US Reports*

(continued)

Exhibit 1.1   (Continued)

- Most work is appellate; only approximately 150 original jurisdiction cases have been decided in the Court's history
- Holds power of *judicial review* (i.e., power to invalidate acts of Congress, the executive branch, and state and local governments)
- No evidence is presented; appeal, conducted primarily by the attorneys in writing or short appearances before the Court.

US Circuit Courts of Appeal

- Official reporter: *Federal Reporter*
- 11 numbered Circuits plus the District of Columbia and the Federal Circuits (13 circuits)
- Every state and territory of the United States belongs to one of the eleven judicial circuits
- Hears appeals from US district courts and various federal administrative and regulatory agencies
- Procedural rules promulgated by Supreme Court and supplemented by rules of each individual circuit
- Judges appointed by the president for life
- No evidence is presented; the appeal is conducted primarily by attorneys in writing or in short appearances before the Court
- Generally meets in panels of three judges and reviews written trial record and the documents submitted by lawyers.

US Court of Appeals for the Federal Circuit (12 judgeships)

National Courts Building, 717 Madison Place NW, Washington, DC 20439; (202) 633-6550

US Court of Appeals DC Circuit (12 judgeships)

US Courthouse, 333 Constitution Ave NW, Washington, DC 20001-2082; (202) 273-0300

US Court of Appeals 1st Circuit (6 judgeships)

Maine, New Hampshire, Massachusetts, Rhode Island and Puerto Rico

1606 John W. McCormack, PO & Courthouse, Boston, MA 02109; (617) 223-9057

US Court of Appeals 2nd Circuit (13 judgeships)

Vermont, Connecticut and New York

US Courthouse, Foley Square, New York, NY 10007; (212) 791-0103

US Court of Appeals 3rd Circuit (14 judgeships)

New Jersey, Pennsylvania, Delaware and the Virgin Islands

Independence Mall West, 601 Market St., Room 21000, Philadelphia, PA 19106; (215) 597-2995

US Court of Appeals 4th Circuit (15 judgeships)

Maryland, West Virginia, Virginia and North Carolina

US Courthouse, 10th & Main Streets, Richmond, VA 23219; (804) 771-2213

US Court of Appeals 5th Circuit (17 judgeships)

Mississippi, Louisiana and Texas

US Courthouse, Room 102, 600 Camp St., New Orleans, LA 70130; (504) 589-6514

Exhibit 1.1 (Continued)

US Court of Appeals 6th Circuit
(16 judgeships)

Ohio, Michigan, Kentucky and Tennessee

US Courthouse, Room 524, Potter Stewart, Cincinnati, OH 45202; (513) 684-2953

US Court of Appeals 7th Circuit
(11 judgeships)

Indiana, Illinois and Wisconsin

US Courthouse, 219 South Dearborn St., Chicago, IL 60614; (312) 435-5850

US Court of Appeals 8th Circuit
(11 judgeships)

Minnesota, Iowa, Missouri, Arkansas, Nebraska, North Dakota and South Dakota

US Court & Custom House, 1114 Market Street, St. Louis, MO 63101; (314) 539-3600

US Court of Appeals 9th Circuit
(28 judgeships)

California, Oregon, Nevada, Montana, Washington, Idaho, Arizona, Alaska, Hawaii, territories of Guam, and Northern Mariana Islands

6th floor, 121 Spear St., San Francisco, CA 94105; (415) 744-9800

US Court of Appeals 10th Circuit
(12 judgeships)

Colorado, Wyoming, Utah, Kansas, Oklahoma and New Mexico

Byron White US Courthouse, 1823 Stout St., Denver, CO 80257; (303) 844-3157

US Court of Appeals 11th Circuit
(12 judgeships)

Alabama, Georgia and Florida

56 Forsyth St. NW, Atlanta, GA 30303; (404) 331-6187

US Court of Federal Claims
(16 judgeships)

717 Madison Place NW, Washington DC 20005-1011; (202) 219-9657

- Official Reporter: *US Claims Court Reporter*
- Nationwide jurisdiction
- Judges appointed by the president for 15-year terms
- Cases heard at locations convenient to the parties involved
- Proceedings in accordance with rules of practice and procedure established by US Court of Federal Claims in agreement with Federal Rules of Evidence and the Federal Rules of Civil Procedure.

US Tax Court (19 judgeships)

400 2nd St. NW, Washington DC 20217-0002; (202) 606-8754

- Official reporter: *Reports of the US Tax Court*
- Judges appointed by the President for 15 year terms
- Hears cases in approximately 80 cities
- Tax Court rules promulgated by the court
- Judges of the court elect one of their number to serve a two-year term as chief judge
- Required by statute to comply with Federal Rules of Evidence & rules for the US district court for the District of Columbia
- Follows Rules of Practice and Procedure of the United States Tax Court

(continued)

Exhibit 1.1   (Continued)

District Bankruptcy Courts
(92 courts)

- Official reporter: *West Bankruptcy Reporter*
- Judges appointed by US Circuit Courts of Appeal for 14-year terms
- Almost always follows federal rules of bankruptcy procedure along with local bankruptcy rules (LBRs) in accordance with local rules of the district courts, and Federal Rules of Civil Procedure
- At least one Federal bankruptcy court is in each federal district except for Guam and the Northern Mariana Islands
- Required by statute to comply with Federal Rules of Evidence

US district courts

- Official reporter: *Federal Supplement*
- Federal courts of original jurisdiction (i.e., Federal trial courts)
- Located in every state and territory of the United States and the District of Columbia
- Jurisdiction
  - Cases involving federal law (including antitrust and ERISA cases which are subject to challenge by the IRS the Dept. of Labor and beneficiaries)
  - Some state cases involving citizens of different states or where amount in controversy exceeds a certain statutory amount: case starts out in state court, is removed to the district courts on a statutory "petition for removal;" court will apply appropriate state laws and federal rules of civil procedure
- Each district court may make and amend rules governing its practice with the boundaries of the Federal Rules of Civil Procedure

- Judges appointed by the president for life
- Required by statute to comply with Federal Rules of Evidence
- List of US District Courts:

  Alabama (Northern, Middle, Southern)
  Alaska
  Arizona
  Arkansas (Eastern, Western)
  California (Northern, Eastern, Central Southern)
  Colorado
  Connecticut
  Delaware
  District of Columbia
  Florida (Northern, Middle, Southern)
  Georgia (Northern, Middle, Southern)
  Guam
  Hawaii
  Idaho
  Indiana (Northern Southern)
  Iowa (Northern, Southern)
  Kansas
  Kentucky (Eastern, Middle, Western)
  Louisiana (Eastern, Middle, Western)
  Maine
  Maryland
  Massachusetts
  Michigan (Eastern, Western)
  Minnesota
  Mississippi (Northern, Southern, Eastern Western)
  Montana
  Nebraska
  Nevada
  New Hampshire
  New Jersey
  New Mexico
  New York (Northern, Southern, Eastern Western)

Exhibit 1.1 (Continued)

North Carolina (Eastern, Middle, Western)	Texas (Northern, Southern, Eastern, Western)
North Dakota	Utah
Northern Mariana Islands	
Ohio (Northern, Southern)	***Other Special Federal Courts***
Oklahoma (Northern, Eastern, Western)	• Created and done away with by Congress from time to time
Oregon	
Pennsylvania (Eastern, Middle, Western)	• Jurisdiction determined by statute.
Puerto Rico	
Rhode Island	United States Court of International Trade
South Carolina	United States Court of Military Appeals
South Dakota	
Tennessee (Eastern, Middle, Western)	District of Columbia Superior Court

Source: Shannon Pratt's Business Valuation Update® (October 1996): 11–13. Figure from *Concepts of Taxation,* 1995 edition, by Ray M. Sommerfeld, Silvia A. Madeo, Kenneth E. Anderson, and Betty R. Jackson. First edition by Sommerfeld. Reprinted with permission of Southwestern, a division of Thomson Learning: *www.thomsonrights.com.* Fax (800) 730-2215. See also Linda L. Kruschke, "An Overview of the U.S. Court System for Non-Lawyers," Special Report in *Shannon Pratt's Business Valuation Update®* (October 2002): 11–13.

Revenue Rulings (RRs)

- Official pronouncements of the national office of the IRS.
- Designed to provide interpretations of the tax law.
- Do not carry the legal force and effect of regulations.
- Although regulations are approved by the Secretary of the Treasury, revenue rulings are not.
- Revenue rulings relevant to business valuation include:
  - **RR59-60:** Valuation of closely held common stock (the most widely referenced revenue ruling, also often referenced for nontax valuations).
  - **RR65-193:** Eliminates wording about separate appraisals of tangible and intangible assets from RR59-60.
  - **RR68-609:** Excess earnings method (also called formula method or treasury method). (Should be used *only* if no better method is available; supersedes RR65-192; confirms that RR59-60 is applicable to business interests of all types.)

- **RR77-287:** Discounts for lack of marketability. (Recognizes private placement studies as relevant empirical data for guidance in quantifying discounts for lack of marketability; issued before pre–initial public offering [IPO] studies existed; pre-IPO studies recognized along with private placement studies in *Estate of Mandelbaum v. Commissioner.*)
- **RR83-120:** Valuation of preferred stock.
- **RR85-75:** Taxpayer is subject to penalty if he or she adopts overstated amount on estate tax return for section 1014 basis.
- **RR93-12:** Minority stockholder of family-controlled company is *not* subject to family attribution. (Reversed RR81-283.)

Note: Major revenue rulings are elaborated on in Chapter 23. References to topics addressed in RR59-60, RR68-609, RR77-287, RR83-120, and RR93-12 are noted wherever relevant topics are discussed throughout this book.

Revenue Procedures (RPs)

- Issued in the same manner as revenue rulings.
- Deal with IRS internal management practices and procedures.
- Revenue procedures relevant to business valuation:
  - **RP66-49:** Procedures and report content for contributions of noncash property.
  - **RP77-12:** Fair market value of assets purchased through liquidation of a subsidiary.
  - **RP98-34:** Option valuation.

Private Letter Rulings (PLRs)

- Issued at taxpayer's request about how IRS will treat a proposed transaction.
- Apply only to taxpayer who requests and obtains ruling but may provide substantial authority for avoiding accuracy-related penalties.
- Useful as indicator of IRS position on key valuation issues.

Technical Advice Memorandums (TAMs)

- Released by IRS national office weekly.
- PLRs pertain to *proposed transactions*; TAMs pertain to *completed transactions.*
- Unlike PLRs, which are initiated by taxpayers *not* under audit, TAMs arise from questions raised by IRS personnel during audits.
- May not be cited or used as precedent but may provide substantial authority in avoiding accuracy-related penalties.

Field Service Advice Memorandums (FSAs)

- Provide nonbonding advice, guidance, and analysis in response to questions from IRS agents, attorneys, and appeals officers on both substantive and procedural issues.
- Like TAMs and PLRs, may not be cited as precedent or authority but represent the current thinking of the IRS.

IRS Valuation Training for Appeals Officers Coursebook

- Internal manual used in training course for IRS appeals officers.
- May not be cited as authority but useful in understanding IRS thinking on valuation issues.
- Updated periodically (latest edition 1997); latest edition available for reading and/or downloading at *BVLibrary.com*sm; also available in print from CCH, Incorporated.

IRS Business Valuation Guidelines

- Draft issued in May 2001; revised guidelines issued in October 2001.
- Available to download from *BVLibrary.com*sm (at Free Downloads section).
- Contain guidelines for developing value, resolution of value, reporting, and a report checklist.

References to Legal and Regulatory Environment

FBVI Ch. 2, Appendix C
Guide 901.10, 901.11, 901.17–901.19
IBA2 Ch. 12
IBA3 Ch. 1
Lawyer pp. 15–19
NACVA BV Ch. 2, App. 3
NACVA Sect. 2
NACVA CA Sect. 2
VSB3 pp. 9–13, 17, 20, 24–25, 39–40, 56, Ch. 46

Chapter 2

Business Valuation Professional Environment

Although businesses and business interests have been valued for many decades, most of the evolution of business appraisal as a profession has occurred in the 1980s and 1990s.

THE APPRAISAL FOUNDATION

Background and Structure

- Founded in 1986 by a group of professional appraisal organizations involved with real estate, personal property, and businesses.
- Congress established an appraisal subcommittee to monitor and recommend federal financing for foundation activities related to real estate.
- Funded by member organizations, Congress, and donations.
- Governed by a board of trustees of approximately 32 members.

- Two advisory councils:
  - The Appraisal Foundation Advisory Council (TAFAC)—composed of non-profit organizations and government agencies.
  - Industry Advisory Council (IAC)—composed of for-profit organizations such as independent appraisal firms, certified public accountant (CPA) firms, and lenders.
- Appoints members to two independent boards:
  - Appraisal Standards Board (ASB)—issues *Uniform Standards of Professional Appraisal Practice* (USPAP), updated annually in November.
  - Appraiser Qualifications Board (AQB)—sets qualifications for appraisers (has set qualifications for real estate appraisers; working on qualification criteria for personal property appraisers; as of 2002, no plans to set criteria for business appraiser qualifications).

Uniform Standards of Professional Appraisal Practice (USPAP)

- Exhibit 2.1 is the table of contents for USPAP '02.
- Compliance with USPAP is legally mandatory for all real estate transactions of more than $250,000 involving federally related agencies and for conversions of mutual savings and loans to stock companies.
- Sections of USPAP that are most directly applicable to appraisers of businesses and intangible assets:
  - Prefatory material (preamble, ethics provision, competency provision, departure provision, jurisdictional exceptions, supplemental standards, and definitions), which applies to appraisals of all types of property.
  - Standard 9, which includes procedural requirements for appraising a business, business interest, or intangible property.
  - Standard 10, which includes requirements for reporting an appraisal of a business, business interest, or intangible property.
- Business appraisers also should be familiar with USPAP standards for appraising other types of property, because other property often is included as part of a business.
- The edition of USPAP that applies to any particular appraisal is *the edition for the year in which the appraisal is performed, not* the effective date of the appraisal in the case of retrospective appraisals.

Major Provisions of USPAP Standards 9 and 10 (per USPAP '02)

Note: The following listing contains only the basic provisions. The provisions also are supplemented by comments, and the appraiser should read and understand the standards as a whole.

Exhibit 2.1   Table of Contents of *Uniform Standards of Professional Appraisal Practice* 2002

TABLE OF CONTENTS
Uniform Standards of Professional Appraisal Practice

Standards and Standards Rules

Statements on Appraisal Standards

Exhibit 2.1 (Continued)

ADDENDA
REFERENCE MATERIAL
(for guidance only)

Advisory Opinions

Source: *The Uniform Standards of Professional Appraisal Practice* (USPAP). Copyright © 2002 by The Appraisal Foundation. Additional copies of USPAP (including Advisory Opinions and Statements) are available for purchase from The Appraisal Foundation, 1029 Vermont Avenue N.W., Suite 900, Washington, DC 20005-3517, (202) 347-7722.

Standards Rule 9-1

In developing a business or intangible asset appraisal, an appraiser must:

(a) be aware of, understand, and correctly employ those recognized methods and procedures that are necessary to produce a credible appraisal;

(b) not commit a substantial error of omission or commission that significantly affects an appraisal; and

(c) not render appraisal services in a careless or negligent manner, such as by making a series of errors that, although individually might not significantly affect the results of an appraisal, in the aggregate affect the credibility of those results.

Standards Rule 9-2

In developing a business or intangible asset appraisal, an appraiser must identify:

(a) the client and any other intended users of the appraisal and the client's intended use of the appraiser's opinions and conclusions;

(b) the purpose of the assignment, including the standard of value (definition) to be developed;

(c) the effective date of the appraisal;

(d) the business enterprises, assets, or equity to be valued;

    (i) identify any buy-sell agreements, investment letter stock restrictions, restrictive corporate charter or partnership agreement clauses, and any similar features or factors that may have an influence on value; and

    (ii) ascertain the extent to which the interests contain elements of ownership control.

(e) the scope of work that will be necessary to complete the assignment;

(f) any extraordinary assumptions necessary in the assignment; and

(g) any hypothetical conditions necessary in the assignment.

Standards Rule 9-3

In developing a business or intangible asset appraisal relating to an equity interest with the ability to cause liquidation of the enterprise, an appraiser must investigate the possibility that the business enterprise may have a higher value by liquidation of all or part of the enterprise than by continued operation as is. If liquidation of all or part of the enterprise is the indicated basis of valuation, an appraisal of any real estate or personal property to be liquidated may be appropriate.

Standards Rule 9-4

In developing a business or intangible asset appraisal, an appraiser must collect and analyze all information pertinent to the appraisal problem, given the scope of work identified in accordance with Standards Rule 9-2(e).

(a) An appraiser must develop value opinion(s) and conclusion(s) by use of one or more approaches that apply to the specific appraisal assignment; and

(b) include in the analyses, when relevant, data regarding:
- (i) the nature and history of the business;
- (ii) financial and economic conditions affecting the business enterprise, its industry, and the general economy;
- (iii) past results, current operations, and future prospects of the business enterprise;
- (iv) past sales of capital stock or other ownership interests in the business enterprise being appraised;
- (v) sales of similar businesses or capital stock of publicly held similar businesses;
- (vi) prices, terms, and conditions affecting past sales of similar business equity; and
- (vii) economic benefit of intangible assets.

Standards Rule 9-5

In developing a business or intangible asset appraisal, an appraiser must reconcile the indications of value resulting from the various approaches to arrive at the value conclusion.

Standards Rule 10-1

Each written or oral business or intangible asset appraisal report must:

(a) clearly and accurately set forth the appraisal in a manner that will not be misleading:

(b) contain sufficient information to enable the intended user(s) to understand it and note any specific limiting conditions concerning information; and

(c) clearly and accurately disclose any extraordinary assumption or hypothetical condition that directly affects the appraisal and indicate its impact on value.

Standards Rule 10-2

Each written business valuation or intangible asset appraisal report must be prepared in accordance with one of the following options and prominently state which option is used: Appraisal Report or Restricted Use Appraisal Report.

(a) The content of an Appraisal Report must be consistent with the intended use of the appraisal and, at a minimum:
- (i) state the identity of the client and any intended users, by name or type;
- (ii) state the intended use of the appraisal;
- (iii) summarize information sufficient to identify the business or intangible assets appraised;

(iv)   state as relevant to the assignment, the extent to which the business interest or the interest in the intangible asset appraised contains elements of
ownership control, including the basis for that determination;

(v)   state the purpose of the appraisal, including the standard of value (definition) and its source;

(vi)   state the effective date of the appraisal and the date of the report;

(vii) summarize sufficient information to disclose to the client and any intended
users of the appraisal the scope of work used to develop the appraisal;

(viii) state all assumptions, hypothetical conditions, and limiting conditions that
affected the analyses, opinions, and conclusions;

(ix)   summarize the information analyzed, the appraisal procedures followed,
and the reasoning that supports the analyses, opinions, and conclusions;

(x)   state and explain any permitted departures from specific requirements of
STANDARD 9 and the reason for excluding any of the usual valuation approaches; and

(xi)   include a signed certification in accordance with Standards Rule 10-3.

(b) The content of a Restricted Use Appraisal Report must be for client use only and
consistent with the intended use of the appraisal and, at a minimum:

(i)   state the identity of the client;

(ii)   state the intended use of the appraisal;

(iii) state information sufficient to identify the business or intangible asset
appraised.

(iv)   state as relevant to the assignment, the extent to which the business interest or the interest in the intangible asset appraised contains elements of
ownership control, including the basis for that determination;

(v)   state the purpose of the appraisal, including the standard of value (definition) and its source;

(vi)   state the effective date of the appraisal and the date of the report;

(vii) state the extent of the process of collecting, confirming, and reporting data
or refer to an assignment agreement retained in the appraiser's workfile
that describes the scope of work to be performed;

(viii) state all assumptions, hypothetical conditions, and limiting conditions that
affect the analyses, opinions, and conclusions;

(ix)   state the appraisal procedures followed, state the value opinion(s) and con-
clusion(s) reached, and reference the workfile;

(x)   state and explain any permitted departures from applicable specific requirements of STANDARD 9; state the exclusion of any of the usual valuation approaches; and state a prominent use restriction that limits use of
the report to the client and warns that the appraiser's opinions and conclusions set forth in the report cannot be understood properly without additional information in the appraiser's workfile; and

(xi)   include a signed certification in accordance with Standards Rule 10-3.

Standards Rule 10-3

Each written business or intangible asset appraisal report must contain a signed certification that is similar in content to the following form:

I certify that, to the best of my knowledge and belief:

—the statements of fact contained in this report are true and correct.

—the reported analyses, opinions, and conclusions are limited only by the reported assumptions and limiting conditions, and are my personal, impartial, and unbiased professional analyses, opinions, and conclusions.

—I have no (or the specified) present or prospective interest in the property that is the subject of this report, and I have no (or the specified) personal interest with respect to the parties involved.

—I have no bias with respect to the property that is the subject of this report or to the parties involved with this assignment.

—my engagement in this assignment was not contingent upon developing or reporting predetermined results.

—my compensation for completing this assignment is not contingent upon the development or reporting of a predetermined value or direction in value that favors the cause of the client, the amount of the value opinion, the attainment of a stipulated result, or the occurrence of a subsequent event directly related to the intended use of this appraisal.

—my analyses, opinions, and conclusions were developed, and this report has been prepared, in conformity with the *Uniform Standards of Professional Appraisal Practice.*

—no one provided significant business valuation assistance to the person signing this certification. (If there are exceptions, the name of each and the significant business valuation assistance must be stated.)

Standards Rule 10-4

An oral business or intangible asset appraisal report must, at a minimum, address the substantive matters set forth in Standards Rule 10-2(a).

Standards Rule 10-5

An appraiser who signs a business or intangible asset appraisal report prepared by another, even under the label "review appraiser," must accept full responsibility for the contents of this report.

Other USPAP Provisions

Statements on Appraisal Standards

Statements on appraisal standards, authorized by the by-laws of The Appraisal Foundation, have as their purpose clarification, interpretation, explanation, or elaboration of USPAP. Statements have the full weight of a standards rule and can be adopted by the ASB only after exposure and comment. To date, the ASB has adopted 10 statements.

Advisory Opinions

In addition to statements on appraisal standards, the ASB also issues advisory opinions. This type of communication by the ASB does not establish new standards or interpret existing standards. Advisory opinions, which do not constitute legal opinions of the ASB, are issued to illustrate the applicability of appraisal standards in specific situations and to offer ASB advice for the resolution of appraisal issues and problems.

Note: USPAP is revised annually in November.

PROFESSIONAL BUSINESS APPRAISAL ORGANIZATIONS

Organizations Offering Business Valuation Certifications

* Four professional organizations in the United States and one in Canada offer some type of professional certification in the field of business appraisal:
    1. The American Institute of Certified Public Accountants (AICPA) (see Exhibit 2.2).
    2. The American Society of Appraisers (ASA) (see Exhibit 2.3).
    3. The Institute of Business Appraisers (IBA) (see Exhibit 2.4).
    4. The National Association of Certified Valuation Analysts (NACVA) (see Exhibit 2.5).
    5. The Canadian Institute of Chartered Business Valuators (CICBV) (see Exhibit 2.6).
* The appraiser should be generally aware of all of these organizations and their perspectives and standards, even though not necessarily bound by them, because issues may arise in litigation with an opposing expert from another organization; various courts have accorded notice to such standards.
* All of the listed organizations offer both formal courses and periodic professional seminar meetings on business valuation.

Business Valuation Professional Association Standards

American Institute of Certified Public Accountants (AICPA)

* The AICPA currently has a committee working on formulating business valuation standards, which are expected to be finalized in 2003.
* The AICPA publishes standards on consulting services generally, which are applicable when CPAs perform business valuation services.

See Chapter 4 for details on the AICPA consulting engagement standards.

Exhibit 2.2   American Institute of Certified Public Accountants (AICPA)
201 Plaza Three, Jersey City, New Jersey 07311-3881, (201) 938-3000

Date formed:	1887 Ownership: Organization sponsored
Description:	Multidisciplinary professional organization of CPAs that recognizes business valuation as a CPA service niche and confers an accreditation reflecting this recognition for those in public practice, industry, government, and education
Certifications offered:	*ABV—Accredited in Business Valuation:*

	Prerequisite:	AICPA member with current CPA license
	Courses/exams:	One-day exam
	Reports:	None
	Experience requirement:	Involvement in at least 10 business valuation engagements

Reaccredidation:	Three-year reaccredidation cycle requires average of 20 hours of business valuation education per year and involvement in at least five business valuation engagements during the cycle
Courses:	Two three-day courses (FBVI, FBVII) plus several one-day advanced elective courses; two-day ABV exam review course, one-day ESOP course
One-day advanced elective courses:	Advanced Cost of Capital Computations in a Complex World (ACCC) Discounts and Premiums in a Business Valuation Environment (ADP)
	Research & Analysis: Critical Techniques in a Business Valuation Engagement (ARA)
	Splitting Up Is Hard to Do: Advanced Valuation Issues in Divorce and Other Litigation Disputes (AVI)
	Divorcing Clients: The CPA's Role (DCCPA)
	Exploring Issues in Valuing Stock Options and Other Assets You Can't See (EIVOS)
	An ESOP Company: What's It Worth? (ESOP)
	An Exciting Insight Into the Health Care Industry and Medical Practice Valuation (HVIC)
	Small Business Valuation Case Study: Let's Work Through the Issues! (SBCS)
Seminars and conferences:	Annual National Business Valuation Conference
Publications:	*CPA Expert*, a quarterly newsletter
	ABV E-Valuation Alert, a monthly e-newsletter to practitioners on technical valuation issues and valuation news
	CPA Consultant, a quarterly newsletter for BV and other CPA consulting practitioners

Exhibit 2.3   American Society of Appraisers (ASA)
P.O. Box 17265, Washington, D.C. 20041, (703) 478-2228 or (800) ASA-VALU
[278-8258]

Date formed:	1936	Ownership:	Owned by members
Description:	Multidisciplinary professional organization offering courses and exams leading to designations in the appraisal of real estate, machinery and equipment, personal property, gems and jewelry, businesses and business interests (including intangible assets), and certain technical specialties		
Certifications offered:	*AM—Accredited Member:*		
	Educational Requirement:	College degree or equivalent	
	Courses/exams:	Completion of four courses of three days each, with successful completion of one half-day exam following each of the three courses and a full-day exam following BV204, or successful completion of an all-day challenge exam; successful completion of an ethics exam	
	Reports:	Submission of two actual appraisal reports to satisfaction of board of examiners	
	Experience requirement:	Two years full-time or full-time-equivalent work (e.g., five years of 400 hours business appraisal work per year equals one year full-time equivalent)	
	Related experience offset:	One full year of the experience requirement is granted to anyone who has any of the following three designations with five years of practice in that respective field: certified public accountant (CPA), chartered financial analyst (CFA), or certified business intermediary (CBI)	
	ASA—Accredited Senior Appraiser:		
		Has met all requirements listed plus an additional three years of full-time or full-time-equivalent experience	
	FASA—Fellow of the American Society of Appraisers:		
		Has met all requirements listed plus is voted into the college of fellows on the basis of technical leadership and contribution to the profession and the society	

Exhibit 2.3 (Continued)

Courses:	Each of the core courses (BV201–204) is three days; BV201 to 203 are followed by a half-day exam, and BV204 is followed by a full-day exam; BV205 and 206 are two days each
	BV201: Introduction to Business Valuation, part I
	BV202: Introduction to Business Valuation, part II
	BV203: Business Valuation Case Study
	BV204: Business Valuation Selected Advanced Topics
	BV205: Appraisal of Small Businesses and Professional Practices
	BV206: Employee Stock Ownership Plans: valuing ESOP Shares
Seminars:	Seminars on specialized topics lasting from two hours to two days are sponsored by various groups within the ASA
	Center for Advanced Valuation Studies (CAVS):
	A series of advanced-level seminars targeted toward seasoned professionals
	The Valuation of Family Limited Partnerships (one day)
	Discounts and Premiums (one day)
	Real Options and the Value of Uncertainty (two days)
	Cost of Capital (two days)
	The Public Guideline Company Method (two days)
Conferences:	Annual interdisciplinary meeting with two and a half days of technical presentations on each of the society's appraisal disciplines
	Annual Advanced Business Valuation Conference with two or two and a half days of advanced business valuation papers, presentations, and discussion
Publications:	*Business Valuation Review*, quarterly professional journal with articles accepted based on peer review: published at 2777 South Colorado Boulevard, Suite 200, Denver, Colorado 80222, (303) 758-8818; the other valuation disciplines also have professional journals, similar to *Business Valuation Review*
	Valuation, published on an irregular basis, contains articles on all of the disciplines of valuation within the ASA; published at ASA headquarters

Exhibit 2.4   Institute of Business Appraisers (IBA)
P.O. Box 17410, Plantation, Florida 33318, (954) 584-1144, www.go-iba.org

Date formed:	1978
Ownership:	Florida not-for-profit Corporation (privately owned)
Description:	Offers programs of interest to members whose business valuation activities are less than full time and/or whose practice includes valuation of small to midsize businesses
Certifications offered:	*CBA—Certified Business Appraiser:*

Educational requirement:	College degree or equivalent
Courses/exams:	Exam of six hours
Reports:	Submission of two business appraisal reports demonstrating professional level of competence
Experience requirement:	10,000 hours (or 90 hours advanced business appraisal courses)

FIBA—Fellow of the Institute of Business Appraisers:

	Has met all requirements listed plus is voted into the college of fellows on the basis of technical leadership and contribution to the profession and the institute

MCBA—Master Certified Business Appraiser:

Educational requirement:	Four-year college degree and two-year postgraduate degree or equivalent
Appraisal experience:	Ten years of full-time experience as business appraiser
Tenure:	Not less than five years holding CBA designation
Other designations:	At least one other journeyman-level designation awarded by professional business appraisal societies

AIBA—Accredited by IBA:

Educational requirement:	College degree or equivalent
Courses/exams:	Successful completion of 64-hour workshop (and pass written exam) or possess a BV designation from AICPA, ASA, or NACVA
Reports:	One report demonstrating competence as business appraiser

Exhibit 2.4 (Continued)

	Professional development:	Proof of 24 hours of advanced BV education; or submission of another report; or pass CBA exam

BVAL—Business Valuator Accredited for Litigation:

Educational requirement:	None	
Courses/exams:	Successful completion of 56-hour IBA-7001 workshop (and pass four-hour written exam)	
Experience requirement:	Demonstrate presentation and process competency during testimony clinics	
Other designations:	Hold a BV designation from IBA, ASA, AICPA, or NACVA; or a CBA candidate who has passed CBA exam	

Courses:	1006:	Preparation for the CBA exam (1 day)
	1007:	Fractional interest premiums and discounts (1 day)
	1020:	Business appraisal for divorce (1 day)
	1018:	Analyzing financial statements (1 day)
	1008:	Discount and capitalization rates (2 days)
	1010:	Report writing, review and analysis (2 days)
	1012:	Fundamentals of BV and the direct market data method (2 days)
	1013:	Case studies (2 days)
	1017:	The guideline public company method and the multiple period discounting method (2 days)
	1019:	Litigation support (2 days)
	8001:	Mastering appraisal skills workshops (64 hours)
	7001:	Expert witness skills workshop (56 hours)

Seminars and conferences:	Seminars on business valuation held at various locations around the United States; annual business valuation conference
Publications:	*IBA News*, bimonthly newsletter
	Business Appraisal Practice, quarterly professional journal with academic-level peer-review editor selection process
	Technical Studies of the IBA Database, articles reviewing statistical and technical aspects of transaction data
	Business Appraisal Reports Library, two volumes of eight appraisal reports illustrating a variety of work products for typical appraisal engagements

Exhibit 2.5   National Association of Certified Valuation Analysts (NACVA)
1111 Brickyard Road, Suite 200, Salt Lake City, Utah 84106, (801) 486-0600

Date formed:	1991
Ownership:	Group of shareholders
Description:	NACVA is an association of CPAs, government valuation analysts, and other professionals who perform valuation services; its purpose is to promulgate the members' status, credentials, and esteem in the field of performing valuations of closely held businesses

Certifications offered:	*CVA—Certified Valuation Analyst*:	
	Educational requirement:	CPA
	Courses/exams:	Forty-hour training course; four-hour proctored exam; and a take-home case study that is estimated to take 40 to 60 hours to complete
	Reports:	Only for sample case on exam
	Experience requirement:	Experience required for certification as CPA
	AVA—Accredited Valuation Analyst:	
	Educational requirement:	Business degree or MBA from an accredited college or university
	Courses/exams:	Five-day training program and a comprehensive two-part exam consisting of a full-day proctored exam and a 40-to-60-hour take-home/in-office exam that incorporates a standardized case study (provided by NACVA) that requires performing a complete business valuation
	Reports:	Only for sample case on exam
	Experience requirement:	Substantial experience in business valuation demonstrated with business references or attestations
	GVA—Government Valuation Analyst:	
	Educational requirement:	College degree
	Courses/exams:	Forty-hour training course; four-hour proctored exam; and a take-home case study that is estimated to take 40 to 60 hours to complete
	Reports:	Only for sample case on exam
	Experience requirement:	Employed by government agency, GS-12 or higher, two years' full-time business valuation experience

Exhibit 2.5 (Continued)

Courses:	Five-day certification training consisting of the following:

Days 1–2:	Fundamentals, Techniques, and Theory
Day 3:	Case Analysis No. 1 and Report Writing
Day 4:	Using Valuation Master 4.0 Software
Day 5:	Working Effectively in the Litigation Environment

	Career Development Institute—Advanced Business Valuation Training—consists of various classes ranging from four to 16 hours, each over five days
Seminars and conferences:	Annual business valuation conference; one- and two-day seminars on key valuations topics, including symposiums
Publications:	*The Valuation Examiner*, a bimonthly magazine

Exhibit 2.6 The Canadian Institute of Chartered Business Valuators (CICBV) 277 Wellington St. West, Toronto, Ontario, Canada M5V3H2 (416) 204-3396

Date formed:	1971
Ownership:	Nonprofit federally incorporated corporation owned by members
Description:	The CICBV is the largest professional valuation organization in Canada. It was established to promote high standards in business and securities valuations; members are entitled to use the professional designation CBV (chartered business valuator) following completion of rigorous study and practical experience requirements; the institute's 650 members and 350 students provide a broad range of business valuation services to Canada's business, legal, investment, banking, and governmental communities
Certifications offered:	*CBV—Chartered Business Valuator*:

Educational requirement:	College degree or equivalent
Courses/exam:	Successful completion of a program of six courses including assignments and examinations for each course plus the required experience, followed by the writing of the membership entrance examination; writing of this examination can be challenged without successful completion of the six courses, provided the applicant has at least five years of full-time experience in the field of business valuation

(continued)

Exhibit 2.6   (Continued)

	Experience requirement:	Two years of full-time experience or the equivalent of part-time experience obtained over a five-year period, attested to by a sponsoring CICBV member
Courses:		All courses are provided by correspondence, including mandatory assignments with proctored examinations; the courses offered are introductory business and security valuations, law and valuation, intermediate business and security valuations, taxation in business valuation, special topics, and litigation
Seminars and conferences:		Seminars and workshops are offered monthly in major cities across Canada
		Biennial national conferences (2 full days)
		Regional conferences (one to one and one-half days)
Publications:		*The Valuation Law Review* is published twice yearly with three sections: corporate securities law, family law, and taxation
		Business Valuation Digest is published twice yearly and consists of articles on business valuations
		The Journal of Business Valuation contains the proceedings of the institute's biennial conferences
		The Business Valuator is a quarterly publication dealing with the activities of the institute

American Society of Appraisers (ASA)

The ASA publishes:

- Principles of Appraisal Practice and Code of Ethics.
- Business Valuation Standards.
  - BVS-I, General Requirements for Developing a Business Valuation.
  - BVS-II, Financial Statement Adjustments.
  - BVS-III, Asset-Based Approach to Business Valuation.
  - BVS-IV, Income Approach to Business Valuation.
  - BVS-V, Market Approach to Business Valuation.
  - BVS-VI, Reaching a Conclusion of Value.
  - BVS-VII, Valuation Discounts and Premiums.
  - BVS-VIII, Comprehensive Written Business Valuation Report.

These standards were discussed at length earlier, but note particularly the USPAP comment to Standards Rule 9–1(a):

Comment: Changes and developments in the economy and in investment theory have a substantial impact on the business appraisal profession. Important changes in the financial arena, securities regulation, and tax law and major new court decisions may result in corresponding changes in business appraisal practice.

In other words, information relied on in an appraisal must be timely relative to the valuation date.

Institute of Business Appraisers (IBA)

The IBA publishes the following:

- Report Writing Standards.
- Technical Standards.
  - 1.0, Oral Professional Conduct and Ethics
  - 2.0, Oral Appraisal Reports
  - 3.0, Expert Testimony
  - 4.0, Letter Form Written Appraisal Reports
  - 5.0, Formal Written Appraisal Reports
  - 6.0, Preliminary Reports

National Association of Certified Valuation Analysts (NACVA)

NACVA publishes:

- General Standards.
- Development Standards.
- Reporting Standards.
- Other Guidelines and Requirements.
- Standards for Limited Scope Reports.
- Other Guidelines.

Association for Investment Management and Research (AIMR)

- Awards the professional designation of Chartered Financial Analyst (CFA), requires three comprehensive exams, one year apart.
- Oriented primarily to public securities markets, but required readings include materials on valuation of closely held companies.
- Includes valuation of closely held companies as one of the practice categories that members may indicate in the membership directory.

Other Relevant Associations

- Canadian Institute of Chartered Business Valuators (CICBV)
  - Awards the professional designation of Chartered Business Valuator (CBV).
  - Oriented primarily to professional business valuators.
  - Issues Practice Standards and a Code of Ethics.
- Employee Stock Ownership Plan (ESOP) Association
  - Membership includes companies that have ESOPs and professional advisors to ESOPs, including ESOP stock appraisers.
  - Through its advisory committee on valuation, issues various publications offering ESOP valuation guidance, including *Valuing ESOP Shares* and position papers on discounts for lack of marketability and control premiums.
  - Does not award any professional designation.
- Institute of Certified Business Counselors (ICBC)
  - Awards the professional designation Certified Business Counselor (CBC).
  - Oriented primarily to business intermediaries, but membership includes professional advisors such as business appraisers.
- International Business Brokers Association (IBBA)
  - Awards the professional designation of Certified Business Intermediary (CBI).
  - Oriented primarily to business intermediaries, but membership includes professional advisers such as business appraisers.
  - Two business appraisal courses of two days each required toward CBI designation.

References to BV Professional Environment

FBVI Ch. 2
FBVII Appendixes C-J
Guide Ch. 1
Lawyer Ch. 2
VAB4 Ch. 1
VSB3 Ch. 1

Chapter 3

Business Valuation Engagement

ELEMENTS OF A BUSINESS VALUATION ENGAGEMENT

- Names of client and appraiser.
- Date of retention.
- Definition of property to be valued.
- Definition (standard) of value sought.
- Effective date of valuation.
- Purpose of valuation (intended use).
- Representations expected, if applicable.
- Contingent and limiting conditions.
- Scope of work product.
- Scheduling.
- Fees.
- Indemnification.
- Resolution of disputes.

NAME OF CLIENT AND APPRAISER

- Must specify client, such as:
  - Company.
  - Owner.
  - Board of directors.
  - Committee of board.
  - Potential buyer.
  - Dissenting shareholder.
  - Divorcing spouse.
  - Government agency (e.g., Internal Revenue Service [IRS], state department of revenue).
  - Lender.
  - Trustee.
  - ESOP.
  - Law firm.
  - Executor.
- Must specify appraiser, such as:
  - Firm.
  - Individual (or group).

DATE OF RETENTION

- Usually the date engagement letter is signed by client.
- May be when retainer is received.
- Often is a question raised by opponents in litigation.

DEFINITION OF PROPERTY TO BE VALUED

Business Entity

- Name of entity (both formal name and doing-business-as [d/b/a] name, if applicable).
- Form of organization (e.g., C corporation, S corporation, limited partnership).
- State or country of registration.
  - May be companies with identical names in different states.
  - State laws may affect valuation (e.g., minority stockholder rights, liquidation or withdrawal rights, majority voting requirements).

Interest to Be Valued

- Definition of subject interest as it relates to the whole (e.g., class of ownership interest, number of shares or units of ownership, percentage).
  - Should be sufficient to define degree of minority/control.
  - Better if also know who holds other shares, but may come later in engagement.
  - Identify rights attendant to the interest.
- Marketability:
  - Public or private.
  - Any options to buy or sell or any transfer restrictions.
- Any special agreements:
  - Noncompete covenant.
  - Employment agreement.
  - Shareholder agreement.

Note: Such special agreements may or may not be part of the property to be valued, and the impact on value of including or excluding them can be significant, especially for smaller companies and companies of a service nature.

DEFINITION OF VALUE SOUGHT

Sources of Instructions as to Definitions of Value

- Statutes.
- Regulations.
- Precedential case law.
- Contractual definition.
- Agreement of parties.
- Direction from court.
- Direction from client or attorney.
- RR59-60, although without force of law, often looked to for guidance.

Commonly Used Standards of Value

Fair Market Value

- Defined in Treasury Regulation §20.2031-1(b):

   The price at which the property would change hands between a willing buyer and a willing seller when the former is not under any compulsion to buy and the latter is not under any compulsion to sell, both parties having reasonable knowledge of relevant facts.

- Some minor variations in definition for certain venues (e.g., some state ad valorem tax definitions).
- Standard of value for virtually all tax matters and many other contexts.
- Characteristics of fair market value:
  - Buyer and seller are hypothetical parties, *not* specific parties.
  - Buyer and seller are typically motivated (e.g., no special motivations such as family ties or synergies).
  - Both parties have reasonable knowledge of the relevant facts.
  - Parties act rationally.
  - Parties are able and willing to consummate the transaction.
  - A reasonable time is allowed for exposure in the open market.
  - Terms are cash or cash equivalent (not affected by special financing or other special terms).
  - Seller must be willing to accept the price available under prevalent economic, industry, and market conditions as of the effective date (*not* "I am willing, but not now, because I cannot get what I want under current conditions").
  - Based on information known, knowable, or reasonably foreseeable as of the effective date but *not* events subsequent to the valuation date that may have affected the value.
- Treatment of subsequent events:

- Criterion is known or knowable (e.g., financial statements as of effective date but not yet finalized, audited, or filed usually are allowable because they contain information knowable at effective date).
- Events in close proximity to valuation date that provide *evidence of value* (e.g., subsequent sale of a comparable property) that did not *affect* value usually are allowable. (Many appraisers believe that some recent court decisions have taken this to an unreasonable extreme.)
- Although appraisers normally are not expected to consider subsequent events not known or foreseeable at effective date, courts have criticized appraisers for not *reconciling* effective date valuation with subsequent transaction price.
- Subsequent events that affected value generally are *not* allowable.
- *Caution:* Unfortunately, some judges (e.g., California family law) have used the term *fair market value* loosely, and in some cases the standard of value actually applied contradicts the traditional definition of *fair market value* as widely interpreted in U.S. Tax Court decisions.

Fair Market Value References

ASA BVS
BV203 Ch. 1 p. 3
BV204 Module 1
CoC2 Ch. 7, 15
FBVI Ch. 1 p. 16
Guide 201.4
IBA1 A.2
IBA6
Lawyer pp. 4–6
QMD p. 7
RR59-60; RR66-49
VAB4 pp. 28–30, 34, 194–195, 219, 228, 261–262, 349–350, 375, 670–671, 726, 817–818, 834
VSB3 pp. 38–41, 53, 56, 61, 230, 248, 265, 270, 274, 313, 336, 409, 436, 535, 682–683, 725
VT Lesson 1, 7

Investment Value

- The definition of *investment value* in business valuation is essentially the same as the definition in the Appraisal Institute's *The Dictionary of Real Estate Appraisal,* 3d ed. (1993):

  The specific value of an investment to a particular investor or class of investors based on individual investment requirements; distinguished from market value, which is impersonal and detached.

- Often applies in strategic acquisitions in which some of the synergies with the buyer may be reflected in acquisition (transaction) price (the price paid may be greater than fair market value because of benefits unique to the particular buyer).
- Often reflected (whether or not explicitly recognized) in marital dissolution cases in which value to the individual, including relationships with other owners, may be taken into account.
- Characteristics of investment value:
  - Main difference between investment value and fair market value is focus on *specific* buyer or seller as opposed to *hypothetical* buyer or seller.
  - May focus *exclusively* on either buyer or seller without giving weight to positions of both.
  - Often tends to emphasize income approach over other approaches.
  - Certain acquisitions discovered through the market approach may reflect investment value premiums over fair market value.
- Some reasons why investment value differs from fair market value:
  - Individual party's future expectations.
  - Individual party's perceived risk.
  - Individual party's tax situation.
  - Individual party's anticipated synergistic benefits.

Investment Value References

BV204 Module 1
Guide 201.8, 1502.19
Lawyer pp. 8–9
VAB4 pp. 30–31, 350–351, 376, 792, 804–805, 817, 834–835

Fair Value

- Defined in the Revised Model Business Corporation Act as
    The value of the shares immediately before the effectuation of the corporate action to which the dissenter objects, excluding any appreciation or depreciation in anticipation of the corporate action unless exclusion would be inequitable.
- A majority of states have adopted the preceding or a very similar definition.
- Some states have adopted the preceding definition but without the clause "unless exclusion would be inequitable."
- Other states (including Delaware) have added the clause "in determining such fair value, the court should take into account all relevant factors."
- Fair value standard is applicable in almost all states for dissenting stockholder matters (buyer willing but seller forced to sell).
- Fair value standard usually applies in states that address value in minority oppression statutes.

- *May* consider fairness to a specific class of sellers (e.g., if bought on going-concern basis, fair value may be on going-concern basis; bought in on control basis, fair value may be on control basis).
- Characteristics of fair value:
  - Only a little more than half of the states have precedential cases interpreting the fair value standard.
  - Of those that have such precedential cases, certain issues, particularly applicability of discounts for minority interest and lack of marketability, vary widely.
  - Some states (including Delaware) do not allow discounts for either minority interest or lack of marketability. (Delaware tends to emphasize the value of a proportionate share of a going concern.)
  - Some states either consistently apply or consistently reject discounts for marketability or minority interest.
  - Some states have said that the treatment of minority and marketability discount is left to the discretion of the court to be determined on a case-by-case basis.
  - Although the seller may not be assumed to be knowledgeable, the valuation will be based on the assumption that the seller or the seller's representative has reasonable knowledge.
- The term *fair value* is sometimes found in accounting literature, but in the context of accounting literature the definition is entirely different from the definitions or court interpretations pursuant to state valuation statutes.
  - In the context of Statement of Financial Accounting Standard (SFAS) 142, "Goodwill and Other Intangible Assets," *fair value* has a very different meaning. It is defined in Appendix F of SFAS 142 as:

    The amount at which [an] asset (or liability) could be bought (or incurred) or sold (or settled) in a current transaction between willing parties, that is, other than in a forced or liquidation sale.

  - This sounds somewhat akin to fair market value, but it actually incorporates some aspects of fair market value and some aspects of investment value. Exhibit 3.1 compares fair market value with fair value in the context of SFAS 142.

Fair Value References

BV204 Module 1
FBVI Ch. 1 p. 18
Guide 201.05, Section 1502
IBA1 A.2, A.11
IBA7
Lawyer pp. 7–8
QMD p. 12
VAB4 pp. 32–33, 351–352, 376, 790–796, 800
VSB3 pp. 27, 45–46, 60, 274, 434, 438, 722–723, 725–726

Exhibit 3.1   Comparison of Fair Market Value with Fair Value

Fair Market Value	Fair Value
Hypothetical willing buyers and sellers	Identifiable buyers and sellers
No compulsion on part of either buyers or sellers	No compulsion (to liquidate) on the part of sellers
	Definition and comments do not preclude consideration of compulsion on part of buyers
Both parties have reasonable knowledge of the relevant facts	Silent on knowledge, but reasonable knowledge (at least) is implied
Financial capacity to engage in transaction is implied	Financial capacity is implied
Hypothetical transaction	Hypothetical transaction
Grounded in time as of the specified valuation date	Grounded in time as of the specified valuation date
Generally considered to be value based on financial returns to acquirer and seller	SFAS 142 implies that fair value is investment value to a particular purchaser

Intrinsic Value (Fundamental Value)

- *Kohlers Dictionary for Accountants* defines *intrinsic value* as the amount that an investor considers, on the basis of an evaluation of available facts, to be the "true" or "real" worth of an item, usually an *equity security*. The value that will become the market value when other investors reach the same conclusions.

- Addresses what the value *ought to be* based on fundamental security analysis, the conclusion of which may or may not coincide with actual market value at any given time.

- Akin to a security analyst's value and not frequently referred to as a legal standard of value.

- This value is not market driven. Buyers and sellers may have a different perception of value. Coincidentally, fair market value may be the same as intrinsic value.

Intrinsic Value References

FBVI Ch. 1. p. 18
Guide 201.09
IBA6
IBA7
Lawyer pp. 9–10
VAB4 pp. 31–32, 351, 376, 818
VSB3 pp. 43–45, 53, 431–432

Transaction Value (Acquisition Value)

- The price at which an actual transaction occurred, defined by the International Business Brokers Association (Business Brokers Glossary) as follows:

  The total of all consideration passed at any time between the buyer and seller for an ownership interest in a business enterprise and may include, but is not limited to, all remuneration for tangible and intangible assets such as furniture, equipment, supplies, inventory, working capital, non-competition agreements, employment, and/or consultation agreements, licenses, customer lists, franchise fees, assumed liabilities, stock options, stock or stock redemptions, real estate, leases, royalties, earn-outs, and future considerations.

- Some definitions would exclude the value of noncompetition agreements and/or employment agreements on the basis that they are contingent on future personal performance.

- Specifically refers to *price* as opposed to *value;* empirical (historical) in nature, not a legal standard of value. (*Price* is the face value at which a specific transaction occurred. It may have been arrived at arbitrarily, by negotiation, by contract, by court order, or by some other means. It may or may not comport to any definition of value discussed herein.)

- Characteristics of transaction value (acquisition value):
  - Usually quoted at face value, without adjustment to cash or cash equivalent value.
  - Usually impounds motivations or circumstances of specific buyer and/or seller (e.g., synergies or compulsion).

- Use of transaction values in valuation:
  - A source of empirical data for market approach.
  - If used to estimate fair market value, must analyze and consider adjustment from transaction terms to cash or cash equivalent value.
  - Difficult to adjust prices for extent of acquired synergies but should be considered.
  - Financial buyer transactions typically will not include synergistic value and therefore may be more useful in market approach where fair market value is sought.
  - As the number of buyers increases, this approach becomes more useful where fair market value is sought.

Transaction Value References

IBA6
Lawyer pp. 12, 14
Market pp. 141–142
VSB3 p. 41

Converting Transaction Value to Cash Equivalent Value References

Guide 1002.4–1002.10
VSB3 Ch. 27

Synergistic Value

- A potential price reflecting the extent of the value of synergistic benefits for which a buyer may be willing to pay.
- In this sense, reflects a level of value that is above fair market value and may comport to investment value (may be considered a subset of investment value).
- Many, if not a majority, of the mergers and acquisitions among public companies in the 1990s were driven by synergistic value.

Standard of Value General References

CoC2 Ch. 7, 15
FBVI Ch. 1 p. 10–18
Guide 201.3–201.13
IBA1 A.2, A.11
IBA2 Ch. 2
IBA3 B.1
IBA7
Lawyer p. 14
NACVA Sect. 1, 2, 7
NACVA-BV Ch. 2, 9
RR59-60
VAB4 pp. 28–34, 52
VSB3 Ch. 3, 40, 41, pp. 21, 39, 40, 63, 247, 265, 274, 313, 335–336, 373–376, 430–432
VT Lessons 1, 7

EFFECTIVE DATE OF VALUATION (VALUATION DATE)

- Most engagements call for valuation as of a specific effective date:
  - Estate tax: date of death or "alternate valuation date" (six months later).
    Note: All property in estate must use the same valuation date.
  - Dissenting stockholder appraisal action: the day immediately preceding the triggering event (e.g., merger).
- Some valuation assignments could call for multiple valuation dates:
  - Series of gifts, if valuation engagement is done retrospectively.
  - Marital dissolution, which may be valued at date of marriage, date of separation, date of filing for divorce, date of trial, or other dates.

- In some cases, either internal or external factors may cause values to vary materially from one date to another, even over very short periods of time.
- Courts expect valuation work and data in as close time proximity as possible to effective valuation date:
  - Site visits.
  - Management interviews.
  - If standard is fair market value, public guideline company prices as of effective date, *not* an average over some period of time.
- Engagement letters normally specify that the valuation is applicable only to the effective date or dates specified in the engagement letter.

Effective Date References

ASA 201G p. 153
ASA 202G p. 153
ASA BVS p. 18
FBVI Ch. 1 p. 6
Guide 1503.1, 1505.33
IRS BV 2.2
VAB4 pp. 26–27, 612, 626, 819

PURPOSE OF VALUATION (INTENDED USE)

- As noted in Chapter 1, the intended use of the valuation usually determines the standard of value and sometimes mandates factors that must or may not be taken into consideration.
- Exhibit 3.2 gives examples of matching the purpose of the valuation with the applicable standard of value.
- Engagement letters usually state that valuation is valid only for the use or uses specified in the engagement letter (as well as only for the effective valuation date).

References Regarding Purpose of Engagement

BV201 "Defining the Appraisal Assignment," III pp. 16–19
BV203 Ch. 1 p. 13
FBVI Ch. 1 p. 9
Guide 204.10, 301.5
IBA1 A.7; IBA2 Ch. 4
IRS BV 2.2
NACVA Sect. 2
NACVA-CA Sects. 2 and 7, example
NACVA-BV Ch. 1, 9, example

Exhibit 3.2   Matching the Standard of Value with the Purpose of the Valuation

Purpose of Valuation	Applicable Standard of Value
Purchase or sale	Generally fair market value, but in many instances investment value, reflecting unique circumstances or motivations of a particular buyer or seller.
Gift, estate, and inheritance taxes and charitable contributions	Fair market value.
Divorce	No statutory standards of value. Courts have wide discretion to achieve equitable distribution. Requires careful study of relevant case law.
Buy-sell agreements	Parties can do anything they want. Very important that all parties to the agreement understand the valuation implications of the wording in the agreement.
Dissenting stockholder actions	Fair value in almost all states. Must read both relevant statute and case law to determine how interpreted in the particular state.
Minority oppression action	Generally, fair value in those states that address it at all. Not always interpreted the same as fair value for dissenting stockholder actions.
Employee stock ownership plans (ESOPs)	Fair market value.
Ad valorem (property) taxes	Generally, fair market value with varied nuances of interpretation. In many states, intangible portion of value excluded by statute.

Source: Shannon P. Pratt, Robert F. Reilly, and Robert P. Schweihs, *Valuing Small Businesses and Professional Practices*, 3rd ed., 1998. McGraw-Hill Companies. Used with permission.

USPAP SMT 9
VAB4 pp. 27–28, 34, 507
VSB3 Ch. 2 p. 20, Ch. 4 p. 63

REPRESENTATIONS

- Valuation engagements normally do not include auditing or investigation for possible fraud; for many valuation engagements, the appraiser may request a representation letter from the client, the company, or an attorney verifying the accuracy of some or all of the factual material and/or assumptions relied on.
- The appraiser also may request a letter of understanding and agreement with the terms and details of the engagement.

- After the preliminary report is rendered, the appraiser may require a representation letter to the effect that the client has read the report and all facts are accurate and no facts have been omitted that would materially affect the values.
- The engagement letter may state that the final report will contain a statement of contingent and limiting conditions similar to that provided with the engagement letter plus any other matters that arise during the course of the engagement.

CONTINGENT AND LIMITING CONDITIONS

- It is good practice to include the general statement of contingent and limiting conditions in both the engagement agreement and the final report.
- Exhibit 3.3 is a sample statement of contingent and limiting conditions.
- If additional contingent and limiting conditions arise during the course of the engagement (e.g., inadequate access to company data), it is a good idea to memorialize them in writing.

SCOPE OF WORK PRODUCT

Written Valuation Reports

A full narrative valuation opinion report typically includes:

- A valuation opinion letter or introductory section summarizing the appraisal procedures and the valuation conclusions.
- Company description.
- Several sections summarizing the relevant valuation theory, methodology, procedures, analyses, and conclusions (including financial statement analysis and relevant industry/economic analysis).
- A valuation synthesis and conclusion.
- An exhibit section presenting a summary of the quantitative and qualitative appraisal analyses. (Qualitative factors may be covered in general text.)
- A listing of the data and documents the appraiser relied on.
- A statement of the contingent and limiting conditions of the appraisal.
- An appraisal certification.
- The professional qualifications of the principal analysts.

Oral Reports and Testimony

Oral reports are expected to include the same analysis and supporting data as written reports. If subject to USPAP, the same minimum requirements for support as for written reports apply.

Exhibit 3.3   Statement of Contingent and Limiting Conditions

This appraisal is made subject to the following general contingent and limiting conditions:

1. We assume no responsibility for the legal description or matters including legal or title considerations. Title to the subject assets, properties, or business interests is assumed to be good and marketable unless otherwise stated.

2. The subject assets, properties, or business interests are appraised free and clear of any or all liens or encumbrances unless otherwise stated.

3. We assume responsible ownership and competent management with respect to the subject assets, properties, or business interests.

4. The information furnished by others is believed to be reliable. However, we issue no warranty or other form of assurance regarding its accuracy.

5. We assume no hidden or unapparent conditions regarding the subject assets, properties, or business interests.

6. We assume that there is full compliance with all applicable federal, state, and local regulations and laws unless the lack of compliance is stated, defined, and considered in the appraisal report.

7. We assume that all required licenses, certificates of occupancy, consents, or legislative or administrative authority from any local, state, or national government, or private entity or organization have been or can be obtained or reviewed for any use on which the opinion contained in this report is based.

8. Unless otherwise stated in this report, we did not observe, and we have no knowledge of, the existence of hazardous materials with regard to the subject assets, properties, or business interests. However, we are not qualified to detect such substances. We assume no responsibility for such conditions or for any expertise required to discover them.

9. Possession of this report does not carry with it the right of publication. It may not be used for any purpose by any person other than the client to whom it is addressed without our written consent, and, in any event, only with proper written qualifications and only in its entirety.

10. We, by reason of this opinion, are not required to furnish a complete valuation report, or to give testimony, or to be in attendance in court with reference to the assets, properties, or business interests in question unless arrangements have been previously made.

11. Neither all nor any part of the contents of this report shall be disseminated to the public through advertising, public relations, news, sales, or other media without our prior written consent and approval.

12. The analyses, opinions, and conclusions presented in this report apply to this engagement only and may not be used out of the context presented herein. This report is valid only for the effective date(s) specified herein and only for the purpose(s) specified herein.

Source: Shannon P. Pratt, Robert F. Reilly, and Robert P. Schweihs, *Valuing Small Businesses and Professional Practices*, 3rd ed., 1998, McGraw-Hill Companies. Used with permission.

Work Product References

FBVI Ch. 1 p. 11
FBVII Ch. 4 p. 8
Guide Ch. 9
IBA1 Ch. 4
IBA2 Ch. 12, 16
IBA7 Ch. 7, 11
IRS BV 4
NACVA-BV Ch. 8, 9
NACVA-CA Sect. 7
VAB4 pp. 35–36, Ch. 20
VSB 3 pp. 29–30, 33–36, Ch. 20
VT Lesson 16

SCHEDULING

- Clients and attorneys should be encouraged to bring the appraiser in as early as possible to provide guidance in structuring the engagement and to allow maximum lead time for the appraisal process.
- The engagement letter should indicate that meeting prescribed due dates depends on timely receipt of documents and necessary information.

FEES

Basis for Fees

- Fee arrangements allowed by USPAP:
  - Hourly.
  - Fixed fee.
  - Combination of fixed fee and time (e.g., fixed fee for written report; hourly for attorney meetings, testimony, testimony preparation, and review of opposing side's materials).
- Fee arrangements not allowed by USPAP:
  - Percentage of value.
  - Contingent on outcome.

Fee Terms

- Retainer payment usually required at time of retention; usually applied to final billing.
- Timeliness of collection:

- Engagement letter usually states that work will continue only if accounts are current.
- Completion of work product and release to client generally depends on all current fees collected. (appraiser would not wish to release work product if the work is incomplete.)
- Before testimony, all fees for work performed should be collected plus enough retainer to cover all expected trial time.

Note: The fee terms are extremely important, because the opposing attorney usually asks about fee collection. If it is not all collected, attorney may raise implication of payment being dependent on the outcome of trial.

INDEMNIFICATION

- Most engagement letters contain indemnification clauses protecting appraisers in case of lawsuits regarding appraisal.
- Indemnification is generally accepted practice with national appraisal and accounting firms.

RESOLUTION OF DISPUTES

- Most engagement letters have clauses regarding resolution of disputes.
- Dispute clauses often specify procedures for arbitration. (Note, however, that the arbitrating clause may void applicability of a malpractice policy.)

Engagement Letter References

BV201 p. 18
BV202 pp. 83–84
BV203 p. 18
Guide 301.5, Section 304, 1313.18, App. 3B, VAL-4
IBA1 A.2, A.7, A.11, Ch. 4
IBA2 Ch. 2, 16, 18
IBA3 B.1
IBA7 Ch. 6
NACVA Sect. 1, 2, 7
NACVA-BV Ch. 2, 8, 9
RR59-60
VAB4 pp. 37–38, 862
VSB3 pp. 21, 28, 46–49, 63, 247, 265, 274–276, 313–314, 335–336, 373–376, 430–432; Ch. 2, 3, 40, 41, 44

Chapter 4

Litigation Service Engagements

By Michael J. Mard, CPA/ABV, ASA

Professional Standards and Rules
    American Institute of Certified Public Accountants (AICPA)
    American Society of Appraisers (ASA)
    Institute of Business Appraisers (IBA)
    National Association of Certified Valuation Analysts (NACVA)
Legal Process and Terms
    Federal Court System
    State Court Systems
    Alternative Dispute Resolution
        Arbitration
        Minitrials
        Mediation
    Pleadings
Discovery
    Fundamental Processes of Discovery
        Interrogatories
        Document Requests
        Depositions
    Tools to Facilitate Discovery
        Requests for Admission
        Subpoenas
Steps in the Trial Process
    Hearings
    Final Hearings
    Triers of Fact
Testimony
    Voir Dire

Direct Examination
Cross-Examination
Redirect Examination
Re–Cross-Examination
Hypothetical Questions
Legal Standards and Rules
Federal Rules of Evidence
Federal Rules of Civil Procedure

An expert's goal should be to clearly and concisely present relevant facts and reasonable opinions in a manner that truly assists the trier of fact. A qualified expert's testimony may be the most demanding professional service a business valuator can provide.

A business appraiser offering litigation services must be classified as either a consultant (providing advice but not offering opinion) or an expert (offering opinion). A business appraiser offering litigation services relative to a business appraisal is ethically bound by professional and legal standards and rules.

PROFESSIONAL STANDARDS AND RULES

The ethical standards applicable to an accredited member of a professional organization obviously apply to the valuator.

American Institute of Certified Public Accountants (AICPA)

The CPA practicing as a business valuator offering expert testimony must adhere to a number of professional standards and rules. These standards include the practitioner's relevant state board of accountancy rules and regulations, which extend from appraisal standards to prohibitions for litigation fees based on commissions. Members of the AICPA are bound by the AICPA's standards and rules, which include:

- Statement on Standards for Consulting Services No. 1 promulgated by the management advisory services division of the AICPA.
- The AICPA Code of Professional Conduct rules 201 and 102.
- Business valuation standards will be released in 2003 and will provide detailed guidance to CPAs with regard to the practice of business valuation.

Each of these standards requires the CPA to perform litigation and consulting services while adhering to the following:

- Professional competence—undertake only those professional services that the member or the member's firm can reasonably expect to be completed with professional competence.
- Due professional care—exercise due professional care in any performance of professional services.
- Planning and supervision—adequately plan and supervise the performance of professional services.
- Sufficient relevant data—obtain sufficient relevant data to afford a reasonable basis for conclusion or recommendation in relation to any professional services performed.

In addition, the AICPA Code of Professional Conduct rule 202, applicable to all consulting services, requires a clear relationship with the client as follows:

- Client interest—serve the client interest by seeking to accomplish the objectives established by the understanding with the client while maintaining integrity and objectivity.
- Understanding with the client—establish with the client a written or oral understanding about the responsibilities of the parties and the nature, scope, and limitations of services to be performed and modify the understanding if circumstances require significant change during the engagement period.
- Communication with the client—inform the client of conflicts of interest pursuant to interpretations concerning the scope or benefits of the engagement and significant engagement findings or events.

The AICPA Code of Professional Conduct rule 102 is binding on the CPA. In the performance of any professional service, a member shall maintain objectivity and integrity, shall be free of conflicts of interest, and shall not knowingly misrepresent facts or subordinate his or her judgment to others.

Objectivity is the quality or state of being free from the influence of emotion, surmise, and bias. Integrity is the quality or state of being undivided, of adhering firmly to a code or standard of values. Independence is the quality or state of being free from the influence, guidance, or control of others.

Article IV of the Code of Professional Conduct differentiates between *objectivity* and *independence* as follows:

> Objectivity is a state of mind, a quality that lends value to a member's services. It is a distinguishing feature of the profession. The principle of objectivity imposes the obligation to be impartial, intellectually honest, and free of conflicts of interest. Independence precludes relationships that may appear to impair a member's objectivity in rendering attestation services.

For members of the AICPA, *independence* is a technical term applying to attest (audit) engagements in which the member is free of influence by familial relations or financial interest with the attest client. For litigation services, however, the trier of fact relates independence with intellectual honesty, both apparent and actual. Most often in a court of law, a lack of independence refers to a lack of objectivity.

Additional background and requirements applicable to the licensee are provided by the AICPA Consulting Engagement Practice Aid Special Report 93-1, *Application of AICPA Professional Standards in the Performance of Litigation Services,* and the AICPA Consulting Engagement Practice Aid Special Report 93-2, *Conflicts of Interest in Litigation Services Engagements.* A flow chart delineating the CPA's responsibilities related to conflicts of interest is presented as Exhibit 4.1.

The AICPA Small Business Consulting Practice Aid 93-3, *Conducting a Valuation of a Closely Held Business,* provides the CPA performing a business valuation with a good introduction to the fundamentals necessary for this practice area. This practice aid has become an official rule and regulation for CPAs in the state of Florida.

The AICPA Technical Consulting Practice Aid 93-4, *Providing Litigation Services,* assists the CPA to understand the legal process, terms, standards, and rules applicable to a CPA performing consulting services in a litigation environment and expert testimony.

American Society of Appraisers (ASA)

- Ethical Standards
- Appraisal Standards

    (See Chapter 2.)

Institute of Business Appraisers (IBA)

- Ethical Standards
- Report Writing Standards
- Technical Standards

    (See Chapter 2.)

National Association of Certified Valuation Analysts (NACVA)

- General and Ethical Standards
- Development Standards
- Reporting Standards

Note: Since a person must be a certified public accountant (CPA) to be an accredited member of NACVA, these members also are bound by the standards of the AICPA. (See previous section; see also Chapter 2.)

LEGAL PROCESS AND TERMS

In the legal arena, an expert is a witness—qualified by knowledge, skill, experience, training, or education—who may be allowed to testify in the form of an opinion if the scientific, technical, or other specialized knowledge will assist the trier of fact to understand the evidence or to determine the fact in issue. A testifying expert's work is fully discoverable, and the expert is expected to testify at trial. Conversely, a consultant's work and work papers generally are considered attorney work product and generally are not discoverable since the consultant's work is used to assist the attorney. Because a consultant is assisting the attorney, the consultant is acting as an advocate and generally is not allowed to testify or offer opinion.

Our judicial system, the ultimate arbiter of disputes, can be divided into three categories: the federal courts, the state courts, and alternative dispute resolution.

Federal Court System

The federal court system is divided into 12 circuits including the District of Columbia, with each circuit supported by a federal district court. The federal district court renders decisions that can be appealed to the federal court of appeals for that circuit. If a party disagrees with the federal court of appeals decision, it can petition the U.S. Supreme Court to review the decision. However, a party has no absolute right of appeal to the U.S. Supreme Court, because the Court generally accepts only cases relevant to all U.S. citizens.

Exceptions to the federal circuit court process include special federal courts requiring specialized knowledge:

- *Tax Court:* Exists only to resolve disputes between the Internal Revenue Service (IRS) and taxpayers. The procedural requirements for filing in Tax Court differ from those in district courts (i.e., the taxpayer can dispute the amount owed before paying the tax). However, the taxpayer carries the burden of proof related to the dispute.
- *Patent Court of Appeals:* Federal district courts hear all patent issues, but appeals from district court decisions on patent cases do not go up to the corresponding circuit court of appeals but rather to the special U.S. Court of Appeals for the federal circuit in Washington, D.C.
- *U.S. Court of Claims:* Created to hear claims against the United States based on the Constitution, acts of Congress, regulation of an executive department, contracts with the United States, or damages in tort cases. In some cases it also hears federal tax matters, in which the taxpayer has already paid the amount of tax levied.
- *Bankruptcy Courts:* Each federal district has a corresponding bankruptcy court to hear cases pertinent to Title 11 of the U.S. Code, which covers bankruptcy matters.

Exhibit 4.1   Conflict of Interest Decision Tree

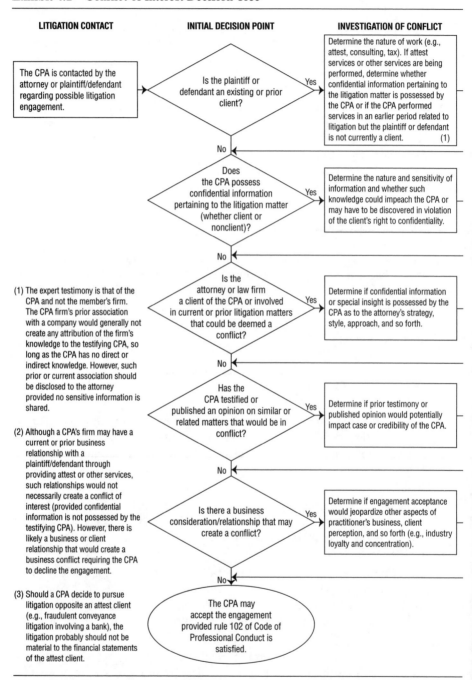

LITIGATION CONTACT | INITIAL DECISION POINT | INVESTIGATION OF CONFLICT

The CPA is contacted by the attorney or plaintiff/defendant regarding possible litigation engagement.

Is the plaintiff or defendant an existing or prior client?

Yes → Determine the nature of work (e.g., attest, consulting, tax). If attest services or other services are being performed, determine whether confidential information pertaining to the litigation matter is possessed by the CPA or if the CPA performed services in an earlier period related to litigation but the plaintiff or defendant is not currently a client.   (1)

No

Does the CPA possess confidential information pertaining to the litigation matter (whether client or nonclient)?

Yes → Determine the nature and sensitivity of information and whether such knowledge could impeach the CPA or may have to be discovered in violation of the client's right to confidentiality.

No

(1) The expert testimony is that of the CPA and not the member's firm. The CPA firm's prior association with a company would generally not create any attribution of the firm's knowledge to the testifying CPA, so long as the CPA has no direct or indirect knowledge. However, such prior or current association should be disclosed to the attorney provided no sensitive information is shared.

Is the attorney or law firm a client of the CPA or involved in current or prior litigation matters that could be deemed a conflict?

Yes → Determine if confidential information or special insight is possessed by the CPA as to the attorney's strategy, style, approach, and so forth.

No

Has the CPA testified or published an opinion on similar or related matters that would be in conflict?

Yes → Determine if prior testimony or published opinion would potentially impact case or credibility of the CPA.

No

(2) Although a CPA's firm may have a current or prior business relationship with a plaintiff/defendant through providing attest or other services, such relationships would not necessarily create a conflict of interest (provided confidential information is not possessed by the testifying CPA). However, there is likely to be a business or client relationship that would create a business conflict requiring the CPA to decline the engagement.

Is there a business consideration/relationship that may create a conflict?

Yes → Determine if engagement acceptance would jeopardize other aspects of practitioner's business, client perception, and so forth (e.g., industry loyalty and concentration).

No

(3) Should a CPA decide to pursue litigation opposite an attest client (e.g., fraudulent conveyance litigation involving a bank), the litigation probably should not be material to the financial statements of the attest client.

The CPA may accept the engagement provided rule 102 of Code of Professional Conduct is satisfied.

Source: "Conflicts of Interest in Litigation Services Engagements chart," *AICPA Consulting Engagement Practice Aid Special Report No. 93-2.* Copyright © 1993 by the American Institute of Certified Public Accountants, Inc. Reprinted with permission.

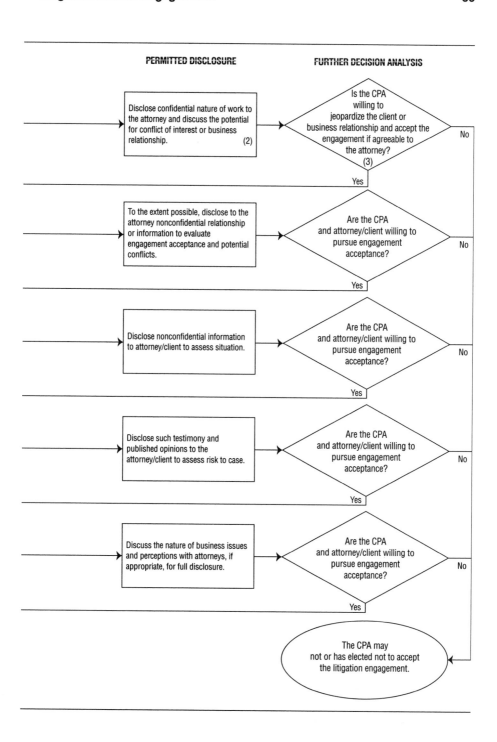

PERMITTED DISCLOSURE

FURTHER DECISION ANALYSIS

Disclose confidential nature of work to the attorney and discuss the potential for conflict of interest or business relationship. (2)

Is the CPA willing to jeopardize the client or business relationship and accept the engagement if agreeable to the attorney? (3)

No

Yes

To the extent possible, disclose to the attorney nonconfidential relationship or information to evaluate engagement acceptance and potential conflicts.

Are the CPA and attorney/client willing to pursue engagement acceptance?

No

Yes

Disclose nonconfidential information to attorney/client to assess situation.

Are the CPA and attorney/client willing to pursue engagement acceptance?

No

Yes

Disclose such testimony and published opinions to the attorney/client to assess risk to case.

Are the CPA and attorney/client willing to pursue engagement acceptance?

No

Yes

Discuss the nature of business issues and perceptions with attorneys, if appropriate, for full disclosure.

Are the CPA and attorney/client willing to pursue engagement acceptance?

No

Yes

The CPA may not or has elected not to accept the litigation engagement.

State Court Systems

Similar to the federal system, state court systems generally have three levels: trial courts, courts of appeal, and the state supreme court. The court systems are structured to have limited and unlimited jurisdiction. Limited jurisdiction may include limiting civil damages to some dollar amount and criminal cases to misdemeanors. Unlimited jurisdiction includes civil courts for monetary damages exceeding the limits of the lower court or for criminal matters including felonies.

Alternative Dispute Resolution

Alternative dispute resolution has come into vogue in recent years as a way to resolve disputes while avoiding the often slow and generally expensive court system. The alternative dispute resolution process is gaining in popularity for two prominent reasons: the parties have some influence over selecting who will decide the matter and decisions remain private. The three most popular methods of alternative dispute resolution are arbitration, minitrials, and mediation.

Arbitration

Arbitration can be binding or nonbinding:

- *Binding arbitration:* The arbitrator's decision is final and binding on the parties (subject to the appellate process agreed to beforehand).
- *Nonbinding arbitration:* The arbitrator's decision is influential and may facilitate settlement; generally the arbitrator's nonbinding decision is a written one forwarded to the judge who has jurisdiction over the matter.

Minitrials

Minitrials have no formal rules of procedure or evidence but rather depend on commonsense arguments and a few key witnesses. This process is most successful for business disputes in which the person hearing the matter is experienced in the subject business.

Mediation

Mediation is considerably different from the trial-like processes of arbitration and minitrials. Mediation involves a process of recognizing strengths and weaknesses, and a mediator works to reconcile the differences and resolve the dispute by compromise. The process can result in a binding agreement. However, if an agreement is not reached, no documents or verbal statements that are designated "For Mediation Purposes Only" can be used against either party at trial.

Pleadings

The legal process starts with pleadings, which have three components:

1. A *complaint* presents the plaintiff's position of being wronged; the complaint lists the individuals who committed the wrong, names the jurisdiction, specifies the laws and legal theories allowing the plaintiff to recover damages, and states whether the plaintiff demands a jury.
2. A *demurrer* is a defendant's response to a plaintiff's complaint when the defendant believes the plaintiff has not met the legal standard for a proper complaint; a demurrer asks the judge to dismiss the complaint because there is no issue of law and no legal liability of the defendant.
3. An *answer* is a formal response by the defendant to the plaintiff's complaint.

DISCOVERY

Discovery, the process of gathering facts and formulating theories, takes place between the filing of the original pleadings and the trial.

Fundamental Processes of Discovery

Interrogatories

Interrogatories are questions the plaintiff or defendant can ask of the other party. These questions must be answered in writing and under oath.

Document Requests

Document requests require one side to provide documents to the other side as long as the request specifies the name of the document and the document is relevant to the issue being litigated.

Depositions

A deposition is an oral testimony of a witness under oath questioned by an attorney. Generally the opposing attorney demands the deposition testimony from an expert witness.

Tools to Facilitate Discovery

Several tools allow attorneys to facilitate discovery.

Requests for Admission

Requests for admission help narrow the factual issues to be litigated. If both parties agree to certain facts before trial, these admissions do not have to be argued and decided by the judge.

Subpoenas

Subpoenas are authorized by an attorney and require the person subpoenaed to appear in court or at a deposition. There are two types of subpoenas:

1. *Subpoena ad testificandum* commands a person to appear and testify as a witness.
2. *Subpoena duces tecum* commands a person to produce documents (e.g., work papers) at the deposition or to the court.

Lawyers, under the power granted from their state licenses, have the power to issue subpoenas. Subpoenas should be distinguished from summons, which are writs signed by a judge directing a sheriff or other officer of the court to notify an individual to appear in court. Subpoenas are more easily quashed (i.e., challenged) than summonses.

References: Legal Documents and Discovery

Guide Sections 1301, 1304
IBA7 Ch. 2, 3, 8, 13, 15
Lawyer Ch. 4
NACVA Sect. 2
NACVA-BV Ch. 8
VAB4 pp. 865–868, 871–872, 880–882
VSB3 Ch. 41 (marital), 46, 48

STEPS IN THE TRIAL PROCESS

The trial process involves a number of steps, including hearings, final hearings, and triers of fact.

Hearings

Hearings are single-issue disputes held in abbreviated fashion in front of the judge by the two attorneys.

One common type of hearing that appraisers may be involved in is a hearing on a *motion in limine* to exclude the testimony and report of the appraiser based on:

- Federal Rule of Evidence 702.
- *Daubert v. Merrel Dow Pharmaceuticals, Inc.,* 509 U.S. 579, 113 S.Ct. 2786 (1993).
- *Kumho Tire Company v. Carmichael,* 526 U.S. 137, 119 S.Ct. 1167 (1999).

The four *Daubert* factors that are considered in determining the admissibility of an expert's report and testimony are:

- Whether the theory or technique can be (or has been) tested.
- Whether the theory or technique has been subjected to peer review and publication.
- Whether there is a known potential rate of error.
- Whether the theory or technique enjoys general acceptance within the relevant professional community.

Final Hearings

Final hearings are conducted by the judge and allow the hearing of all relevant testimony. The judge renders decisions based on findings of fact in final hearings.

Triers of Fact

The two basic types are judge and jury:

1. The *judge* in a *bench trial* has the final authority, including rendering the findings of fact.
2. A *jury* renders the ultimate findings of fact based on the evidence the judge determines the jury will use.

TESTIMONY

A business valuator offering expert opinion testimony should be aware of certain rules of evidence, including those for voir dire, direct examination, cross-examination, redirect examination, re–cross-examination, and hypothetical questions.

Voir Dire

Voir dire, strictly interpreted, means to inquire. However, the term generally is used by the court to allow an opposing attorney to question a witness after the expert's qualifications have been presented to the court but before the court has decided to qualify the witness as an expert. Under voir dire, the opposing attorney may challenge the witness's qualifications, including education, skill, and experience.

Direct Examination

Direct examination is the first examination of a witness by the attorney for the party who is calling the witness. Through this direct testimony, the expert offers the opinion and the facts and processes on which the opinion is based. Through direct examination, the expert's written report, if any, is offered into evidence and should contain:

- A complete statement of all opinions.
- The basis and facts for all opinions.
- Data or other information considered by the expert.
- Exhibits used in support of the opinion.
- The expert's qualifications.
- The expert's signature or identification of the responsible expert.

During direct examination the attorney may not ask leading questions that suggest the answer but must ask open-ended questions. Generally, a fact witness may not base conclusions on hearsay, which is evidence not based on the witness's personal knowledge but rather on something the witness heard someone say (rumor). A qualified expert may base the opinion on evidence gained from interviewing others. The information gained must be the type that experts in the field normally rely on (this is known as the *hearsay exception*).

Cross-Examination

Cross-examination is a series of questions asked by the opposing attorney based on issues raised in direct examination of the witness. Cross-examination rules permit the attorney to ask leading questions that suggest the answer. Further, cross-examination rules allow the attorney to be forceful and to introduce the expert's prior deposition or other testimony or writings in an attempt to impeach (i.e., discredit) the expert.

Redirect Examination

Redirect examination is the process immediately following cross-examination in which the expert's client's attorney may clarify additional issues, but only those brought up in cross-examination. The attorney may not ask about issues not covered in cross-examination.

Re–Cross-Examination

Re–cross-examination follows redirect examination and again is limited to issues raised in redirect examination.

Hypothetical Questions

During testimony an expert may be asked hypothetical questions, which are a combination of facts and circumstances represented by the attorney as assumed truth. The attorney then asks the expert a question related to these assumed facts and the expert must respond. That response can be used by the attorney to support or contradict the expert's opinion on direct examination.

After the plaintiff has presented all of his or her evidence, the defense can move for a directed verdict in which the court may decide to render a summary judgment, essentially recognizing that the plaintiff's case was not proven and the defendant wins by default.

LEGAL STANDARDS AND RULES

Federal Rules of Evidence

An expert testifying in state court must adhere to that jurisdiction's legal standards and rules, which are typically modeled after the Federal Rules of Evidence:

Rule 701—Opinion Testimony by Lay Witnesses

If the witness is not testifying as an expert, the witness's testimony in the form of opinions or inferences is limited to those opinions or inferences which are (a) rationally based on the perception of the witness, (b) helpful to a clear understanding of the witness's testimony or the determination of a fact in issue, and (c) not based on scientific, technical, or other specialized knowledge within the scope of Rule 702.

Rule 702—Testimony by Expert

If scientific, technical, or other specialized knowledge will assist the trier of fact to understand the evidence or to determine a fact in issue, a witness qualified as an expert by knowledge, skill, experience, training, or education, may testify thereto in the form of an opinion or otherwise, if (1) the testimony is based upon sufficient facts or data, (2) the testimony is the product of reliable principles and methods, and (3) the witness has applied the principles and methods reliably to the facts of the case.

Rule 703—Bases of Opinion Testimony by Experts

The facts or data in the particular case upon which an expert bases an opinion or inference may be those perceived by or made known to the expert at or before the hearing. If of a type reasonably relied upon by experts in the particular field in forming opinions or inferences upon the subject, the facts or data need not be admissible in evidence in order for the opinion or inference to be admitted. Facts or data that are otherwise inadmissible shall not be disclosed to the jury by the proponent of the opinion or inference unless the court determines that their probative value in assisting the jury to evaluate the expert's opinion substantially outweighs their prejudicial effect.

Rule 704—Opinion on Ultimate Issue

(a) Except as provided in subdivision (b), testimony in the form of an opinion or inference otherwise admissible is not objectionable because it embraces an ultimate issue to be decided by the trier of fact.

(b) No expert witness testifying with respect to the mental state or condition of a defendant in a criminal case may state an opinion or inference as to whether the defendant did or did not have the mental state or condition constituting an element of the crime charged or of a defense thereto. Such ultimate issues are matters for the trier of fact alone.

Rule 705—Disclosure of Facts or Data Underlying Expert Opinion

The expert may testify in terms of opinion or inference and give reasons therefor without first testifying to the underlying facts or data, unless the court requires otherwise. The expert may in any event be required to disclose the underlying facts or data on cross-examination.

Rule 706—Court-Appointed Experts

(a) Appointment. The court may on its own motion or on the motion of any party enter an order to show cause why expert witnesses should not be appointed, and may request the parties to submit nominations. The court may appoint any expert witnesses agreed upon by the parties, and may appoint expert witnesses of its own selection. An expert witness shall not be appointed by the court unless the witness consents to act. A witness so appointed shall be informed of the witness's duties by the court in writing, a copy of which shall be filed with the clerk, or at a conference in which the parties shall have opportunity to participate. A witness so appointed shall advise the parties of the witness's findings, if any; the witness's deposition may be taken by any party; and the witness may be called to testify by the court or any party. The witness shall be subject to cross-examination by each party, including a party calling the witness.

(b) Compensation. Expert witnesses so appointed are entitled to reasonable compensation in whatever sum the court may allow. The compensation thus fixed is payable from funds which may be provided by law in criminal cases and civil actions and proceedings involving just compensation under the Fifth Amendment. In other civil actions and proceedings the compensation shall be paid by the parties in such proportion and at such time as the court directs, and thereafter charged in like manner as other costs.

(c) Disclosure of appointment. In the exercise of its discretion, the court may authorize disclosure to the jury of the fact that the court appointed the expert witness.

(d) Parties' experts of own selection. Nothing in this rule limits the parties in calling expert witnesses of their own selection.

Federal Rules of Civil Procedure

On December 1, 1993, as approved by the U.S. Supreme Court and Congress, new Federal Rules of Civil Procedure became effective. These new rules reflect the most sweeping changes in more than 50 years and were intended to reduce the effect of trial by ambush by requiring full disclosure by the expert offering an opinion. The rule as it particularly applies to experts is provided in its entirety in Appendix B, but significant sections include the following:

Rule 26(a)(2)(B)—experts may need to submit signed written reports that address:

- A complete statement of all opinions expressed and the underlying bases and reasons.
- The data or other information considered by the witness in forming the opinions.
- Any exhibits to be used as a summary of or support for the opinions.
- Qualifications of the witness, including a list of all publications authored by the witness within the preceding 10 years.
- Compensation to be paid for the study and testimony.
- A listing of any other cases in which the witness has testified as an expert at trial or by deposition within the preceding four years.

The timing of such reports is:

- At the times and in the sequence directed by the court, or
- Absent a stipulation or court order, at least 90 days before trial or, for rebuttal evidence, 30 days after disclosure by the other party.

Rule 26(e)(1)—the expert has a duty to supplement a written report or deposition:

- The expert also must supplement if in some material respect the information disclosed is incomplete or incorrect or if the additional or correct information has not been otherwise made known to the other parties during the discovery process or in writing.
- Such supplements shall be made at appropriate intervals but in any event must be completed at least 30 days before trial.

The complete text of Federal Rules of Civil Procedure Rule 26 is provided in Appendix B.

References for Litigation Service Engagements

FBVII Ch. 5

Guide Ch. 13 (litigation support services)

IBA7 Ch. 1, 2, 8, 10, 14

Lawyer Ch. 4

NACVA Sect. 2

NACVA-BV Ch. 8

VAB4 Ch. 20 (writing the business valuation report), Ch. 21 (sample report), Ch. 22 (reviewing a business valuation report), Ch. 39 (litigation support services), Ch. 40 (expert testimony)

VSB3 Ch. 40 (buyouts and dissolutions), Ch. 41 (marital dissolution), Ch. 46 (litigation), Ch. 47 (damages), Ch. 48 (arbitration/mediation)

PART II

Terminology and Notation

Chapter 5

International Glossary of Business Valuation Terms

The second edition of the International Glossary of Business Valuation Terms *is now out. It contains definitions of 38 additional terms (not in the original edition and denoted here by an asterisk). Definitions of only two terms are changed from the original edition, and the changes are only to clarify the wording, not changing the meaning. The glossary is a joint effort of the American Institute of Certified Public Accountants, the American Society of Appraisers, the Canadian Institute of Chartered Business Valuators, the Institute of Business Appraisers, and the National Association of Certified Valuation Analysts.*

—Shannon Pratt

To enhance and sustain the quality of business valuations for the benefit of the profession and its clientele, the below-identified societies and organizations have adopted the definitions for the terms included in this glossary:

- American Institute of Certified Public Accountants
- American Society of Appraisers
- Canadian Institute of Chartered Business Valuators
- Institute of Business Appraisers
- National Association of Certified Valuation Analysts

The performance of business valuation services requires a high degree of skill and imposes upon the valuation professional a duty to communicate the valuation process and conclusion in a manner that is clear and not misleading. This duty is advanced through the use of terms whose meanings are clearly established and consistently applied throughout the profession.

If, in the opinion of the business valuation professional, one or more of these terms needs to be used in a manner that materially departs from the enclosed definitions, it is recommended that the term be defined as used within that valuation engagement.

This glossary has been developed to provide guidance to business valuation practitioners that constitutes the competent and careful determination of value and, more particularly, the communication of how that value was determined.

Note: The current version of the glossary is available at the Free Downloads section of *BVResources.com*[sm]

Departure from this glossary is not intended to provide a basis for civil liability and should not be presumed to create evidence that any duty has been breached.

*Adjusted Book Value Method—A method within the asset approach whereby all assets and liabilities (including off-balance sheet, intangible, and contingent) are adjusted to their fair market values. *[Note: In Canada on a going concern basis.]*

*Adjusted Net Asset Method—*See* **Adjusted Book Value Method.**

Appraisal—*See* **Valuation.**

Appraisal Approach—*See* **Valuation Approach.**

Appraisal Date—*See* **Valuation Date.**

Appraisal Method—*See* **Valuation Method.**

Appraisal Procedure—*See* **Valuation Procedure.**

*Arbitrage Pricing Theory—A multivariate model for estimating the cost of equity capital, which incorporates several systematic risk factors.

Asset (Asset-Based) Approach—A general way of determining a value indication of a business, business ownership interest, or security using one or more methods based on the value of the assets net of liabilities.

Beta—A measure of systematic risk of a stock; the tendency of a stock's price to correlate with changes in a specific index.

Blockage Discount—An amount or percentage deducted from the current market price of a publicly traded stock to reflect the decrease in the per-share value of a block of stock that is of a size that could not be sold in a reasonable period of time given normal trading volume.

*Book Value—*See* **Net Book Value.**

Business—*See* **Business Enterprise.**

Business Enterprise—A commercial, industrial, service, or investment entity (or a combination thereof) pursuing an economic activity.

*Business Risk—The degree of uncertainty of realizing expected future returns of the business resulting from factors other than financial leverage. *See* **Financial Risk.**

Business Valuation—The act or process of determining the value of a business enterprise or ownership interest therein.

Capital Asset Pricing Model (CAPM)—A model in which the cost of capital for any stock or portfolio of stocks equals a risk-free rate plus a risk premium that is proportionate to the systematic risk of the stock or portfolio.

Capitalization—A conversion of a single period of economic benefits into value.

Capitalization Factor—Any multiple or divisor used to convert anticipated economic benefits of a single period into value.

***Capitalization of Earnings Method**—A method within the income approach whereby economic benefits for a representative single period are converted to value through division by a capitalization rate.

Capitalization Rate—Any divisor (usually expressed as a percentage) used to convert anticipated economic benefits of a single period into value.

Capital Structure—The composition of the invested capital of a business enterprise, the mix of debt and equity financing.

Cash Flow—Cash that is generated over a period of time by an asset, group of assets, or business enterprise. It may be used in a general sense to encompass various levels of specifically defined cash flows. When the term is used, it should be supplemented by a qualifier (for example, "discretionary" or "operating") and a specific definition in the given valuation context.

***Common Size Statements**—Financial statements in which each line is expressed as a percentage of the total. On the balance sheet, each line item is shown as a percentage of total assets, and on the income statement, each item is expressed as a percentage of sales.

Control—The power to direct the management and policies of a business enterprise.

Control Premium—An amount or a percentage by which the pro rata value of a controlling interest exceeds the pro rata value of a noncontrolling interest in a business enterprise, to reflect the power of control.

Cost Approach—A general way of determining a value indication of an individual asset by quantifying the amount of money required to replace the future service capability of that asset.

Cost of Capital—The expected rate of return that the market requires in order to attract funds to a particular investment.

***Debt-free**—*We discourage the use of this term. See* **Invested Capital.**

Discount for Lack of Control—An amount or percentage deducted from the pro rata share of value of 100% of an equity interest in a business to reflect the absence of some or all of the powers of control.

Discount for Lack of Marketability—An amount or percentage deducted from the value of an ownership interest to reflect the relative absence of marketability.

***Discount for Lack of Voting Rights**—An amount or percentage deducted from the per-share value of a minority interest voting share to reflect the absence of voting rights.

Discount Rate—A rate of return used to convert a future monetary sum into present value.

***Discounted Cash Flow Method**—A method within the income approach whereby the present value of future expected net cash flows is calculated using a discount rate.

*Discounted Future Earnings Method—A method within the income approach whereby the present value of future expected economic benefits is calculated using a discount rate.

*Economic Benefits—Inflows such as revenues, net income, net cash flows, etc.

Economic Life—The period of time over which property may generate economic benefits.

Effective Date—*See* **Valuation Date.**

Enterprise—*See* **Business Enterprise.**

*Equity—The owner's interest in property after deduction of all liabilities.

Equity Net Cash Flows—Those cash flows available to pay out to equity holders (in the form of dividends) after funding operations of the business enterprise, making necessary capital investments, and increasing or decreasing debt financing.

Equity Risk Premium—A rate of return added to a risk-free rate to reflect the additional risk of equity instruments over risk-free instruments (a component of the cost of equity capital or equity discount rate).

Excess Earnings—That amount of anticipated economic benefits that exceeds an appropriate rate of return on the value of a selected asset base (often net tangible assets) used to generate those anticipated economic benefits.

Excess Earnings Method—A specific way of determining a value indication of a business, business ownership interest, or security determined as the sum of (a) the value of the assets derived by capitalizing excess earnings and (b) the value of the selected asset base. Also frequently used to value intangible assets. *See* **Excess Earnings.**

Fair Market Value—The price, expressed in terms of cash equivalents, at which property would change hands between a hypothetical willing and able buyer and a hypothetical willing and able seller, acting at arms length in an open and unrestricted market, when neither is under compulsion to buy or sell and when both have reasonable knowledge of the relevant facts. *[Note: In Canada, the term "price" should be replaced with the term "highest price."]*

*Fairness Opinion—An opinion as to whether or not the consideration in a transaction is fair from a financial point of view.

*Financial Risk—The degree of uncertainty of realizing expected future returns of the business resulting from financial leverage. *See* **Business Risk.**

Forced Liquidation Value—Liquidation value at which the asset or assets are sold as quickly as possible, such as at an auction.

*Free Cash Flow—*We discourage the use of this term. See* **Net Cash Flow.**

Going Concern—An ongoing operating business enterprise.

Going Concern Value—The value of a business enterprise that is expected to continue to operate into the future. The intangible elements of going concern value result from factors such as having a trained workforce, an operational plant, and the necessary licenses, systems, and procedures in place.

Goodwill—That intangible asset arising as a result of name, reputation, customer loyalty, location, products, and similar factors not separately identified.

Goodwill Value—The value attributable to goodwill.

***Guideline Public Company Method**—A method within the market approach whereby market multiples are derived from market prices of stocks of companies that are engaged in the same or similar lines of business, and that are actively traded on a free and open market.

Income (Income-Based) Approach—A general way of determining a value indication of a business, business ownership interest, security, or intangible asset using one or more methods that convert anticipated economic benefits into a present single amount.

Intangible Assets—Nonphysical assets such as franchises, trademarks, patents, copyrights, goodwill, equities, mineral rights, securities, and contracts (as distinguished from physical assets) that grant rights and privileges, and have value for the owner.

***Internal Rate of Return**—A discount rate at which the present value of the future cash flows of the investment equals the cost of the investment.

***Intrinsic Value**—The value that an investor considers, on the basis of an evaluation or available facts, to be the "true" or "real" value that will become the market value when other investors reach the same conclusion. When the term applies to options, it is the difference between the exercise price or strike price of an option and the market value of the underlying security.

Invested Capital—The sum of equity and debt in a business enterprise. Debt is typically (a) all interest-bearing debt or (b) long-term interest-bearing debt. When the term is used, it should be supplemented by a specific definition in the given valuation context.

Invested Capital Net Cash Flows—Those cash flows available to pay out to equity holders (in the form of dividends) and debt investors (in the form of principal and interest) after funding operations of the business enterprise and making necessary capital investments.

Investment Risk—The degree of uncertainty as to the realization of expected returns.

Investment Value—The value to a particular investor based on individual investment requirements and expectations. *[Note: in Canada, the term used is "value to the owner."]*

Key Person Discount—An amount or percentage deducted from the value of an ownership interest to reflect the reduction in value resulting from the actual or potential loss of a key person in a business enterprise.

Levered Beta—The beta reflecting a capital structure that includes debt.

***Limited Appraisal**—The act or process of determining the value of a business, business ownership interest, security, or intangible asset with limitations in analyses, procedures, or scope.

Liquidity—The ability to quickly convert property to cash or pay a liability.

Liquidation Value—The net amount that would be realized if the business is terminated and the assets are sold piecemeal. Liquidation can be either "orderly" or "forced."

Majority Control—The degree of control provided by a majority position.

Majority Interest—An ownership interest greater than 50% of the voting interest in a business enterprise.

Market (Market-Based) Approach—A general way of determining a value indication of a business, business ownership interest, security, or intangible asset by using one or more methods that compare the subject to similar businesses, business ownership interests, securities, or intangible assets that have been sold.

*****Market Capitalization of Equity**—The share price of a publicly traded stock multiplied by the number of shares outstanding.

*****Market Capitalization of Invested Capital**—The market capitalization of equity plus the market value of the debt component of invested capital.

*****Market Multiple**—The market value of a company's stock or invested capital divided by a company measure (such as economic benefits, number of customers).

Marketability—The ability to quickly convert property to cash at minimal cost.

Marketability Discount—*See* **Discount for Lack of Marketability.**

*****Merger and Acquisition Method**—A method within the market approach whereby pricing multiples are derived from transactions of significant interests in companies engaged in the same or similar lines of business.

*****Midyear Discounting**—A convention used in the Discounted Future Earnings Method that reflects economic benefits being generated at midyear, approximating the effect of economic benefits being generated evenly throughout the year.

Minority Discount—A discount for lack of control applicable to a minority interest.

Minority Interest—An ownership interest less than 50% of the voting interest in a business enterprise.

*****Multiple**—The inverse of the capitalization rate.

Net Book Value—With respect to a business enterprise, the difference between total assets (net of accumulated depreciation, depletion, and amortization) and total liabilities as they appear on the balance sheet (synonymous with shareholder's equity). With respect to a specific asset, the capitalized cost less accumulated amortization or depreciation as it appears on the books of account of the business enterprise.

Net Cash Flows—When the term is used, it should be supplemented by a qualifier. *See* **Equity Net Cash Flows** and **Invested Capital Net Cash Flows.**

*Net Present Value—The value, as of a specified date, of future cash inflows less all cash outflows (including the cost of investment) calculated using an appropriate discount rate.

Net Tangible Asset Value—The value of the business enterprise's tangible assets (excluding excess assets and nonoperating assets) minus the value of its liabilities.

Nonoperating Assets—Assets not necessary to ongoing operations of the business enterprise. *[Note: in Canada, the term used is "redundant assets."]*

*Normalized Earnings—Economic benefits adjusted for nonrecurring, noneconomic, or other unusual items to eliminate anomalies and/or facilitate comparisons.

*Normalized Financial Statements—Financial statements adjusted for nonoperating assets and liabilities and/or for nonrecurring, noneconomic, or other unusual items to eliminate anomalies and/or facilitate comparisons.

Orderly Liquidation Value—Liquidation value at which the asset or assets are sold over a reasonable period of time to maximize proceeds received.

Premise of Value—An assumption regarding the most likely set of transactional circumstances that may be applicable to the subject valuation; for example, going concern, liquidation.

*Present Value—The value, as of a specified date, of future economic benefits and/or proceeds from sale, calculated using an appropriate discount rate.

Portfolio Discount—An amount or percentage deducted from the value of a business enterprise to reflect the fact that it owns dissimilar operations or assets that do not fit well together.

*Price/Earnings Multiple—The price of a share of stock divided by its earnings per share.

Rate of Return—An amount of income (loss) and/or change in value realized or anticipated on an investment, expressed as a percentage of that investment.

Redundant Assets—*See* Nonoperating Assets.

Replacement Cost New—The current cost of a similar new property having the nearest equivalent utility to the property being valued.

Report Date—The date conclusions are transmitted to the client.

Reproduction Cost New—The current cost of an identical new property.

*Required Rate of Return—The minimum rate of return acceptable by investors before they will commit money to an investment at a given level of risk.

Residual Value—The value as of the end of the discrete projection period in a discounted future earnings model.

*Return on Equity—The amount, expressed as a percentage, earned on a company's common equity for a given period.

*Return on Investment—*See* Return on Equity and Return on Invested Capital.

***Return on Invested Capital**—The amount, expressed as a percentage, earned on a company's total capital for a given period.

Risk-Free Rate—The rate of return available in the market on an investment free of default risk.

Risk Premium—A rate of return added to a risk-free rate to reflect risk.

Rule of Thumb—A mathematical formula developed from the relationship between price and certain variables based on experience, observation, hearsay, or a combination of these; usually industry specific.

Special Interest Purchasers—Acquirers who believe they can enjoy postacquisition economies of scale, synergies, or strategic advantages by combining the acquired business interest with their own.

Standard of Value—The identification of the type of value being used in a specific engagement; for example, fair market value, fair value, investment value.

Sustaining Capital Reinvestment—The periodic capital outlay required to maintain operations at existing levels, net of the tax shield available from such outlays.

Systematic Risk—The risk that is common to all risky securities and cannot be eliminated through diversification. The measure of systematic risk in stocks is the beta coefficient.

***Tangible Assets**—Physical assets (such as cash, accounts receivable, inventory, property, plant and equipment, etc.).

Terminal Value—*See* **Residual Value.**

***Transaction Method**—*See* **Merger and Acquisition Method.**

Unlevered Beta—The beta reflecting a capital structure without debt.

Unsystematic Risk—The portion of total risk specific to an individual security that can be avoided through diversification.

Valuation—The act or process of determining the value of a business, business ownership interest, security, or intangible asset.

Valuation Approach—A general way of determining a value indication of a business, business ownership interest, security, or intangible asset using one or more valuation methods.

Valuation Date—The specific point in time as of which the valuator's opinion of value applies (also referred to as "effective date" or "appraisal date").

Valuation Method—Within approaches, a specific way to determine value.

Valuation Procedure—The act, manner, and technique of performing the steps of an appraisal method.

Valuation Ratio—A fraction in which a value or price serves as the numerator and financial, operating, or physical data serves as the denominator.

Value to the Owner—*[Note: In Canada, see* **Investment Value.***]*

***Voting Control**—*De jure* control of a business enterprise.

Weighted Average Cost of Capital (WACC)—The cost of capital (discount rate) determined by the weighted average, at market value, of the cost of all financing sources in the business enterprise's capital structure.

Chapter 6

Notation System Used in This Book

Value at a Point in Time
Cost of Capital and Rate of Return Variables
Income Variables
Periods or Variables in a Series
Weightings
Growth
Mathematical Functions

A source of confusion for those trying to understand financial theory and methods is the lack of a standard system of notation. The following notation system is adapted from the fourth edition of *Valuing a Business: The Analysis and Appraisal of Closely Held Companies* (2000, McGraw-Hill Companies. Used with Permission), by Shannon P. Pratt, Robert F. Reilly, and Robert P. Schweihs, also found in *Valuing Small Businesses and Professional Practices,* 3rd ed. (1998), by the same authors, published by McGraw-Hill. These texts are used in American Society of Appraisers courses referenced in this book. Also, the American Institute of Certified Public Accountants (AICPA) has adopted this system of notation for its series of business valuation courses. The system is also used in *Cost of Capital: Estimation and Applications,* 2nd ed. (2002) by Shannon Pratt, published by John Wiley & Sons, Inc.

VALUE AT A POINT IN TIME

PV = present value
FV = future value
$MVIC$ = market value of invested capital

COST OF CAPITAL AND RATE OF RETURN VARIABLES

k = discount rate (generalized)

k_e = discount rate for common equity capital (cost of common equity capital); unless otherwise stated, it is generally assumed that this discount rate is applicable to net cash flow available to common equity

$k_{e(pt)}$ = cost of equity before income tax effect

k_p = discount rate for preferred equity capital

k_d = discount rate for debt (net of income tax effect, if any)

(*Note:* Complex capital structures could include more than one class of capital in any of the preceding categories; more subscripts would thus be required.)

$k_{d(pt)}$ = cost of debt before income tax effect

k_{ni} = discount rate for equity capital when net income rather than net cash flow is the measure of economic income being discounted

c = capitalization rate (direct capitalization rate)

c_e = capitalization rate for common equity capital; unless otherwise stated, it is generally assumed that this capitalization rate is applicable to net cash flow available to common equity

c_{ni} = capitalization rate for net income

c_p = capitalization rate for preferred equity capital

c_d = capitalization rate for debt

(*Note:* Complex capital structures could include more than one class of capital in any of the preceding categories; more subscripts would thus be required.)

t = tax rate (expressed as a percentage of pretax income)

R = rate of return

R_f = rate of return on a risk-free security

$E(R)$ = expected rate of return

$E(R_m)$ = expected rate of return on the market (usually used in the context of a market for equity securities, such as the New York Stock Exchange [NYSE] or Standard and Poor's [S&P] 500)

$E(R_i)$ = expected rate of return on security i

B = beta (a coefficient, usually used to modify a rate of return variable)

B_L = levered beta

B_U = unlevered beta

RP = risk premium

RP_m = risk premium for the market (usually used in the context of a market for equity securities, such as the NYSE or S&P 500)

RP_s = risk premium for small stocks (usually average size of lowest quintile or decile of NYSE as measured by market value of common equity) over and above RP_m

RP_u = risk premium for unsystematic risk attributable to the specific company

RP_i = risk premium for the ith security

K_i ... K_n = risk premium associated with risk factors i through n for the average asset in the market (used in conjunction with arbitrage pricing theory)

$WACC$ = weighted average cost of capital

INCOME VARIABLES

E = expected economic income (in a generalized sense; i.e., could be dividends, any of several possible definitions of cash flows, net income, and so on)

NI = net income (after entity-level taxes)

NCF_e = net cash flow to equity

NCF_f = net cash flow to the firm (to overall invested capital, or entire capital structure, including all equity and long-term debt)

PMT = payment (interest and principal payment on debt security)

D = dividends

T = tax (in dollars)

GCF = gross cash flow (usually net income plus noncash charges)

EBT = earnings before taxes (before entity-level income taxes)

$EBIT$ = earnings before interest and taxes (before entity-level income taxes)

$EBDIT/EBITDA$ = earnings before depreciation, interest, and entity-level income taxes (*depreciation* in this context usually includes amortization)

PERIODS OR VARIABLES IN A SERIES

i = ith period or ith variable in a series (may be extended to the jth variable, the kth variable, and so on)

n = number of periods or variables in a series, or the last number in a series

∞ = infinity

0 = period$_0$ is the base period, usually the latest year immediately preceding the valuation date

WEIGHTINGS

W = weight
W_e = weight of common equity in capital structure
W_p = weight of preferred equity in capital structure
W_d = weight of debt in capital structure
(*Note:* For purposes of computing a weighted average cost of capital [*WACC*], it is assumed that preceding weightings are at market value.)

GROWTH

g = rate of growth in a variable (e.g., net cash flow)

MATHEMATICAL FUNCTIONS

Σ = sum of (add all of the variables that follow)
Π = product of (multiply together all of the variables divided by the number of variables)
$\bar{x}$ = mean average (sum of the values of the variables divided by the number of variables)
G = geometric mean (product of the values of the variables taken to the root of the number of variables)

PART III

Valuation Approaches and Methods

Chapter 7

Overview of Valuation Approaches and Methods

APPROACHES, METHODS, AND PROCEDURES

Although by no means universally, business appraisers generally think of the various common business valuation methodologies in terms of a three-tiered hierarchy:

1. *Approaches:* The broadest grouping, generally corresponding roughly to real estate valuation approaches:
   - *Income approach:* Conversion of expected future economic benefits into present value.
   - *Market approach:* Valuation by comparison with transactions in similar businesses or business interests.
   - *Asset-based approach:* Revaluation of the company's assets and liabilities to achieve an adjusted net asset value.

Note: More detailed definitions of each of the preceding approaches are contained in Chapter 5.

2. *Methods:* The primary sets of methodologies used within an approach (e.g., discounting or capitalization methods within the income approach or guideline public company method within the market approach).

3. *Procedures:* Specific valuation techniques applied within each method (e.g., price/earnings multiples or price/sales multiples within the guideline public company method).

CLASSIFICATION OF VALUATION METHODS

There is no right or wrong way to classify business valuation methods. The following generally represents the current consensus.

Income Approach Methods

- *Discounting:* Projecting *all* expected future economic benefits (e.g., net cash flow or some other measure of income) and discounting each expected benefit back to a present value at a *discount rate* that represents the cost of capital for that investment (time value of money plus risk). (Discounting may involve a discrete projection period plus a terminal value.)
- *Capitalization:* Dividing a *single* historical or projected economic benefit (e.g., net cash flow or some other income variable) by a *capitalization rate* that represents the discount rate for that variable less the expected sustainable long-term growth rate in that variable.

Discounted Economic Income Method References

CoC2 Ch. 4
FBVI Ch. 5 pp. 6, 18–34
Lawyer Ch. 8
VAB4 pp. 41, Ch. 9, 209–211, 574

Market Approach Methods

- *Guideline publicly traded company method:* Relating market value multiples for public company stocks (or partnership interests) to fundamental financial variables for the subject company (e.g., price/earnings multiples).
- *Guideline merger and acquisition method:* Relating value multiples from sales of entire companies or controlling interests to fundamental financial variables for the subject company (e.g., price/earnings multiples).

- *Prior transactions, offers, and buy-sell agreements:* Relating ways to reach value based on prior transactions, offers, or agreements in the subject company owner-ship interests to current data for the subject company.

Asset-Based Methods

- *Adjusted net asset method:* Individually adjusting all assets and liabilities (includ-ing those off balance sheet, intangibles, and contingencies) to current values and computing a resulting net asset value.
- *Excess earnings method:* Collective valuation of all intangible assets as a group by capitalizing returns over and above a reasonable rate of return on tangible assets and adding the capitalized value of intangibles thus estimated to the value of tan-gible assets.

   Note: Some prefer to classify the excess earnings method as a *hybrid method,* be-cause it combines asset value with a capitalized earnings component.

Asset-Based Methods References

BV201 "Asset Approach," VII pp. 53–66
FBVI Ch. 1
FBVII Ch. 1 p. 34
Guide 203.5, 203.15–203.19, 204.17, 204.18, 204.21, 204.32, 1402.9, Section 701
IBA1 A.3
IBA2 Ch. 2, 6
IBA3 F.9
Lawyer pp. 82, 84, Ch. 10
VAB4 Ch. 14
VSB3 Ch. 22, 23, p. 485
VT Lesson 7

Rules of Thumb and Industry Formulas

- Folklore (generally based on oral history passed among members of an industry tribe) regarding methods and parameters for valuation of companies in a particular industry or profession.
- Not classified here among preceding methods, because different rules of thumb may invoke accepted or innovative versions of any of the mentioned methods, although some classify them as a market method, implying rules based on mar-ket data.
- Although a widely used industry rule of thumb should not be ignored, such rules generally should *not* be used as the only method (even if dignified by being called a "method").

Rules of Thumb References

> BV201 "Market Approach," VI, H p. 49
> BV202 "Other Considerations," X, J p. 82
> FBVI Ch. 1 p. 34
> FBVII Ch. 2 p. 69
> Guide 203.23, Section 707, App. 7C, 1103.20–1103.21, 1106.21
> IBA1 A.3
> IBA2 Ch. 2
> Lawyer Ch. 12
> Market pp. 44–46, 136, 258–259, 261
> VAB4 pp. 274–275
> VSB3 Ch. 18

VALUING INVESTED CAPITAL OR EQUITY

Any of the methods can be used to value either the entire invested capital or just the equity. If the entire invested capital is valued, the debt can be subtracted to estimate the value of the equity.

Invested Capital

Definition of Invested Capital

- The *International Glossary of Business Valuation Terms* defines *invested capital* as:

> the sum of equity and debt in a business enterprise. Debt is typically (a) all interest bearing or (b) long-term interest-bearing debt. When the term is used, it should be supplemented by a specific definition in the given valuation context.

- There are some ambiguities regarding exactly what is included:
  - Most, but not all, appraisers would include the current portion of long-term debt.
  - Sometimes *all* interest-bearing debt is included in invested capital.

Returns to Invested Capital

- When valuing invested capital, all of the returns available to all of the stakeholders (owners of any debt or equity interests) need to be recognized:
  - Interest on whatever debt is included in the invested capital being valued.
  - Preferred and common dividends.
  - Returns (earnings or cash flow) available to stockholders.

- In the market approach:
  - The numerator for invested capital value ratios is the market value of invested capital (MVIC).
  - The denominator includes returns to all invested capital holders, providers of debt capital as well as equity capital (e.g., earnings before interest and taxes [EBIT] and earnings before interest, taxes, depreciation, and amortization [EBITDA]).

Equity

Definition of Equity

- The *International Glossary of Business Valuation Terms* defines *equity* as:

    the owner's interest in property after deduction of all liabilities (usually referring to market value)

- In spite of the given definition, in the context of valuation, the term *equity* often is used to mean only common equity, with preferred equity treated as part of the senior portion of the capital structure.

Returns to Equity

- When valuing common equity, the returns used should be *net* of returns to senior portions of the capital structure:
  - After interest (net of tax effect).
  - After preferred dividends.
- In the market approach (assuming a ratio of market value to some income variable):
  - The numerator for common equity value ratios is the market value of common equity.
  - The denominator includes only returns related to common equity (e.g., net income and pretax income).

Applicability of Invested Capital versus Equity Valuation Procedures

There are no hard and fast rules, but the following often apply:

- Invested capital procedures tend to be used often for control valuations, because the control buyer may want to value the entire capital structure and then decide how to finance it; also, the acquisition market tends to look at businesses on an invested capital basis.

- Invested capital procedures often are used for highly leveraged capital structures in which small changes in returns can greatly affect equity.
- Equity procedures often are used for minority interest valuations (since a minority owner cannot change the capital structure).
- As with all methods, the more data available and the more reliable the data, the more applicable it is.

CLASSIFICATION OF APPROACHES AND METHODS IS NOT DISCRETE

All of the business valuation methods are somewhat interrelated:

- The income approach derives cost of capital from market data.
- The market approach uses multiples of either income variables or asset values (the multiples are the inverse of capitalization rates for the respective variables).
- The asset-based approach derives asset values from market data.
- The excess earnings method uses income, market, and asset data.

RELATIVE STRENGTHS AND WEAKNESSES OF VARIOUS METHODS

Discounted Economic Income Method

In a generalized sense, the income variable can be net cash flow, net income, pretax income, EBIT, or some other income variable.

Advantages of Discounting Method

- Theoretically most pure; captures present value of all future realizable cash.
- Widely used in the financial markets for pricing and decision making.
- Increasing acceptance in the courts.

Disadvantages of Discounting Method

- Requires projections of future economic benefits; may be controversial.
- Requires estimate of appropriate discount rate (cost of capital); also subject to controversy.
- May be difficult to explain to an audience without sufficient financial background.

Capitalization Method

Advantages of Capitalization Method

- Widely used by investors (although probably not as much as discounted cash flow).
- Does not require specific-period, long-term forecasts.
- Simple to understand and explain.
- Used at one time or another in almost all courts.

Disadvantages of Capitalization Method

- Oversimplification of discounting method; future economic benefits are not reflected explicitly and may be difficult or unreasonable to assume a constant growth rate.
- Implicitly assumes that a variable capitalized represents a reasonable base from which future benefits will proceed.
- Both the measure of economic income to be capitalized and the capitalization rate may be controversial.
- Difficult to use in start-up or high-growth companies.

Guideline Public Company Method

Advantages of Guideline Public Company Method

- Many guideline publicly traded companies available for different industries.
- Market regarded as final arbiter of value.
- Prices of guideline publicly traded companies available as of any effective valuation date.
- Excellent quantity and quality of data for each company because of filings with Securities and Exchange Commission (SEC).
- Inexpensive to acquire data with readily available databases and software (although analysis is usually time-consuming if done properly).
- Most investors and judges familiar with the method.
- If using for valuing a minority ownership interest, extensive empirical data available to support quantification of a discount for lack of marketability.
- If company potentially could go public, it is especially relevant.

Disadvantages of Guideline Public Company Method

- Public companies are not available in all industries.
- Often difficult to find adequately similar companies.
- Most public companies are much larger than many private companies being valued.

- Many public companies have higher potential growth than private companies, which may require a difficult adjustment in the comparison.
- Adjustments for relative minority ownership control characteristics between guideline companies and subject may be controversial and difficult to quantify.
- Many public companies not "pure plays" in the industry of interest.
- For very small companies, factors driving value may be different than for public companies.
- If valuing a controlling interest, adjustment for control may be difficult and controversial.
- Some judges (notably California family law judges) have disallowed the guideline public company method for valuing private companies.

Guideline Merger and Acquisition Method

Advantages of Guideline Merger and Acquisition Method

- If valuing a controlling ownership interest, no premium for control needed.
- If the acquired company was public before acquisition, excellent comparative financial data usually available.
- Generally understood and accepted by courts.

Disadvantages of Guideline Merger and Acquisition Method

- In most cases, fewer comparative merger and acquisition transactions than guideline publicly traded companies are available.
- Data are not readily accessible on a single database and thus are more difficult to find than guideline publicly traded company data.
- Not all databases include full terms of deal.
- Transactions are not on the same date as effective valuation date; may require adjustments for differences in time (e.g., changes in industry price/earnings multiples).
- If valuing a minority interest, discounts for minority ownership interest and/or lack of marketability may be controversial and hard to quantify.
- If the acquired company was private before acquisition, financial data are usually limited and may not be possible to fully verify.
- Often includes synergistic or strategic value; therefore may not represent fair market value.

Prior Transactions, Offers, and Buy-Sell Agreements

Advantages of Prior Transactions, Offers, and Buy-Sell Agreements

- If on an arm's-length basis, may be the best evidence of value because they deal directly with the subject itself.

- Accurate, detailed data are often available.
- Courts are receptive of arm's-length basis.

Disadvantages of Prior Transactions, Offers, and Buy-Sell Agreements

- May be difficult to establish arm's-length character.
- Removed in time from effective date of valuation; may require adjustments for differences in time.
- In case of offers and incomplete contracts, may be difficult to establish whether a bona fide offer from a qualified buyer and may include various terms and conditions.

Adjusted Net Asset Value Method

Advantages of Adjusted Net Asset Value Method

- Easy to understand.
- Courts willing to consider it in many cases.
- May be especially relevant in tangible-asset-intensive business if valuing controlling interest.
- If valuing a controlling ownership interest, liquidation value may exceed going-concern value.

Disadvantages of Adjusted Net Asset Value Method

- May be expensive and difficult to get reliable market-derived data for valuation of many assets and liabilities.
- Valuation of many assets and liabilities, especially intangibles and contingent items, may be considered speculative.
- Of questionable relevance in many going-concern premise valuations, especially minority interests.
- Least reliable in business with significant intangible value and/or valuing a minority interest.

Excess Earnings Method

Advantages of Excess Earnings Method

- Seemingly simplistic (although that can be misleading).
- Widely used in family law courts, especially for professional practices and small service businesses.

Disadvantages of Excess Earnings Method

- Wide disagreement in profession as to how it should be implemented:
  - What income variable should be capitalized?

- What assets should be adjusted and/or included in the tangible asset base?

  Note: RR68-609 is silent on these points.

- No empirical basis available for developing or supporting capitalization rate applicable to excess earnings.
- Method does not provide mechanics for incorporating expected growth.
- Not widely used by the financial community.
- Internal Revenue Service (IRS) position (per RR68-609) is that it should be used "only if no better method is available."

Rules of Thumb

Advantages of Rules of Thumb

- Should be considered if they are widely publicized in a particular industry.
- Usually simple to apply.
- May be used as a "sanity check."

Disadvantages of Rules of Thumb

- No empirical verification of the extent to which market actually tends to follow them.
- Usually do not know details of transactions that allegedly underlie the rule (e.g., debt? cash versus terms? noncompete? what transferred?).
- For most industries, the various sources of rules of thumb usually produce a very wide range of potential values.

Relative Strengths and Weaknesses of Various Methods References

FBVII Ch. 2 p. 69
Guide Sections 203, 204, 205
IBA1 B. 7
IBA3 Ch. D, F
IBA6 Ch. 1, 2
RR59–60
VAB4 Ch. 19
VSB3 Ch. 12, 26, 31
VT Lesson 7

Advantages of Rules of Thumb References

> BV201 "Business Valuation Theory," II. G-H pp. 9–11
> FBVII Ch. 2 p. 70
> IBA2 Ch. 3
> VAB4 pp. 274–275

Disadvantages of Rules of Thumb References

> FBVII Ch. 2 p. 69
> Guide App. 7C
> IBA1 A. 3
> IBA2 Ch. 7
> IBA3 F. 8
> VAB4 pp. 274–275
> VSB3 pp. 289–290

APPLICABILITY OF VARIOUS METHODS

Control versus Minority Valuation

Discounted or Capitalized Cash Flow or Other Economic Income Measure

- Can be used for either control or minority valuation:
  - If control valuation basis, benefit stream would reflect control-type adjustments, such as excess compensation.
  - If minority ownership basis, economic benefit stream generally would not reflect control-type adjustments.
- Discount for lack of marketability applicable for minority ownership valuation, possibly for control basis valuation (but likely would be considerably smaller, if applicable, for control valuation).
- Little or no difference in the discount or capitalization rate between control and minority valuation, though for control, assumed capital structure change could change weighted average cost of capital.

Guideline Public Company Method

- Can be used for either control or minority ownership basis valuation:
  - If control, there *may* be some control premium warranted (also possibly discount for lack of marketability).

- If minority, there *may* be a minority interest discount, even though public stock transactions are minority interests (although this is a controversial point, and some say it would never be applicable).

Note: The control-minority issue with the guideline public company method is controversial (see Chapter 11).

- Discount for lack of marketability applicable if minority valuation, possibly if control valuation.

Guideline Merger and Acquisition Method

- Good for control valuations, because based directly on other control transactions.
- If used for minority valuation, usually would have to discount for *both* minority interest and lack of marketability.

Prior Transactions, Offers, and Buy-Sell Agreements

- May be difficult to discern whether transactions were arm's length.
- Depends on whether they were applicable to control or minority transactions.
- Adjustments may be necessary; sometimes perhaps too speculative to handle if deal is not comparable to subject transaction from control-minority perspective.
- Must consider adjustments for difference in time, if applicable.

Asset-Based Methods

- Generally used for control basis valuations, since minority interest holders have no direct claim on the assets and cannot force their disposition or utilization.
- If used for minority interest valuation, usually would have to discount for *both* lack of control and lack of marketability.

Excess Earnings Method

- Generally used for control ownership valuations (if used for minority, consider both minority and marketability discounts).
- Could be used for minority valuations, depending on assumption about level of economy's income capitalized and possibly adjustments for minority and/or lack of marketability status.

Rules of Thumb

- Universally relate to control value.
- If using for minority, need to consider adjustments for minority and/or lack of marketability.

For a summary of how methodology affects control versus minority value, see Exhibit 7.1.

How Purpose of Valuation and Definition of Value Affect Selection of Methods

The purpose of the valuation usually determines the applicable definition of value, which in turn affects which methods may be most appropriate. The legal context of the valuation may also control, or at least influence, the selection of methods.

Tax-Related Valuations (Including Employee Stock Ownership Plans)

- Standard is fair market value.
- RR59-60 is strong on guideline public company method.
- IRS tends to favor the market approach:
  - Considers market approach most directly representative of market value.
  - Considers income approach more susceptible to manipulation of data than market approach.
- Tax Court also often favors the market approach.
- Nevertheless, income approach is often used and accepted in court.
- If a controlling interest and liquidation value may exceed going-concern value, then asset-based approach is also appropriate.

Exhibit 7.1   Summary of How the Valuation Methodology Affects the Resulting Value

Approach/Method	Assumptions	Resulting Value
Income approach	Control cash flows	Control[a]
	Minority cash flows	Minority, marketable
Guideline merged & acquired company method	Control transacted	Control[a]
Guideline publicly traded company method	Trading at or above control level	Control
	Trading below control value	Minority, marketable
Asset accumulation method	Control over assets	Control
Excess earnings method	Control over assets	Control

Source: Shannon P. Pratt, *Business Valuation Discounts and Premiums* (New York: John Wiley & Sons, Inc., 2001). Copyright © 2001, John Wiley & Sons, Inc. This material is used by permission of John Wiley & Sons, Inc.

[a]If synergies involved, could be acquisition value.

- Discounted net cash flow to invested capital often is used for leveraged employee stock ownership plans (ESOPs) to help avoid distortions arising from the leverage.
- Market approach using returns to invested capital also sometimes used to deflect effects of leverage.

Marital Dissolutions

- Standard of value not specified in state statutes.
- Most family law courts have broad discretion to choose the method or methods on a case-by-case basis.
- Excess earnings method is widely used in family law courts, especially for professional practices.
- Discounted cash flow is gradually becoming more accepted in family law courts because of recognition of its wide use in the professional financial community.
- Market approach often is used, but some California family law judges have said that there are too many differences between public and private companies to use the publicly traded guideline company method for valuation of a private company. (Many appraisers disagree with that conclusion.)
- Case law should be studied carefully (e.g., even if the term *fair market value* is used, actual methods and procedures often depart from a strict fair market value standard).
- Valuation practitioners should confirm the proper standards of value with legal counsel for the client.

Dissenting Stockholder and Minority Oppression Actions

- Standard of value in most cases is fair value.
- Must look to state precedential cases to see how interpreted.
- Most states will give some weight to each of three major approaches—income, market, and asset. (The mathematical weighting of value indications from each of these three approaches is known as the *Delaware Block Method.*)
- Delaware court said in 1997 opinion that the discounted cash flow method is becoming its preferred method of choice in dissenting stockholder actions.

Availability of Data

- For any method considered, adequacy of available data must be assessed (e.g., reliable projections for discounted cash flow method, sufficient transactions for market approach).
- Sometimes conceptually preferable methods cannot be used because of inadequacy of data.

Chapter 8

Income Approach: Cost of Capital

COST OF CAPITAL BASICS

Why Cost of Capital Is Essential to Business Valuation

- Cost of capital is at the very heart of business valuation.
- "Value today always equals future cash flow discounted at the opportunity cost of capital" (Paul Samuelson and William Nordhaus, *Economics,* 14th ed., 1992, quoted in VAB3).

Definition of Cost of Capital

- *Cost of capital* is the expected rate of return that the market requires to attract funds to a particular investment.
- In economic terms, it is an *opportunity cost*—that is, the cost of forgoing the next best alternative investment (equivalent risk at higher expected return or lowered risk at same expected return).
- Cost of capital is based on the *principle of substitution*—an investor will not invest in a particular asset if there is a more attractive substitute (as defined previously).
- Cost of capital is *market driven*—the competitive rate of return available in the market on a comparable investment.
- The most important component of comparability is *risk*.
- *Risk* is the degree of uncertainty that the investor will realize the expected returns at the times specified.
- Since risk cannot be observed directly, analysts have developed several ways to estimate it using available market data (generally based on some past period of time).

- Each component of a company's capital structure (e.g., debt and equity) has a cost of capital.
- The blended average of the costs of these components is the company's weighted average cost of capital (WACC; defined in later section).

Components of Cost of Capital

- Three basic components of cost of capital:
  1. The "real" rate of return that investors expect in exchange for letting someone else use their money on a riskless basis.
  2. Expected inflation—the expected depreciation in purchasing power while the money is tied up.
  3. Risk—the uncertainty about when and how much cash flow or other economic income will be received.

The combination of the first two items is sometimes referred to as the time value of money, which is the same for all investments of the same expected duration. Although these expectations may vary for different investors, the market tends to form a consensus. The analysis of the many factors causing uncertainty of returns determines the cost of capital for investments of varying levels of risk.

Cost of Capital Equals Discount Rate

- Also referred to as the *required rate of return.*
- A *discount rate* is an annually compounded percentage rate of return by which each increment of expected future return is discounted back to a present value.
- The essence of the cost of capital (discount rate) is that it is the percentage rate of return that equates expected future increments of income with present value.
- The discount rate (cost of capital) equals the *total* expected rate of return—that is, dividends or withdrawals plus expected annually compounded change in the value of the investment over the life of the investment.

Note: The relationship between *discount rates* and *capitalization rates* is covered in Chapter 10.

Characteristics of Cost of Capital

Cost of Capital Is Forward-Looking

- Cost of capital represents investors' *expectations.*
- Actual past returns are relevant to an estimate of cost of capital only to the extent that there is reason to believe that they are representative of future expectations.

Cost of Capital Is a Function of the Investment

- Cost of capital depends on the investment, *not* the investor—that is, it depends on how the capital is used.
- Cost of capital for a given investment (e.g., acquisition or expansion) may be at, above, or below a company's overall cost of capital, depending on relative riskiness.
- If a discount rate other than that appropriate for the investment on a stand-alone basis is used to discount expected returns, the resulting indication of value can be considered *investment value* rather than *fair market value,* because the result depends on the circumstances or perspective of a *particular* investor rather than the *hypothetical* investor contemplated in the definition of fair market value; this investment value phenomenon often is reflected in acquisition prices, in which a buyer uses its own company's cost of capital to discount expected cash flows from the acquiree.
- If valuing subsidiaries, each may have a different cost of capital on a stand-alone basis depending on the relative risk.

Cost of Capital Is Based on Market Value, Not Book Value

- Cost of capital is based on *expected returns relative to market prices.*
- For example, the yield to maturity shown in the bond quotations in the financial press is based on the market price of the bond, not its face value.
- Similarly, the implied cost of capital for a publicly traded stock is based on the market price of that stock, *not* on the company's book value per share of stock.

Cost of Capital Is Usually Stated in Nominal Terms

- As noted earlier, one of the components of the cost of capital is expected inflation.
- This assumes, of course, that the expected returns to be discounted also will be estimated by reflecting the effect of expected inflation (normally the case in developed economies with predictable inflation rates).
- For countries with hyperinflation, it is usually more reliable to state both projections and discount rates in real rather than nominal terms.

Cost of Capital Basics References

CoC2 Ch. 1
FBVI Ch. 5 pp. 46–69
NACVA Sect. 1
NACVA-BV Ch. 4, 5
NACVA-CA Sect. 6
VAB4 Ch. 9
VSB3 Ch. 13

COST OF CAPITAL BY CAPITAL STRUCTURE COMPONENT

Cost of Debt

- If a company is borrowing at current rates, the actual rate that the company is paying is usually the pretax cost of debt.
- If there is some long-term debt at rates different from the prevailing market, market rates may be estimated by risk analysis of the subject compared with yields on public debt of comparable risk.
- Since interest on debt is tax deductible, after-tax cost of debt (market rate multiplied by one minus the company's tax rate) is a relevant cost to the company.
- Sometimes there are hidden costs that should be considered, such as:
  - Points up front (a percentage of the loan paid as part of the loan fee).
  - Compensating bank balance requirements.
  - Personal guarantees (to date, no generally accepted method to measure its cost, but insurers of seller paper usually have charged about 3%).

Cost of Debt Reference

VAB4 Ch. 23

Cost of Preferred Equity

- If dividend yield is at market rate for preferred stocks of equivalent risk, then that yield usually represents cost of preferred equity.
- If yield different from prevailing market rate, market rate may be estimated by risk analysis of the subject compared with yields of public preferred equity of equivalent risk.
- In considering yield rates for preferred stocks of equivalent risk, also must consider equivalent terms, because terms of preferred stocks vary greatly.

Cost of Preferred Equity Reference

VAB4 Ch. 24

Cost of Common Equity

- Unlike costs of debt and preferred equity, cost of common equity is not directly observable in the market, because there are no stated amounts of expected returns to which market price can be related.

- Spectrum conceivably could span from less than 10% to more than 50% of the cost of equity capital.
- Cost of equity covers a wide band of required rates of return because of the wide range of risk:
  - Large, stable company with consistently predictable and significant dividends.
  - More cyclical or erratic company; more of expected return depends on stock price increases than on dividends.
  - Small company with no dividends.
  - Start-up company with no track record or venture capital.
- Analysis of risk to place company's cost of equity within this wide band is arguably the most challenging exercise in business valuation.

WEIGHTED AVERAGE COST OF CAPITAL

Definition of WACC

Weighted average cost of capital (WACC) is the blended costs of the company's capital structure components, each weighted by the *market value* of that component.

Computation of WACC

- The formula for WACC, using the notation system in Chapter 6, is:

$$WACC = (k_e \times W_e) + (k_p \times W_p) + (k_{d(pt)}[1 - t] \times W_d)$$

where

$WACC$ = weighted average cost of capital
  k_e = cost of common equity capital
  W_e = percentage of common equity in the capital structure, at market value
  k_p = cost of preferred equity
  W_p = percentage of preferred equity in the capital structure, at market value
  $k_{d(pt)}$ = cost of debt pretax
  t = tax rate
  W_d = percentage of debt in the capital structure, at market value

- Preceding computation example in tabular form:

Capital Component	Percentage of Capital Component in Capital Structure[a]	Cost of Capital Component		Weighted Cost of Capital Component
Debt	0.30	$0.10 - 0.03^{b}$	=	0.021
Preferred Equity	0.10	0.12	=	0.012
Common Equity	0.60	0.20	=	0.120
	1.00			
	Weighted Average Cost of Capital		=	0.153

[a]At market value
[b]Assuming 30% tax rate

- Since percentage of each capital component is at *market* value, which is the unknown value for the equity, it is usually necessary to start by *estimating* the percentages of the capital components, then iterating (repeating) the process as many times as necessary (can be done almost instantaneously with contemporary electronic spreadsheet programs).
- For an example of the iterative process to develop WACC using CAPM, see Appendix E in *Cost of Capital: Estimation and Applications,* 2nd edition.

Company Actual versus Hypothetical Capital Structure

Minority Interest Basis

If valuation is on minority interest basis, the company's actual capital structure usually is used since a minority stockholder cannot change the capital structure.

Control Basis

If valuation is on a control basis, a case can be made for using a hypothetical capital structure.

- If hypothetical capital structure, industry median or average is most typical.
- Remember, if using industry average, must be at relative market values of components, *not* at book values:
  - *Sources based on balance sheet numbers usually are not satisfactory* because they are at book values (e.g., Risk Management Association's [formerly Robert Morris Associates] *Annual Statement Studies, Financial Studies of the Small Business, Almanac of Business and Industrial Financial Ratios*).
  - *Better to use source where capital structure percentages are computed based on market values* (e.g., *Cost of Capital Yearbook*).
  - Could also develop own set of guideline public or merged and acquired companies to get average capital structures.

Weighted Average Cost of Capital References

BV203 "Discount Rates," IV. E pp. 33–36; Ch. 8, pp. 5–7
BV204 Module 2
CoC2 Ch. 7
FBVI Ch. 5 p. 61
Guide 501.33, 506.9–506.11
IBA2 Ch. 8, 14
IBA3 Ch. L
Lawyer pp. 128–131
NACVA-BV Ch. 4, 5
VAB4 pp. 184–185, 190–191, 319

ESTIMATION OF COST OF EQUITY CAPITAL

Elements Reflected in Cost of Equity

Risk-Free Rate

- Rate of return available on a security considered free of default risk, usually a U.S. Treasury security. (Ibbotson recommends using the 20-year maturity.)
- The U.S. government does not issue a 20-year Treasury security, making a 30-year security with 20 years to maturity, as listed in the *Wall Street Journal,* as a good option.
- A good source of finding a 20-year maturity is the Web site of the Federal Reserve Bank in St. Louis, *www.frb.org/stl.*
- Risk-free rate actually includes some degree of *maturity risk* (also called *horizon risk* or *interest rate risk*), the risk that the market value of the security will fluctuate with changes in the general level of interest rates.

Equity Risk Premium

The equity risk premium (ERP) is the return over and above the risk-free rate that investors require to incur the risk of investing in an equity security instead of a risk-free security. The equity risk premium may include any or all of the following elements:

- *General equity risk premium:* The expected return above the risk-free rate available by investing in common stocks of companies such as those included in the Standard and Poor's 500 Index (S&P 500).
- *Size premium (small stock premium):* Additional expected return for incurring additional risk of investing in companies smaller than the "market index" (which, for Ibbotson Associates data, is the S&P 500).

- *Company-specific risk premium:* Additional return required if risks of subject company greater than those reflected in companies on which earlier risk premium elements are based. (Company-specific component *could* be a negative risk premium adjustment.)

Note: All of the various models for estimating cost of equity include the previously mentioned elements, either explicitly or implicitly.

Capital Asset Pricing Model

Description of CAPM

The structure of the Capital Asset Pricing Model (CAPM) is that the cost of equity capital is the risk-free rate plus a linear function of a measure of *systematic risk* times the general equity risk premium.

- *Systematic risk* is the sensitivity (measured by coefficient of variation) of returns above the risk-free rate for the subject security to returns above the risk-free rate for a market average (e.g., the S&P 500).
- *Beta,* the measure of systematic risk, is computed by regressing returns on a security or portfolio on returns for the market index.
- The reason CAPM includes only systematic risk as a factor in determining required rate of return is that theoretically *unsystematic risk* (risk unique to a company or industry) can be eliminated by holding a fully diversified portfolio of securities.
- Since a private company does not have a track record of regular price changes (part of the return measure included in the calculation of beta), to use CAPM for estimating the cost of a private company's capital, betas usually are derived from public company average betas for a relevant industry group.

Computing a CAPM Estimate of Cost of Equity Capital

- Basic CAPM formula:

$$E(R_i) = R_f + B(RP_m)$$

where

$E(R_i)$ = expected return (cost of capital) for an individual security
R_f = rate of return available on a risk-free security (as of the valuation date)
B = beta
RP_m = equity risk premium for the market as a whole (or, by definition, the equity risk premium for a security with a beta of 1.0)

Note: The RP_m is an *estimated* market risk premium, which may be estimated in several different ways, as summarized in subsequent sections of this chapter.

- Example in tabular form:

Risk-free rate		6.0%
General equity risk premium	7.5%	
Times security beta	1.2	
Equity risk premium for subject		9.0
Cost of equity capital for subject		15.0%

Modified (Expanded) CAPM Cost of Equity

- Empirical tests of CAPM have found that CAPM does not fully explain the returns exhibited in the market, particularly for small companies. Therefore, modified CAPM models have been developed.
- The CAPM formula often is expanded to include size effect and company-specific risk:

$$E(R_i) = R_f + B(RP_m) + RP_s + RP_u$$

where

  $E(R_i)$ = expected return (cost of capital) for an individual security i
  R_f = rate of return available on a risk-free security (as of the valuation date)
  RP_m = equity risk premium for the market as a whole (or, by definition, the equity risk premium for a security with a beta of 1.0)
  RP_s = risk premium for small stock size
  RP_u = risk premium attributable to the specific company (u stands for unsystematic risk)
  B = beta

- Computational example in tabular form:

Risk-free rate		7.0%
General equity risk premium	8.0%	
Times beta	1.3	
Equity risk premium including beta		10.4
Small stock size premium (10th decile)		5.8
Specific risk premium		1.0
Cost of equity capital for subject		24.2%

Selection of Risk-free Rate

- Usually based on short-term (30-day), intermediate-term (5-year), or long-term (20-year) U.S. Treasury security yield to maturity. (The selected term should match the time horizon of the subject investment.)
- General preference for 20-year rate:
  - Matches long-term horizon of equity investment.
  - Subject to less volatility than shorter-term rates.
- If using Ibbotson data for equity risk premium, should match risk-free rate selection with short-, intermediate-, or long-term equity risk premium.
- The risk-free rate should be the rate existing in the market as of the effective valuation date.
- Also, if using Ibbotson historical data, choose between:
  - Arithmetic average historical equity risk premium (recommended by Ibbotson): (The reason that Ibbotson recommends the arithmetic average as the best estimate of the expected risk premium is because there is no autocorrelation; that is, the returns are random [independent of each other]; the next year's return is unrelated to the prior year. For a more complete explanation see Ibbotson Associates' *Stocks, Bonds, Bills, and Inflation Valuation Edition* 2002 *Yearbook,* pp. 153–154.)
  - Geometric average historical equity risk premium.

Selection of Equity Risk Premium

- May be based on:
  - Ibbotson historical risk premium data from *Stock, Bonds, Bills, and Inflation* yearbooks.
  - Discounted cash flow (DCF) method (see later section).
- If using Ibbotson data, match equity risk premium to risk-free rate:
  - Long-term premium (based on 20-year bond yields).
  - Intermediate-term premium (based on 5-year bond yields).
  - Short-term premium (based on 30-day note yields).

Selection of Size Effect Premium

- Ibbotson data show that small companies require returns over and above those that would be reflected by their specific betas.
- If using CAPM, use only size premium data *in excess of CAPM return* or total return in excess of the risk-free rate for the relevant size decile.
- The size premium is *not* multiplied by beta. (Beta is applied only to the *general* equity risk premium.)

Note: All Ibbotson return data are *after* entity-level income taxes.

Company-Specific Risk Premium

Estimation of company-specific risk premium is subjective, based on analysis of the characteristics of the subject company relative to companies from which other risk premium data are drawn (not captured in either beta or size premium). Factors could include:

- Smaller than the smallest premium group.
- Industry risk not fully reflected in beta.
- Relative volatility of returns.
- Leverage (but may be adjusted using levered and unlevered betas).
- Concentration of customer base.
- Key person dependence or small management base.
- Key supplier dependence.
- Abnormal present or pending competition.
- Pending regulatory changes.
- Pending lawsuits.
- Relatively undiversified operations:
  - Products.
  - Geographically.
- Special environmental problems.
- Unrecorded liabilities.

Levered and Unlevered Betas

- Betas published by the various reporting services reflect whatever leverage the respective companies have.
- The estimated effect of leverage can be removed by *unlevering* the betas.
- Then the beta can be *relevered* to reflect any desired degree of leverage.
- Can be used for valuing either invested capital or equity but used primarily for valuing invested capital.
- Formula for unlevering beta (beta assuming 100% equity in capital structure, known as the *Hamada formula* after the man who originated it):

$$B_u = \frac{B_L}{1 + (1 - t)(W_d / W_e)}$$

where

B_u = beta unlevered
B_L = beta levered
t = tax rate for the company
W_d = Percentage of debt in the capital structure (at market value)
W_e = Percentage of equity in the capital structure (at market value)

- Example:

  Assume the following for guideline company A:

  　　Levered (published) beta: 1.2

  　　Tax rate: 40%

  　　Market value capital structure: 30% debt, 70% equity

$$B_u = \frac{1.2}{1 + (1 - 0.40)(0.30 / 0.70)}$$

$$= \frac{1.2}{1 + 60(0.429)}$$

$$= \frac{1.2}{1.257}$$

$$= 0.95$$

- Formula for relevering beta:

$$B_L = B_u [1 + (1 - t)(W_d/W_e)]$$

where the definitions of the variables are the same as in the formula for computing unlevered betas.

- Example:

  Assume the following for the subject company:

  Unlevered beta: .90

  Tax rate: .30

  Capital structure: 60% debt, 40% equity

$$B_L = 0.90[1 + (1 - 0.30)(0.60/0.40)]$$

$$= 0.90[1 + 0.70(1.5)]$$

$$= 0.90\,(2.05)$$

$$= 1.85$$

Assumptions Underlying CAPM

The assumptions underlying CAPM are:

- Investors are risk averse. (For each increment of risk, an increment of expected return is required to induce the investor to choose the higher-risk investment.)
- Rational investors seek to hold efficient portfolios (i.e., portfolios that are fully diversified).
- All investors have identical investment time horizons (i.e., expected holding periods generally speaking, indefinitely long term).

- All investors have identical and reasonable expectations about such variables as rates of return and how capitalization rates are generated.
- There are no transaction costs (e.g., transaction costs are ignored in the model).
- There are no investment-related taxes at the investor level; that is, all such consequences are ignored (but there may be corporate income taxes).
- The rate received from lending money is the same as the cost of borrowing money.
- The market has perfect divisibility and liquidity (i.e., investors can readily buy or sell any desired fractional interest).

Obviously, the extent to which these assumptions are met in the real world affects the application of CAPM for the valuation of closely held businesses, business interests, or investment projects. For example, although the perfect divisibility and liquidity assumption approximates reality for publicly traded stocks, it does not hold for privately held companies. Consequently, the company-specific, nonsystematic risk factor may be required in expected returns for closely held companies even if it is not for public companies.

Since much of the return for public companies depends on changes in market price, and closely held companies lack these observable market price changes, we have no way to measure betas directly for closely held companies. As a (somewhat imperfect) proxy, we use average betas for similar public companies.

Build-Up Model

Build-Up Like CAPM, with Beta Assumed to Be 1.0

The build-up model is identical in form to the extended version of CAPM, except that the beta factor is not incorporated (implicitly assuming that beta equals 1.0). Since the build-up model is merely a proxy for the extended model, it is important to note that the same assumptions and limitations of the extended model may be applicable.

Effect of No Beta on Other Elements of Cost of Capital

Note: IBBOTSON ASSOCIATES HAS CHANGED ITS RECOMMENDED METHOD OF MEASURING THE SIZE PREMIUM SINCE THE FIRST EDITION OF THIS BOOK.

Ibbotson Associates now distinguishes between what it calls a *size premium* and what it refers to as a "small stock premium." In the build-up method, Ibbotson advocates using the "size premium," which is "returns in excess of CAPM" (the same as used in the CAPM model). In the build-up model, however, Ibbotson advocates modifying it by an industry adjustment factor, which Ibbotson provides for about 300 Standard Industrial Classification (SIC) codes in Chapter 3 of its *Stocks, Bonds, Bills and Inflation Valuation Edition 2002 Yearbook.*

What Ibbotson Associates now calls the *small stock premium* is simply the arithmetic average of historical rates of return for the size category that the subject company falls into, less the arithmetic average of historical rates of return for the S&P 500. In earlier years Ibbotson advocated this method, and some analysts still believe it is better.

Discounted Cash Flow Method of Estimating Cost of Equity

Theory of the DCF Method

- The discounted cash flow (DCF) method can be used to estimate cost of capital by using the present value formula in reverse; stock prices are assumed to reflect the present value of expected returns, so the rate of return the market requires can be computed by implication.
- A private company can use the method to estimate cost of equity for public companies in the same industry to use as a proxy for the private company.

Single-Stage DCF Model

- The single-stage DCF model is based on an algebraic manipulation of the constant growth capitalization model; the formula is:

$$PV = \frac{NCF_0(1+g)}{k-g}$$

where

PV = present value

NCF_0 = net cash flow in period 0, the period immediately preceding the valuation date

k = discount rate (cost of capital)

g = expected long-term sustainable growth rate in net cash flow to investor

- When the present value (i.e., the market price) is known, but the discount rate (i.e., the cost of capital) is unknown, the preceding formula can be rearranged to solve for the cost of capital:

$$k = \frac{NCF_0(1+g)}{PV} + g$$

where the variables have the same definitions as before.

- Example: Substituting in the given formula to estimate the cost of equity capital for Morton's Restaurant Group as of December 31, 1996:

NCF_0 = free cash flow $0.522 per share (from Compustat PC Plus version 6.01, a product of Standard & Poor's)

g = analysts' consensus growth rate of 8.4% (reported by Morningstar Stock Tools, supplied by Zack's)

PV = stock price of $16.875 per share (as of December 31, 1996)

$$k = \frac{0.522(1+0.84)}{16.875} + 0.084$$

$$k = \frac{0.522(1.084)}{16.875} + 0.084$$

$$k = \frac{0.566}{16.875} + 0.084$$

$$k = 0.034 + 0.084$$

$$k = \underline{0.118}$$

Note: The preceding example used free cash flow as calculated by Compustat. Other renditions use dividends plus some estimate of long-term dividend growth.

Multistage DCF Model

- Multistage DCF models may have two stages of growth plus a terminal stage.
- A three-stage model would be:

$$PV = \sum_{n=i}^{5} \frac{\left[NCF_0(1+g_1)^n\right]}{(1+k)^n} + \sum_{n=6}^{10} \frac{\left[NCF_5(1+g_2)^{n-5}\right]}{(1+k)^n} + \frac{\dfrac{NCF_{10}(1+g_3)}{k-g_3}}{(1+k)^{10}}$$

where

PV = present value

NCF_0 = net cash flow (or dividend) in the immediately preceding period

NCF_5 = expected net cash flow (or dividend) in the fifth year

NCF_{10} = expected net cash flow (or dividend) in the tenth year

g_1, g_2, and g_3 = expected growth rates in NCF (or dividends) through each of stages 1, 2, and 3, respectively

k = cost of capital (discount rate)

The above "stages" can be done in three-year increments or in increments of any number of years. Also, the length of the second stage can differ from the length of the first stage.

- Multistage models generally are much more reliable than single-stage models, since single-stage models reflect only short-term growth expectations.
- The given DCF model formulation estimates the entire cost of equity capital without identifying how much of it is attributable to which elements (i.e., risk-free rate, general equity risk premium, size premium, and/or company-specific risk factors).
- To estimate the company's total equity risk premium, subtract the risk-free rate as of the same date that the total DCF method cost of equity capital was estimated.

Arbitrage Pricing Model

Arbitrage Pricing Model Theory

The arbitrage pricing model can be thought of as a multivariate extension of CAPM, incorporating several systematic risk factors, one of which may be sensitivity to market returns as defined in CAPM.

Arbitrage Pricing Model Formula

- The econometric estimation of cost of capital by the arbitrage pricing model takes the form:

$$E(R_i) = R_f + (B_{i1}K_1) + (B_{i2}K_2) + \dots + B_{in}K_n)$$

where

$E(R_i)$ = expected rate of return on the subject security
R_f = rate of return on a risk-free security
$K_i \dots K_n$ = risk premium associated with factor K for the average asset in the market (general macroeconomic factors such as changes in investor confidence, inflation, etc.)
$B_{i1} \dots B_{in}$ = sensitivity of security i to each risk factor relative to the market average condition to that factor

- The variables used generally are based on measures of macroeconomic risk factors expected to have different impacts on different companies.
- The arbitrage pricing model is not used widely today; usually it is used for very large companies.

Income Approach: Cost of Capital References

BV202 "Discount Rates," IV. B-C pp. 20–33
BV204 Module 2
CoC2 all chapters
FBVI Ch. 5
Guide Ch. 5
IBA1 B.15
IBA2 Ch. 8
IBA3 Ch. L
IBA4 Ch. 10, 11, 13, 15
IBA6 Ch. 2
NACVA Sect. 1
NACVA-BV Ch. 4, 5
NACVA-CA Sect. 3, 6, App.
VAB4 Ch. 9
VSB3 Ch. 15, 27, App. A

Chapter 9

Income Approach: Discounting Method

THEORY OF THE DISCOUNTED ECONOMIC INCOME METHOD

- Also called the "multiperiod income discounting model."
- The discounted economic income method is based on the premise that a financial investment is worth the sum of all of the future benefits it will provide to its

owner, each discounted to a present value at a discount rate that reflects the time value of money and the degree of risk (uncertainty) of receiving the benefits when and in the amounts expected.

- In economic theory, the discounted economic income method is the proper way to value any investment.
- It requires:
  - Projections of timing and amounts of *future expected returns.*
  - A *discount rate* that reflects the *cost of capital* for the type of investment and returns contemplated.
- Although discounted economic income is theoretically the best valuation method, it has obvious problems:
  - Reliability of amounts of income projected.
  - Deciding number of years to project discretely before estimating a terminal value.
  - Uncertainty about the choice of measure of economic income to be projected.
  - Selection of discount rate.
  - Whether return should be assumed at end of each year or more frequently.
- In presenting the discounting methodology, we use the term *economic income* as a general expression without specifying the definition of the economic benefits (returns) to be discounted, recognizing that there is not total agreement on this (or any other) term that is intended to be general without specifying which of the many possible measures of income we choose to use in the model.
  - There is a tendency to use *net cash flow* as a measure of economic income within the income approach, but other measures of return, such as net income, also are used.
  - As outlined in the next section, the economic income can be either that available only to common equity or to all invested capital.

Theory of Discounted Economic Income Method References

BV201 "Business Valuation Theory," II.B.3, p. 6
BV202 "Income Base Approach," III, pp. 12–17
BV203 "Income Approach-Multi-period," Ch. 8, pp. 1–30
BV204 Module 3
FBVI Ch. 5 pp. 18–24
Guide 500.1–500.2 500.4, 500.6, 505.1–505.2
IBA1 A.3
IBA2 Ch. 2, 8
IBA3 F.10
IBA4 Ch. 4, 5, 12
IBA6 Ch. 2

Lawyer pp. 105–108
NACVA-CA Sect. 6
VAB4 pp. 45–46, 152–154
VSB3 pp. 484–485, 552–555, Ch. 13, 14, 15, 42
VT Lesson 7

DISCOUNTING METHOD CAN BE USED FOR EITHER COMMON EQUITY OR INVESTED CAPITAL

Using Discounting Method for Common Equity

- Returns discounted must be those available to common equity owners. (This means returns *after* entity-level income taxes, whether actual or imputed, and *before* personal income taxes.)
- Discount rate should be equity cost of capital. (See Chapter 8.)
- Equity value may be estimated by discounting returns available to all invested capital and subtracting the market value of senior capital (preferred stocks and interest-bearing debt).

Using Discounting Method for Invested Capital

- Returns discounted should be those available to all invested capital holders (after tax-affecting the tax-deductible interest cost of debt).
- Discount rate should be weighted average cost of capital (WACC), based on market value weightings. (See Chapter 8.)

NET CASH FLOW IS PREFERRED MEASURE OF ECONOMIC INCOME IN INCOME APPROACH

Definition of Net Cash Flow

Net Cash Flow to Equity

Net income (after entity-level income tax, usually after any normalizing adjustments)

- + noncash charges (e.g., depreciation, amortization, addition to deferred revenue, and deferred taxes, assuming that they were subtracted in arriving at net income)
- − capital expenditures*
- − additions to net working capital*
- ± changes in long-term debt *(add cash from borrowing, subtract repayments)*

= net cash flow to equity

*Only amounts necessary to support projected operations

Net Cash Flow to Invested Capital

Net income (after entity-level income tax, usually after any normalizing adjustments)

+ noncash charges (e.g., depreciation, amortization, additions to deferred revenue, and deferred taxes)

− capital expenditures*

− additions to net working capital*

± interest expense *(net of the tax deduction resulting from interest as a tax-deductible expense)**

= net cash flow to invested capital

*Only amounts necessary to support projected operations

Reason for Preference for Net Cash Flow

- Net cash flow is the amount available to take out of the business or use on a discretionary basis without jeopardizing the ongoing operations or achievement of the projected future net cash flows of the business.
- The Ibbotson empirical data often used for estimating cost of capital is based on total cash returns available to the investor (dividends plus capital appreciation—and net cash flow similarly represents the amount of cash return that is available for investors to take out of the business).

Net Income as an Alternative Measure

- Net income does not measure amounts of income actually available to the investor.
- For a growing company, capital expenditures are likely to exceed depreciation and net additions to working capital needed, so net cash flow is likely to be lower than net income.
- For a cyclical company, net income must be higher in some years and net cash flow higher in other years.
- The discount rate derived from cash flow data (e.g., Ibbotson data) may be adjusted to be applied to net income, but this procedure is not fully satisfactory because the relationship between net cash flow and net income is rarely constant over time.

Note: Ibbotson data returns include dividends plus changes in market value. These are the amounts available to the investors because the public stocks are highly liquid and the capital can be liquidated at any time. When valuing on control basis, the net cash flow is the amount that can be taken out by the owners of the capital at any time without jeopardizing the operation of the business.

Reason for Preference for Net Cash Flow References

BV202 "Single Period Income" pp. 42–46; "Multi Period Income" pp. 47–61
CoC2 Ch. 2, 3, 21, App. D
FBVI Ch. 5 p. 33
IBA2 Ch. 8
Lawyer pp. 131–132
VSB3 pp. 217–220, 238–246

PRESENT VALUE DISCOUNTING FORMULA

$$PV = \frac{NCF_1}{(1+k)} + \frac{NCF_2}{(1+k)^2} + \ldots + \frac{NCF_n}{(1+k)^n}$$

where

PV = present value
$NCF_1 \ldots NCF_n$ = net cash flow (or other measure of economic income) expected in each of the periods 1 through n, n being the final cash flow in the life of the investment
k = cost of capital applicable to the defined stream of net cash flow

The analyst must match the cost of capital estimate to the definition of the economic income stream being discounted. Estimating the cost of capital accurately is largely a function of reflecting in the cost of capital estimate the degree of risk inherent in the expected cash flows being discounted.

Example: Valuing a Bond

1. The bond has a face value of $1,000.
2. It pays 8% interest on its face value.
3. The bond pays interest once a year, at the end of the year. (This, of course, is a simplifying assumption; some bonds and notes pay only annually, but most publicly traded bonds pay interest semiannually.)
4. The bond matures exactly three years from the valuation date.

5. As of the valuation date, the market yield to maturity (total rate of return, including interest payments and price appreciation) for bonds of the same risk grade as the subject bond is 10%.

Note the important implications of this scenario:

1. The issuing company's *embedded cost of capital* for this bond is only 8%, although the *market cost of capital* at the valuation date is 10%. This difference may result because the general level of interest rates was lower at the time of issuance of this particular bond or because the market's rating of the risk associated with this bond increased between the date of issuance and the valuation date.

2. If the issuing company wanted to issue new debt on comparable terms as of the valuation date, it presumably would have to offer investors a 10% yield, the current market-driven cost of capital for bonds of that risk grade, to induce investors to purchase the bonds.

3. For purposes of valuation and capital budgeting decisions, when we refer to cost of capital, we mean market cost of capital, not embedded cost of capital.

Substituting numbers derived from the preceding assumptions into the formula gives:

$$PV = \frac{\$80}{(1+0.10)} + \frac{\$80}{(1+0.10)^2} + \frac{\$80}{(1+0.10)^3} + \frac{\$1,000}{(1+0.10)^3}$$

$$= \frac{\$80}{1.10} + \frac{\$80}{1.21} + \frac{\$80}{1.331} + \frac{\$1,000}{1.331}$$

$$= \$72.73 + \$66.12 + \$60.10 + \$751.32$$

$$= \underline{\$950.27}$$

In this example, the fair market value of the subject bond as of the valuation date was $950.27, the amount a willing buyer would expect to pay and a willing seller would expect to receive (before taking into consideration any transaction costs).

This computation is sometimes presented in tabular form, after converting the denominator applicable to each expected cash flow in the equation to a *discount factor,* by which each expected cash flow can then be multiplied.

The discount factor is computed by dividing 1 by the amount of each denominator:

$$\frac{1}{1.10} = 0.90910; \frac{1}{1.21} = 0.82645; \frac{1}{1.331} = 0.75132$$

The preceding computations can be presented in tabular form as:

Year	Projected Net Cash Flow		Discount Factor		Discounted Value
1	$80	×	0.90910	=	$72.73
2	$80	×	0.82645	=	$66.12
3	$80	×	0.75132	=	$60.10
Terminal (also year 3)	$1,000	×	0.75132	=	$751.32
			Total present value		$950.27

NET CASH FLOWS SHOULD BE PROBABILITY-WEIGHTED EXPECTED VALUES

Net cash flows to be discounted or capitalized should be *expected values*—that is, *probability-weighted* cash flows. While valuation analysts typically do not have the luxury of a distribution of possible cash flows for each future period, it is useful to understand the concept. It may lead the analyst to adjust a projected number if a skewness of possible outcomes is suspected.

If the distribution of possible cash flows in each period is symmetrical above and below the most likely cash flow in that period, then the most likely cash flow is equal to the probability-weighted cash flow (the mathematically expected value of the distribution). However, many distributions of possible cash flows are skewed. The following table tabulates the probability-weighted expected values of projected cash flows under a symmetrically distributed scenario and a skewed distribution scenario. Exhibit 9.1 portrays the information graphically.

Scenario A—Symmetrical Cash Flow Expectation

Midpoint of Range	Probability of Occurrence	Weighted Value
$1,600	0.01	$16
$1,500	0.09	$135
$1,300	0.20	$260
$1,000	0.40	$400
$ 700	0.20	$140
$ 500	0.09	$45
$ 400	0.01	$4
	1.00	$1,000

Exhibit 9.1   Symmetrical and Skewed Cash Flow Expectations

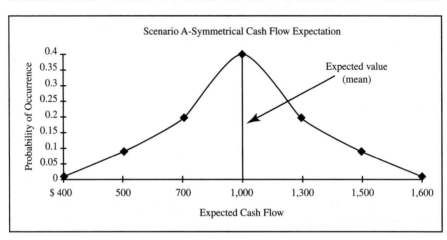

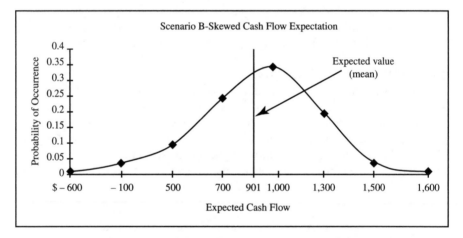

Note: In both scenario A and scenario B, the most likely cash flow is $1,000. In scenario A, the expected value (probability weighted) is also $1,000. But in scenario B, the expected value is only $901. In scenario B, the $901 is the figure that should appear in the numerator of the discounted cash flow formula, not $1,000. Most analysts do not have the luxury of a probability distribution for each expected cash flow but should be aware of the concept when deciding on the amount of each expected cash flow to be discounted

Scenario B—Skewed Cash Flow Expectation

Midpoint of Range	Probability of Occurrence	Weighted Value
$1,600	0.01	$16
$1,500	0.04	$60
$1,300	0.20	$260
$1,000	0.35	$350
$ 700	0.25	$175
$ 500	0.10	$50
$ (100)	0.04	$ (4)
$ (600)	0.01	$ (6)
	1.00	$901

ESTIMATING TERMINAL VALUE

Concept of Terminal Value

- Most equity investments are regarded as having a perpetual life.
- For most equity investments, it is practical to project reasonably reliable specific-period future cash flows (or other returns) only for a limited time period, often three to 10 years.
- The present value of the expected future cash flows (or other returns) beyond the specific projection period is captured by estimating a terminal value, and discounting that terminal value to a present value for the number of years of the specific projection period. (The *terminal value* is the estimated value as of the *end* of the specific projection period, or, in other words, the *beginning* of the company's life immediately following the specific projection period. Therefore, the terminal value is discounted to present value by the number of years in the specific projection period, *not n + 1*. This is true even if the terminal value is estimated by capitalizing the returns expected in the year following the specific projection period.)

Methods of Estimating Terminal Value

Liquidation or Salvage Method

In situations in which the investment is assumed to have a finite life, the estimated liquidation or salvage value at the end of the finite life is the terminal value.

Liquidation or Salvage Method References

FBVI Ch. 1 p. 21
VSB3 p. 28, Ch. 22, 40

Market Multiple Method

- Terminal value is sometimes estimated as a multiple of some income variable (e.g., for equity, a price/earnings multiple; for invested capital, a multiple of market value of invested capital to earnings before interest and taxes [MVIC/EBIT] or market value of invested capital to earnings before interest, taxes, depreciation, and amortization [MVIC/EBITDA]).
- The market multiple method has major weaknesses:
  - Mixes market approach with income approach; terminal value is often a large part of present value, especially with a short, specific projection period, resulting in a major part of what is attributed to income approach actually being based on the market approach method.
  - Requires predicting market multiples as of the end of a specific projection period, which requires a high degree of clairvoyance. (The idea of the market approach is to use observed multiples as of the valuation date. But using market multiples for the terminal value means guessing at multiples as of some time in the future that cannot be observed as of the valuation date.)

Capitalization Method

Generally preferred method is capitalization of cash flow expected in the year following a specific projection period, usually by the Gordon Growth Model (explained in Chapter 10).

MIDYEAR DISCOUNTING CONVENTION

Midyear Convention Concept

Preceding computations have assumed receipt of cash flows at the end of each year. This may be appropriate when you are valuing a seasonal business that receives most of its cash flow toward the end of the year (e.g., Christmas products). If cash flows are received evenly throughout the year, computations can be modified to assume cash flow for the year received at the middle of the year rather than at the end of the year by subtracting 0.5 from the exponent applied to the discount rate.

Formula for Midyear Discounting Convention

$$PV = \frac{NCF_1}{(1+k)^{0.5}} + \frac{NCF_2}{(1+k)^{1.5}} + \dots + \frac{NCF_n}{(1+k)^{n-0.5}}$$

where the variables are defined the same as before.

Effect of Midyear Conventions on Indicated Value

- The midyear convention always results in a higher present value than the year-end convention because it assumes that cash flows are received earlier. (In effect, the result approximates continuous compounding.)
- Since the discount rate is compounded for a half a year *less* for each projected increment, effectively including the terminal values, the *discount factor* is higher, resulting in a higher value for each increment of benefit projected.

Midyear Discounting Convention References

BV204 Module 3
CoC2 pp. 30–31
FBVI Ch. 5 p. 21
Guide 505.58–505.62
Lawyer pp. 132, 135, 136
VAB4 pp. 187–188
VSB3 pp. 246, 261–262, 264

ADJUSTMENTS TO VALUE INDICATED BY DISCOUNTING METHOD

Minority-Control Issue

- Because all of the empirical methods for estimating cost of capital are based on data from minority public stock transactions, many people mistakenly think that the DCF method should produce a minority value, but this is not necessarily true.
- Most investors take the position that *whether the investment is minority or control has little or possibly no impact on the cost of capital (discount rate).*
- The difference between minority and control value is mostly in the projections— the numerator in the present value method, *not* the denominator (discount rate).
- Thus, DCF can produce either a minority or a control value, depending primarily on whether the economic benefit stream projected is that available to a minority owner or a control owner. (There *may* be little or no difference in a company that is managed to its maximum potential and benefits are distributed pro rata to all owners.)
- However, even without expecting any immediate cash flow benefits, *some* investors might pay a premium for the rights to make certain control decisions (e.g., go public, merge, declare dividends, or make acquisitions). (One might argue that a premium paid for these reasons would make the resulting price representative of *investment value* rather than *fair market value.*)

- Some minority owners might pay a portion of a control premium for a swing vote block.

Discount for Lack of Marketability

- Because the discount rates are derived from highly liquid public market transactions, a discount for lack of marketability should be considered.
- Discounts for lack of marketability attributable to minority interests usually are substantial—20 to 50% is common. (See Chapter 16.)
- Discounts for lack of marketability for controlling interests are considered on a case-by-case basis; if applied, they would be significantly less than for minority interests.

Income Approach: Discounting Method References

BV203 Ch. 5 pp. 6–11
BV204 Module 3
CoC2 all chapters
D&P pp. 29–31, Ch. 5, 9
FBVI Ch. 5 p. 18
Guide Ch. 5
IBA1 C.2
IBA2 Ch. 10
IBA3 Ch. M
IBA4 Ch. 7
Lawyer Ch. 8
NACVA Sect. 3
NACVA-BV Ch. 7
QMD Ch. 1, 5–14, App. A, App. B
RR59-60; RR77-287; RR83-120
VAB4 Ch. 9, pp. 209–211, 574, 608, 672–673, 804, 806–807, 822
VSB3 Ch. 25, 34
VT Lesson 7

Chapter 10

Income Approach: Capitalization Method

THEORY OF THE CAPITALIZATION METHOD

The capitalization method is really a short-cut version of the discounting method. Instead of projecting each year's specific expected amount of economic return, capitalization starts with a base amount and implicitly assumes that that amount will remain constant or will increase or decrease at some predictable average rate in perpetuity.

CAPITALIZATION METHOD CAN BE USED FOR EITHER COMMON EQUITY OR INVESTED CAPITAL

Using Capitalization Method for Common Equity

- Returns capitalized should be those available to common equity owners.
- Capitalization rate should be derived from equity cost of capital. (See later sections regarding adjusting from equity cost of capital to a capitalization rate.)

- May estimate equity value by capitalizing economic returns available to all invested capital and subtracting value of senior capital (debt and preferred stock in capital structure).

Using Capitalization Method for Invested Capital

- Returns capitalized should be those available to all invested capital holders (after taking into account the tax-deductible interest cost of debt, recognizing that the focus is on returns *after* entity-level income taxes but *before* personal income taxes).
- Capitalization rate would reflect weighted average cost of capital (WACC; see later sections regarding adjusting from WACC to a capitalization rate for invested capital).

DIFFERENCE BETWEEN CAPITALIZATION RATE AND DISCOUNT RATE

- In the capitalization method, some base amount of return is divided by a rate called a *capitalization rate.*
- In the capitalization method, all changes in expected future increments of return are captured in the capitalization rate (the denominator) rather than in the specific projected economic returns (the numerator) in the discounting method.
- The changes in future returns are captured in the capitalization method by starting with a *discount rate* and *subtracting the projected sustainable average annual rate of growth* in the variable being capitalized. (See Gordon Growth Model in a later section.)
- Therefore,

$$c = k - g$$

where

c = capitalization rate
k = discount rate (cost of capital)
g = growth rate (expected long-term sustainable rate of growth, theoretically in perpetuity, in the net cash flow or other economic income variable being capitalized)

- Mathematically, in a perfect world, if the growth rate is estimated accurately, the capitalization method will produce an indicated value exactly the same as that produced by the discounting method.

- The relationship between the discount rate and the capitalization rate is the same whether capitalizing returns to equity or returns to all invested capital.
- Therefore, since WACC is the discount rate for returns to all invested capital,

$$c_f = WACC - g$$

where

c_f = capitalization rate for returns to all invested capital
$WACC$ = weighted average cost of capital
g = growth rate (expected long-term sustainable rate of growth, theoretically in perpetuity, in the net cash flow or other economic income variable representing returns available to all invested capital)

- If very high growth is expected in the short term followed by a slower growth period, then the discounting method may be preferred; otherwise, a growth rate that blends the short- and long-term expectations must be estimated. (High market P/Es obviously imply high expected growth rates, but timing of expected growth is speculative.)
- As in the discounting method, net cash flow (as defined in Chapter 9) is rapidly gaining favor among appraisers as the conceptually preferable measure of economic income to capitalize in the context of the income approach. (Other income variables are commonly capitalized in the context of the market approach.)

Difference between Capitalization Rate and Discount Rate References

BV201 "Business Valuation Theory," II.B.3.b, p. 6
BV202 "Income Base Approach," III.B, pp. 14–15; "Discount Rates," IV–V, pp. 19–41
BV203 Ch. 9, pp. 2–4
CoC2 Ch. 1, 2, 4, 18, App. D
FBVI Ch. 5 p. 47
Guide Sections 501, 502, 503, VAL-9a, VAL-9b
IBA1 A.3, B.14-16
IBA2 Ch. 2, 8
IBA3 Ch. K
IBA4 Ch. 3
IBA7 Ch. 12
RR59-60; RR68-609; RR83-120
VAB4 pp. 195–196, 204–210
VSB3 Ch. 13, 14, 15
VT Lesson 7

CAPITALIZATION METHOD FORMULA

No-Growth Formula

$$PV = \frac{NCF_1}{c}$$

where

PV = present value
NCF_1 = net cash flow expected in the first period immediately following
   the valuation date
c = capitalization rate

Example: Valuing a Preferred Stock

Make the following assumptions:

1. The preferred stock pays dividends of $5 per share per year.
2. The preferred stock is issued in perpetuity and is not callable.
3. It pays dividends once a year, at the end of the year. (This, of course, is a simplification; some privately owned preferred stocks pay only annually, but most publicly traded preferred stocks pay dividends quarterly.)
4. As of the valuation date, the market yield for preferred stocks of the same risk grade as the subject preferred stock is 10%. (We also must assume comparable rights, such as voting, liquidation preference, redemption, conversion, participation, cumulative dividends, etc.)
5. There is no prospect of liquidation.

Note: The par value of the preferred stock makes no difference, since it is issued in perpetuity and there is no prospect of a liquidation. The entire cash flow an investor can expect to receive over the life of the investment (perpetuity in this case) is the $5 per-year per-share dividend.

Substituting numbers derived from the preceding assumptions yields:

$$PV = \frac{\$5.00}{0.10}$$
$$= \$50.00$$

In this example, the estimated fair market value of the subject preferred stock is $50 per share, the amount a willing buyer would expect to pay and a willing seller would expect to receive (before considering any transaction costs).

Reflecting Growth in the Capitalization Method: The Gordon Growth Model (Constant Growth Model)

- For many companies, the income available to both equity investors and to all invested capital is expected to grow rather than remain static.
- A common formula for reflecting growth in the capitalization method is the Gordon Growth Model:

$$PV = \frac{NCF_0(1+g)}{k-g}$$

where

PV = present value

NCF_0 = net cash flow in period 0, the period immediately preceding the valuation date

k = discount rate (cost of capital)

g = expected long-term sustainable rate of growth in net cash flow to investor

Note: For this model to make economic sense, NCF_0 should represent a normalized amount of cash flow from the investment for the previous year, from which a steady rate of growth is expected to proceed. It is a simplified version of the discounted cash flow method, assuming constant growth from a base. Therefore, NCF_0 need not be the actual cash flow for period 0 but may be the result of certain normalization adjustments, such as elimination of the effect of one or more nonrecurring factors or adjustment of unusual expenses. Alternatively, the numerator simply could be NCF_1 if there is a good estimate of the net cash flow for the period immediately following the effective valuation date.

In fact, if NCF_0 is the actual net cash flow for period 0, it is incumbent on the valuation analyst to take reasonable steps to be satisfied that NCF_0 is indeed the most reasonable base from which to start the expected growth embedded in the growth rate. Furthermore, the valuation report should state the steps taken and the assumptions made in concluding that last year's actual results are the most realistic base for expected growth. Automatic acceptance of recent results as representative of future expectations without critical analysis is one of the most common errors in implementing the capitalization method of valuation.

Example

Assume:

1. NCF in the period just ended (period 0) was $100.
2. Cost of capital (discount rate, k) is 13%.

3. Sustainable rate of growth in net cash flow from year 0 to perpetuity is expected
    to be 3%.

Calculating the capitalized present value with these assumptions in the Gordon
Growth Model yields:

$$PV = \frac{\$100(1+0.03)}{0.13-0.03}$$
$$= \frac{\$103}{0.10}$$
$$= \underline{\underline{\$1,030}}$$

The investor in the example thus earns a *total* rate of return of 13%, comprised of
10% return in the period immediately preceding the valuation date (the capitalization
rate) plus 3% annually compounded growth in the value of the investment.

MAJOR DIFFERENCE BETWEEN DISCOUNTING AND CAPITALIZING

The difference between discounting and capitalizing is in how the analyst reflects changes over time in expected future cash flows.

- In *discounting*, each future increment of return is estimated separately and put in
  the numerator.
- In *capitalizing*, changes in future returns are estimated in the form of one average
  annual compounded growth rate, which is then subtracted from the discount rate
  in the denominator.

If we assume a constant expected growth rate in net cash flow to the investor in perpetuity, then it is a mathematical truism that the discounting method and the capitalizing method will produce identical values.

USING THE GORDON GROWTH CAPITALIZATION MODEL FOR THE TERMINAL VALUE IN THE DISCOUNTING METHOD (TWO-STAGE MODEL)

For many investments, even given an accurate estimate of the cost of capital,
there are practical problems with either a pure discounting or a pure capitalizing
method of valuation.

- *Problem with discounting:* There are few equity investments for which economic returns for each specific incremental period can be projected with accuracy many years into the future.
- *Problem with capitalizing:* For most equity investments, it is not reasonable to expect a constant growth rate in perpetuity from either the year preceding or the year following the valuation date.

This dilemma is typically dealt with by combining the discounting method and the capitalizing method into a two-stage model. The idea is to project discrete cash flows for some number of periods into the future and then to project a steady growth model starting at the end of the discrete projection period. Each period's discrete cash flow is discounted to a present value, and the capitalized value of the projected cash flows following the end of the discrete projection period is also discounted back to a present value. The sum of the present values is the total present value. The capitalized value of the projected cash flows following the discrete projection period is called the *terminal value,* or *residual value.*

The preceding narrative explanation of a two-stage model is summarized in seven steps:

1. Decide on the reasonable length of time for which discrete projections can be made.
2. Estimate specific amounts of expected cash flow for each of the discrete projection periods.
3. Estimate a long-term sustainable rate of growth in cash flows from the end of the discrete projection period forward.
4. Use the Gordon Growth Model to estimate value as of the end of the discrete projection period.
5. Discount each of the increments of cash flow back to a present value at the discount rate (cost of capital) for the number of periods until it is received.
6. Discount the terminal value (estimated in step 4) back to a present value for the number of periods in the discrete projection period (the same number of periods as the last increment of cash flow).
7. Add the values derived from steps 5 and 6.

These steps can be summarized in the following formula:

$$PV = \frac{NCF_1}{(1+k)} + \frac{NCF_2}{(1+k)^2} + \ldots + \frac{NCF_n}{(1+k)^n} + \frac{\dfrac{NCF_n(1+g)}{k-g}}{(1+k)^n}$$

where

$NCF_1 \ldots NCF_n$ = net cash flow expected in each of the periods 1 through n, n being the last period of the discrete cash flow projections

k = discount rate (cost of capital)

g = expected long-term sustainable growth rate in net cash flow, starting with the last period of the discrete projection as the base year

Example of Two-Stage Model

Although the discrete projection period in the two-stage model is typically between five and 10 years, for simplicity we use a three-year discrete projection period. Assume:

1. Expected net cash flows at the end of years 1, 2, and 3 are $100, $120, and $140, respectively.

2. Beyond year 3, cash flow is expected to increase fairly evenly at a rate of about 5% in perpetuity.

3. The cost of capital for this investment is estimated to be 12%.

Substituting numbers derived from these assumptions yields:

$$PV = \frac{\$100}{(1+0.12)} + \frac{\$120}{(1-0.12)^2} + \frac{\$140}{(1+0.12)^3} + \frac{\dfrac{\$140(1+0.05)}{0.12-0.05}}{(1+0.12)^3}$$

$$= \frac{\$100}{1.12} + \frac{\$120}{1.2544} + \frac{\$140}{1.4049} + \frac{\dfrac{\$147}{0.07}}{1.4049}$$

$$= \$89.29 + \$95.66 + \$99.65 + \frac{\$2,100}{1.4049}$$

$$= \$89.29 + \$95.66 + \$99.65 + \$1,494.77$$

$$= \underline{\underline{\$1,779.37}}$$

Thus, the estimated fair market value of this investment is $1,779.37, the amount a willing buyer would expect to pay and a willing seller would expect to receive (before considering of any transaction costs).

A common error is to discount the terminal value for $n + 1$ periods instead of n periods. The assumption we have made is that the nth-period cash flow is received at the end of the nth period, and the terminal value is the amount for which we estimate we could sell the investment as of the end of the nth period. The end of one period and the beginning of the next period are the same moment in time, so they must be discounted for the same number of periods.

Note that in the preceding example, the terminal value represents 83% of the total present value ($1,494.77 ÷ $1,779.37 = 0.83). The analyst should always keep in mind three relationships when using cost of capital in a two-stage model for valuation:

1. The shorter the projection period, the greater the impact of the terminal value on the total present value.
2. The closer the estimated growth rate is to the cost of capital, the more sensitive the model is to changes in assumptions regarding the growth rate (this is true for the straight capitalization model as well as the two-stage model); of course, if the growth rate exceeds the cost of capital, the model implodes and is useless.
3. For cyclical businesses, it is desirable to cover a complete expected cycle.

Using the Gordon Growth Capitalization Model for the Terminal Value in the Discounting Method References

CoC2 Ch. 14
Guide 505.46–505.49
Lawyer pp. 110–112
VSB3 Ch. 15

MIDYEAR CONVENTION IN THE CAPITALIZATION MODEL

Midyear Version of the Gordon Growth Model

- As in the discounting method, the basic capitalization formula implicitly assumes cash flows received at the end of each year.
- As in the discounting method, the capitalization formula can be modified to reflect the assumption that cash flows are distributed more or less evenly throughout the year.
- The modification is made by accelerating the returns by a half-year in the numerator (by multiplying the first year's expected return by $[1 + k]^{.5}$):

$$PV = \frac{NCF_1(1+k)^{0.5}}{k-g}$$

Note: See article by Todd A. Kaltman, "Capitalization Using a Mid-Year Convention," *Business Valuation Review* (December 1995): 178–182.

- As in the discounting method, this modification has the effect of increasing the indicated value, because it is assumed that the cash flows are received earlier.

MIDYEAR CONVENTION IN THE TWO-STAGE MODEL

Combining discrete period discounting and capitalized terminal value into a two-stage model, the midyear convention in the two-stage equation becomes:

$$PV = \frac{NCF_1}{(1+k)^{0.5}} + \frac{NCF_2}{(1+k)^{1.5}} + \cdots + \frac{NCF_n}{(1+k)^{n-0.5}} + \frac{\dfrac{NCF_n(1+g)(1+k)^{0.5}}{k-g}}{(1+k)^n}$$

Make the following assumptions (for simplicity, using only three years of discrete projections):

1. NCF at year 1, $100; year 2, $120; year 3, $140.
2. Constant growth in NCF following year 3 at 5% compounded annually.
3. Discount rate 12%.

$$PV = \frac{\$100}{(1+0.12)^{0.5}} + \frac{\$120}{(1+0.12)^{1.5}} + \cdots + \frac{\$140}{(1+0.12)^{2.5}} + \frac{\dfrac{\$140(1+0.05)(1+0.12)^{0.5}}{0.12-0.05}}{(1+0.12)^3}$$

$$= \frac{\$100}{1.058} + \frac{\$120}{1.185} + \frac{\$140}{1.328} + \frac{\dfrac{\$155.526}{0.07}}{1.4049}$$

$$= \$94.52 + \$101.27 + 105.42 + \frac{\dfrac{\$2,221.80}{1.4049}}{}$$

$$= \$94.52 + \$101.27 + \$105.42 + \$1,581.46$$

$$= \underline{\underline{\$1,882.67}}$$

Note that this value of $1,882.67 compares with $1,779.37 in the two-stage model with the year-end assumption.

The reader should also be aware that there is an alternative version of the terminal value factor in the two-stage model that actually is equivalent to that used in the preceding formula. Instead of using the modified capitalization equation in the numerator of the terminal value factor, the normal terminal value capitalization equation is used, and the terminal value is discounted by $n - .5$ years instead of n years.

This equation reads as follows:

$$PV = \frac{NCF_1}{(1+k)^{0.5}} + \frac{NCF_2}{(1+k)^{1.5}} + \cdots + \frac{NCF_n}{(1+k)^{n-0.5}} + \frac{\dfrac{NCF_n(1+g)}{k-g}}{(1+k)^{n-0.5}}$$

Using the same numbers as earlier, the equation works out to:

$$PV = \frac{\$100}{(1+0.12)^{0.5}} + \frac{\$120}{(1+0.12)^{1.5}} + \cdots + \frac{\$140}{(1+0.12)^{2.5}} + \frac{\dfrac{\$140(1+0.05)}{0.12-0.05}}{(1+0.12)^{2.5}}$$

$$= \frac{\$100}{1.058} + \frac{\$120}{1.185} + \frac{\$140}{1.328} + \frac{\dfrac{\$147}{0.07}}{1.328}$$

$$= \$94.52 + \$101.27 + \$105.42 + \frac{\$2,100}{1.328}$$

$$= \$94.52 + \$101.27 + \$105.42 + \$1,581.32$$

$$= \underline{\underline{\$1,882.53}}$$

Note: The $0.14 difference is a matter of rounding.

General Capitalized Return Method References

BV204 Module 2
CoC2 all chapters
FBVI Ch. 5 p. 22
Guide Sect. 504
Lawyer Ch. 8
VAB4 Ch. 10
VSB3 Ch. 15

Using Midyear Capitalization Convention References

BV204 Module 3
CoC2 pp. 30–31
FBVI Ch. 5 p. 21
Lawyer pp. 133–134
VAB4 pp. 214–215, 218
VSB3 pp. 261–265

CAPITALIZATION RATE: BUILD-UP SUMMATION METHOD

An alternative method of developing a risk premium to add to the risk-free rate in the income capitalization method is called the *Black/Green Method,* or the *Build-up Summation Method,* taught only by NACVA and not endorsed by any of the other professional organizations. The procedure is as follows:

1. Assign a number up to 10 to each of a list of risk factors within each of four categories:
   - Competition.
   - Financial strength.

- Management ability and depth.
- Profitability and stability of earnings.

2. Assign a weight to each risk factor within each category in step 1.
3. Compute a weighted average of the risk factors within each of the four categories, using the values from step 1 and the weights from step 2.
4. Add the total of the weighted averages for each of the four categories as computed in step 3.

The result is the total risk premium factor, which is added to the risk-free rate to estimate a capitalization rate. An example is shown as Exhibit 10.1.

Exhibit 10.1 Capitalization Rate: Build-Up Summation Method

	Risk Indicator	Weight	Weighted Risk
Competition			
Proprietary content	6.0	1.0	6.0
Relative size of company	2.0	1.0	2.0
Relative product/service quality	4.0	1.0	4.0
Produce/service differentiation	4.0	1.0	4.0
Market strength	2.0	1.0	2.0
Market size and share	2.0	1.0	2.0
Pricing competition	6.0	1.0	6.0
Ease of market entry	2.0	1.0	2.0
Patent/copyright protection	8.0	1.0	8.0
Total weight factors		9.0	36.0
Total weighted average			4.0
Financial Strength			
Total debt to assets	4.0	1.0	4.0
Long-term debt to equity	4.0	1.0	4.0
Current ratio	4.0	1.0	4.0
Quick ratio	4.0	1.0	4.0
Interest coverage	4.0	1.0	4.0
Total weight factors		5.0	20.0
Total weighted average			4.0
Management Ability and Depth			
Accounts receivable turnover	2.0	1.0	2.0
Inventory turnover	2.0	1.0	2.0
Fixed asset turnover	4.0	1.0	4.0
Total asset turnover	4.0	1.0	4.0
Employee turnover	8.0	1.0	8.0
Management depth	8.0	1.0	8.0
Facilities condition	6.0	1.0	6.0

Exhibit 10.1 (Continued)

Family involvement	8.0	1.0	8.0
Books and records quality	6.0	1.0	6.0
Contracts	8.0	1.0	8.0
Gross margin	4.0	1.0	4.0
Operating margin	4.0	1.0	4.0
Total weight factors		12.0	66.0
Total weighted average			5.5
Profitability and Stability of Earnings			
Years in business	2.0	1.0	2.0
Industry life cycle	4.0	1.0	4.0
Return on sales	6.0	1.0	6.0
Return on assets	4.0	1.0	4.0
Return on equity	4.0	1.0	4.0
Other considerations			
Sales growth percentage	6.0	1.0	6.0
Operating earnings growth percentage	5.0	1.0	5.0
Accounts receivable collection days	7.0	1.0	7.0
Accounts payable payment days	3.0	1.0	3.0
Operating cycle	4.0	1.0	4.0
Total weight factors		10.0	45.0
Total weighted average			4.5
Total Risk Premium Factor			18.0

Source: NACVA course, "Development of Capitalization/Discount Rates and Valuation Discounts and Premiums," p. 23.

Note: Risk factor, as well as the weights to each, is totally a function of each individual analyst's judgment, and there is no body of empirical evidence for guidance in quantifying either the risk factor values or the weights applicable to each. Therefore, many consider the method too subjective, recognizing that different analysis may opine to capitalization rates anywhere from 10 to 40% using the method, depending on the factor values and weights assigned.

Chapter 11

Market Approach: Guideline Public Company Method

RATIONALE AND BACKGROUND

- The market approach is based on the assumption that arm's-length transactions of a similar property provide empirical evidence regarding value.
- Almost all transactions in publicly traded securities are at arm's length.
- Can directly observe capitalization rates for public companies.
- In a given industry, risk and growth characteristics may be similar.
- If risk and growth characteristics differ for the subject company, adjustments should be made to pick the right capitalization rate for the subject company.
- RR59-60 strongly advocates the guideline public company method.

- IRS favors the market approach in general and the guideline public company method in particular.
- Tax Court has for decades based many decisions on the guideline public company method.
- Recognizing the uniqueness of different companies, the business valuation community today tends to use the expression *guideline company,* although the term *comparable* is also used.
- Many people erroneously think of *comparable* narrowly in the sense of similar products or the same value drivers, but the term actually refers to companies with similar risk characteristics (e.g., similar supply and demand forces and other economic risk factors; for example, very common in Tax Court to use companies that have similar consumer brand recognition and distribution, even though the products themselves may be different).

AVAILABILITY OF GUIDELINE PUBLIC COMPANY DATA

Population of Companies

- More than 16,000 companies are required to file reports electronically with the Securities and Exchange Commission (SEC):
  - More than 12,000 operating companies.
  - More than 4,000 holding companies (e.g., Real Estate Investment Trusts [REITs], mutual funds).
  - Companies capitalized less than $10 million number more than most people assume.
- Thousands more trade through OTC Bulletin Board or Pink Sheets, but financial data are not as readily available.
- Thousands of limited partnerships are registered with the SEC, hundreds of which transact fairly regularly (although this market is shrinking).

Data Available Easily and Cheaply

- EDGAR (Electronic Data Gathering, Analysis, and Retrieval System): Since May 1996 all companies required to file annual reports with the SEC must file electronically, and access through the Internet is free (several low-cost, enhanced EDGAR services are also available); major SEC filings include:
  - Form 10-K: Annual report.
  - Form 10-Q: Quarterly report.
  - Form 8-K: Significant special events report.
- Many commercial electronic databases, some with long historical information; many ratio calculations offered.

- Many print databases available by subscription and at most public libraries.

Data Scope and Reliability

- Reporting regulations set by the SEC.
- Require many data items not required in nonpublic company audited reports.
- The SEC requires additional data disclosures beyond those required in audited statements of nonpublic companies.

SELECTION OF GUIDELINE PUBLIC COMPANIES

Search Mechanisms for Guideline Public Companies

- EDGAR searchable by Standard Industrial Classification (SIC) code.
- Most commercial electronic databases searchable by SIC code.
- *Directory of Companies Required to File Annual Reports with the SEC* lists all companies required to file both by SIC code and alphabetically.

Criteria for Selection

- RR59-60 advocates use of public companies that are the same or similar to the subject company; *similar* generally has been interpreted to allow wide latitude in guideline company selection (e.g., in *Estate of Gallo v. Commissioner,* there were no good public winemaker comparables, so experts on both sides of the case used brewers, distillers, soft drink bottlers, and high-brand-recognition consumer food packagers); the object is to find companies that experience similar risk characteristics.
- Although the primary criterion is line of business, many other criteria may be considered:
  - Markets served.
  - Type of products.
  - Geographical territory served.
  - Size.
  - Comparability of financial history (e.g., profitability).

Comprehensiveness of Selection

- Define selection criteria.
- Define population from which the companies are selected.
- Select all companies that meet criteria.

- If companies that appear to meet criteria are eliminated, explain why.
- May avoid consolidated data of large conglomerates.

Number of Companies

- The better the comparability, the fewer needed.
- One is better than none, but then the public guideline company method usually cannot be the primary valuation method.
- Three could be sufficient if the companies have very similar risk profiles.
- Five to seven good guideline companies is the goal.
- Number of good companies affects the weight accorded to the method.
- If more than 10 good guideline companies are available, criteria may be tightened to include only those most comparable.

Number of Companies References

IBA2 Ch. 2, 16
IBA6 Ch. 2
Lawyer p. 149
NACVA-CA Sect. 3, App.
VAB4 p. 233
VSB3 pp. 436–438, Ch. 17, App. A

VALUATION METHODOLOGY

Value Multiples Concept

- Based on multiples of publicly traded security prices to company fundamental financial variables (e.g., net income, pretax income, gross cash flow, EBIT, sales).
- The value multiple is the inverse of the capitalization rate for each respective variable.
- Publicly traded security prices as of effective valuation date, applied to fundamental data as close to valuation date as practically possible.
- Value multiples should be applied to subject company fundamental financial variables defined the same as the public company variables on which the guideline company value multiples were based.

Equity Value Multiples

- *Price/earnings:* Stock price divided by after-tax net income per share.
  - Most widely recognized multiple.
  - Good if depreciation generally represents decrement to asset values.

- *Price/gross cash flow:* Stock price divided by net income plus noncash charges per share.
  - Good if depreciation is especially high.
  - Good if companies have varied depreciation policies.
- *Price/pretax income:* Stock price divided by net income per share before taxes.
  - Good if company has abnormal tax rates for limited period of time.
  - S corporations: May use pretax income or may attribute C corporation or personal tax rates.

S Corporations and Other Pass-Through Entities References

Guide 404.46
Lawyer pp. 158–162
VAB4 Ch. 26
VSB3 43, 403, 703
VT Lesson 7

- *Price/sales:* Stock price divided by sales per share.
  - Good if subject and guideline companies are homogeneous in operating characteristics.
  - Often used for service companies with high customer-base persistence.
- *Price/book value:* Stock price divided by book value of equity.
  - Good if asset values have recently been stated at fair market value (e.g., financial institutions, retailers with significant inventories).
  - The closer asset book values are to market values for both subject and guideline companies, the more relevant the multiple is.

Invested Capital Multiples

- *Market value of invested capital (MVIC)/earnings before interest, taxes, depreciation, and amortization (EBITDA):* MVIC divided by EBITDA.
- *MVIC/earnings before interest and taxes (EBIT):* MVIC divided by EBIT.
- *MVIC/book value of invested capital:* MVIC divided by book value of equity plus senior securities.

Note: If valuing equity using invested capital multiples, the value of senior securities needs to be subtracted from the indicated value of MVIC for the subject to obtain the indicated value of common equity for the subject.

Time Periods for Measurement of Financial Variables

- Should be same for subject company as for guideline companies (or as close as possible given available data).
- If book values, use latest comparable date available.
- For income variables, many options:
  - Last 12 months.
  - Last fiscal year.
  - Average of some number of years, such as three or five years, or an estimated cycle for a cyclical industry.
  - Weighted average of some number of years (be sure to justify numbers of years and weights).
  - Projection for coming year.

Adjustments to Guideline Company Financial Statements

Guideline company financial statements should be analyzed and, if necessary, adjusted to be comparable to those of the subject company.

- Eliminate extraordinary and/or nonrecurring items (e.g., fire, flood, or strike) that distorted results.
- Adjust from last-in-first-out (LIFO) to first-in-first-out (FIFO) inventory accounting if guideline companies and subject company are not on same basis.

Adjustments to Guideline Company Financial Statements References

FBVII Ch. 2 p. 43
Guide Section 603
IBA8
Market Ch. 7
VAB4 p. 241
VSB3 Ch. 26

Selection and Weighting of Value Multiples

- Select from multiples for which there are adequate reliable data.
- Lean toward invested capital multiples when valuing controlling interests.
- However, invested capital multiples may also be used for minority interests, especially if capital structures among companies are widely divergent.

- Usually put most weight on multiples with least statistical dispersion among guideline companies (e.g., lowest coefficient of variation; see VAB4 p. 244 and VSB3 p. 362).
- May use either subjective or mathematical weighting of multiples selected.

Selection and Weighting of Value Multiples References

FBVII Ch. 2 pp. 48–50
Guide Sections 604, 605
Lawyer pp. 156–157
Market Ch. 10
VAB4 pp. 242–249
VSB3 Ch. 26

Selection of Multiples from Range Found in Guideline Companies

- Many choices available:
  - Median.
  - Mean.
  - Upper or lower quartile.
  - Top or bottom of range.
  - Outside the observed range.
  - Multiples of guideline companies with characteristics most resembling subject company.
- Multiple selection should be based on an analysis of the fundamentals of the subject company compared with those of the guideline companies.
- Should justify choice of multiples applied to subject relative to observed guideline company ratios.
- Rationale for level of multiples selected based on comparative analysis of guideline companies versus subject company:
  - Relative growth prospects (higher growth rates lead to lower cap rates in income approach, higher multiples in market approach).
  - Relative risk ratios (see Chapter 18).

ADJUSTMENTS FROM INDICATED VALUE

- Publicly traded guideline company transactions are fully marketable minority interests.

- If valuing private company, discount for lack of marketability usually appropriate for minority interests and in some cases even for controlling interests.
- Minority discount or control premium should be considered on a case-by-case basis:
  - To what extent might the private company minority stockholders be disadvantaged compared with the public company stockholders (e.g., money otherwise available for dividends siphoned off in excess compensation to control stockholder and friends)?
  - What could a controlling interest stockholder do to make the control interest more valuable (e.g., improve management)?

Many appraisers now believe that, as in the income approach, whether this method produces a control or minority value is determined by the cash flows used, not by the fact that the value is estimated by reference to publicly traded minority interests.

Note: See Chapter 7 for relative advantages and disadvantages of the guideline public company valuation method.

Adjustments from Indicated Value References

D&P pp. 32–40, Ch. 5, 9
Guide Sections 606, 607
IBA2 Ch. 2, 16
Lawyer p. 219
Market Ch. 11, 12
NACVA-CA Sect. 3, App.
VAB4 p. 252
VSB3 Ch. 17, 27 pp. 436–38 (discounts for lack of control), App. A

Market Approach: Guideline Public Company Method References

BV201 "Data Gathering," "Data Analysis," "Business Valuation Theory," "Market Approach"
BV203 Ch. 6
BV204 Module 1
FBVII Ch. 2
Guide 205.10, Ch. 6, 1002.14, 1101.39, 1103.5, 1103.6, 1103.8, 1103.9, VAL-11
IBA1 A.3, A.12
IBA2 Ch. 2, 7, 16
IBA3 Ch. 6
IBA 6 Ch. 1
Lawyer Ch. 9
Market all chapters
NACVA-BV Ch. 9

NACVA-CA Sect. 3
RR59-60; RR77-287
VAB4 Ch.11, pp. 326–328, 373, 481–485, 497–502, 608–610, 775–781, 805–806, 822
VSB3 Ch. 5, 13, 16–21, 42
VT Lessons 1, 7

Chapter 12

Market Approach: Guideline Merger and Acquisition Method

RATIONALE AND BACKGROUND

- Similar to guideline publicly traded company rationale but deals with ownership transfers of controlling rather than minority interests.
- Need to investigate whether transaction is actually between parties with arm's-length relationship (but almost all of the transactions in the databases are at arm's length).
- If not on arm's-length basis, may represent investment value or some other definition of value rather than fair market value.

AVAILABILITY OF GUIDELINE MERGER AND ACQUISITION DATA

Because of a proliferation in recent years of data on merged and acquired companies, the guideline merger and acquisition method has become much more feasible and widely used of late.

Population of Acquired Public Companies

- Average of about 700 public companies acquired each year.
- Most convenient (and cost-effective) source is *Mergerstat/Shannon Pratt's Control Premium Study*™ (available online at *BVMarketData.com*^{sm}).
  - Data available from 1998 forward (over 3,000 transactions available as of late 2002).
  - Contains transactions in which 50.1% or more of a previously public company was acquired, whether by another public company or in a "going private" transaction.
- Exhibit 12.1 is a transaction report showing the data available for each company online in *Mergerstat/Shannon Pratt's Control Premium Study*™ at *BVMarketData.com*^{sm}.

Exhibit 12.1   Mergerstat/Shannon Pratt's Control Premium Study™ Transaction Report

---

Transaction Details

	Acquiror	Target
SIC	6021 National Commercial Banks	6021 National Commercial Banks
NAICS	52211 Commercial banking	52211 Commercial banking
Name	US Bancorp	Scripps Financial Corp
Business Description	National commercial bank	National commercial bank
Stock Exchange	New York	American
Nation	United States	United States

Premiums

2 Month	1 Month	1 Week	1 Day	MergerStat Control Premium
1.197	0.846	0.792	0.357	0.357

Target Stock Prices (per share)

CUSIP	Target Stock Ticker	Unaffected Price	Announce Day Price	1 Day Price	1 Week Price	1 Month Price	2 Month Price
	SLJ	17.000	17.000	17.000	12.875	12.500	10.500

Sale Details

Date Announced	6/27/00
Date Effective	10/13/00
Deal Value ($mil)	$160
Deal Currency	United States Dollar
% of Shares Acquired	100.0
% of Shares Held at Date Announced	N/A
% of Shares Held after Acquisition	100.0
Purchase Price Per Share ($'s)	$23.07
Common Shares Acquired (mil)	6.918
Deal Exchange Rate	1.000
Purchase Price/Share (Home currency)	23.070
Consideration	S
Attitude	
Form	ACQ
Transaction Purpose	Horizontal

Target Financial Data ($mil)

LTM Net Sales	53.970
LTM EBITDA	23.460
LTM EBIT	21.970
LTM Net Income	4.740
BV Target Common Equity	46.740
Target Invested Capital	160.362
Book Value Per Share	6.757
Common Shares Outstanding (000's)	6.918
Operating Profit Margin	0.407
Net Profit Margin	0.088

Target Pricing Multiples

Implied MVE ($mil)	159.592
Price/Sales	2.957
Price/Income	33.669
Price/Book Value	3.410
Target Invested Capital/EBIT	
Target Invested Capital/EBITDA	

Source: Mergerstat LP: *www.mergerstat.com.*

N/A = Not available

- Additional data may be obtained from filings with the Securities and Exchange Commission (SEC).
- See Chapter 21 for additional sources of public company acquisition data.

Data on Acquisitions of Private Companies

- There has been great progress in collecting reliable data on private company transactions in recent years.
- The most recent is *Pratt's Stats*™, sponsored by the International Business Brokers Association (IBBA).
  - Data collected primarily from intermediaries (brokers); if buyer was a public company, data collected from SEC filings.
  - Over 4,700 transactions as of late 2002.
  - Almost 60 data points for each transaction (e.g., summary income statements, summary balance sheets, 10 valuation multiples, terms, data on noncompete and employment agreements, sale date, location, Standard Industrial Classification (SIC) and North American Industrial Classification System (NAICS) codes, business description, etc.).
  - Exhibit 12.2 is a transaction report showing the data available for each company in *Pratt's Stats*™ at *BVMarketData.com*^sm.
  - Size range < $100,000 to $999 million with emphasis on middle-market companies.
- *BIZCOMPS*®
  - Data collected from business brokers.
  - Over 5,500 transactions as of late 2002.
  - About 20 data points for each transaction (e.g., sales, discretionary earnings, two valuation multiples, terms, sale data, location, SIC and NAICS codes, etc.).
  - Exhibit 12.3 is a transaction report showing the data available for each company in *BIZCOMPS*® at *BVMarketData.com*^sm.
  - Searchable online for any of the above fields.
  - Emphasis on small companies; 97% under $1 million.
- Exhibit 12.4 is a summary as of mid-2002 of *Pratt's Stats*™, the *Public Company Database, BIZCOMPS*®, *Mergerstat/Shannon Pratt's Control Premium Study*™, *The FMV Restricted Stock Study*™, and the *Valuation Advisors' Lack of Marketability Discount Study*™, which can be searched online simultaneously.
- *IBA Market Data Base*
  - Data collected from various sources.
  - Over 23,000 transactions as of late 2002, going back over 20 years.
  - About 15 data points for each transaction (e.g., sales, discretionary earnings, two valuation multiples, sale date, location, SIC codes, etc.).
  - Available to IBA members on request.

Exhibit 12.2   Pratt's Stats™ Transaction Report

Transaction Details

Intermediary Name	N/A
Firm Name	N/A
SIC	7373 Computer Integrated Systems Design
NAICS	451152
Business Description	Design Internet, Intranet and Extranet Systems
Company Name	PC Workstation dba PWR Systems
Sale Location	N/A
Years in Business	N/A
Number Employees	N/A
Report Date	3/27/00

Income Data

Data is "Latest Full Year" Reported	Yes
Data is Restated (see Notes for any explanation)	No
Income Statement Date	12/31/99
Net Sales	$15,928,205
COGS	$13,094,364
Gross Profit	$2,833,841
Yearly Rent	N/A
Owner's Compensation	N/A
Other Operating Expenses	N/A
Noncash Charges	N/A
Total Operating Expenses	$2,454,787
Operating Profit	$379,054
Interest Expenses	$0
EBT	$379,054
Taxes	$12,541
Net Income	$366,513

Asset Data

Data is "Latest Full Year" Reported	Yes
Data is "Purchase Price Allocation agreed upon by Buyer and Seller"	No
Balance Sheet Date	12/31/99
Cash Equivalents	$457,850
Trade Receivables	$3,692,224
Inventory	$567,836
Other Current Assets	$3,426
Total Current Assets	$4,721,336
Fixed Assets	$6,189
Real Estate	N/A
Intangibles	N/A
Other Noncurrent Assets	$18,904
Total Assets	$4,746,429
Long-term Liabilities	N/A
Total Liabilities	N/A

Transaction Data

Date Sale Intiated	N/A
Date of Sale	3/27/00
Asking Price	N/A
Equity Price	$6,200,000
Market Value of Invested Capital	$6,200,000
Liabilities Assumed	N/A
Employment Agreement Value	N/A
Noncompete Value	N/A
Amount of Down Payment	$6,200,000
Stock or Asset Sale	Stock
Company Type	C Corporation
Was there an Employment/Consulting Agreement?	Yes
Was there an Assumed Lease in the sale?	No
Was there a Renewal Option with the Lease?	No

Additional Transaction Information

Was there a Note in the consideration paid?	Yes
Was there a personal guarantee on the Note?	No
Terms	Consideration paid as follows: $1,200,000 cash, note payable of $500,000 payable in 12 monthly installments, and 1,500,000 shares of buyer's common stock valued at $4,500,000.
Balance of Assumed Lease (Months)	N/A
Terms of Lease	N/A
Noncompete Length (Months)	N/A
Noncompete Description	N/A
Employment/Consulting Agreement Description	Entered into 3 employment agreements for Vice Presidents and Executive Officers, each for $200,000 per year and up to $25,000 bonus.
Additional Notes	

Valuation Multiples

Equity Price/Net Sales	0.389
Equity Price/Gross Cash Flow	N/A
Equity Price/EBT	16.357
Equity Price/Net Income	16.916
Equity Price/Book Value of Equity	N/A
MVIC/Net Sales	0.389
MVIC/EBITDA	N/A
MVIC/EBIT	16.357
MVIC/Discretionary Earnings	N/A
MVIC/Book Value of Invested Capital	N/A

Financial Ratios

Net Income/Sales	0.023
EBIT/Sales	0.024
Sales/Total Assets	0.298
Sales/Fixed Assets	0.000
EBIT/Interest Expense	N/A
Long-term Debt/Total Assets	N/A
Return on Assets	0.077
Return on Equity	N/A

Source: BVR website. Copyright © Pacific Services, Inc.

N/A = Not available

Exhibit 12.3 BIZCOMPS® Transaction Report

Transaction Details	
Business Description	Deli-Office Building
SIC	5812 Eating and Drinking Places
NAICS	722211 Limited-service restaurants
Location	Albuquerque, NM
Number Of Employees	N/A

Transaction Data	
Sale Date	5/20/99
Days On Market	202
Ask Price (000)	$20.0
Sale Price (000)	$12.0
Percent Down	100.0%
Terms on Outstanding Consideration	N/A

Income Data ($000s)		Asset Data ($000s)	
Annual Gross Sales	$55.0	Inventory Value	$0.0
Franchise Royalty	N/A	Furniture, Fixtures and Equipment	$7.0
SDCF	$10.0	Value Of Real Estate	N/A

Operating Ratios		Valuation Multiples	
SDCF/Annual Gross Sales	0.182	Sale Price/AnnualGross Sales	0.218
Rent/Annual Gross Sales	6.5%	Sale Price/SDCF	1.200

Copyright © 2002 BIZCOMPS®. All rights reserved. Available at *www.BVMarketData.com.*
(888) BUS-VALU, (503) 291-7693
N/A = Not available

- Exhibit 12.5 is a sample report received from IBA in response to a request for a specific SIC code).
- Mostly small companies.

Data on Acquisitions of Public and Private Companies

- *Done Deals®*
  - Data collected from SEC filings (see Appendix A for access information).
- *Pratt's Stats™* has a public company section, which is being distributed as a part of the subscription to the private company database at press time, but which is anticipated to be renamed and spun off as a separate database in the future.

Nature and Limitations of Guideline M&A Data

- Because it would be an unlikely coincidence that merger and acquisition (M&A) transactions would occur on subject company valuation date, should select a time frame for transactions to consider taking into account:
  - Relevant time frame dependent partly on stability or changes in industry valuation environment (e.g., industries get hot and cold in the market, which affects pricing multiples).

Exhibit 12.4   Data Available from *BVMarketData*^{SM} Databases

Business Valuation_{SM}
R e s o u r c e s

PIONEERING THE FUTURE OF BUSINESS VALUATIONS

BVMarketData^{SM}

| BVResources | BVLibrary | BVStore |

Home
Search All
Pratt's Stats
MergerStat CPS
BIZCOMPS
Public Company
FMV Stock Study
Subscribe
Contribute
About Us
Contact Us
Policies
Help

LOGGED IN

Search All Databases (4 Digit Codes)

Select the count to view more information. By selecting the count, SUBSCRIBERS will view the details of the databases to which they subscribe and VISITORS will view a brief summary of the available information in each database. Click on the subscribe menu to gain instant access to any of the databases.

Search All Databases (4 Digit Codes)

Select the count to view more information. By selecting the count, SUBSCRIBERS will view the details of the databases to which they subscribe and VISITORS will view a brief summary of the available information in each database. Click on the subscribe menu to gain instant access to any of the databases.

Counts

A   Pratt's Stats™
B   Mergerstat / Shannon Pratt's Control Premium Study™
C   BIZCOMPS®
D   Public Company™
E   FMV Restricted Stock Study™
F   Valuation Advisors' Lack of Marketability Study™

SIC	A	B	C	D	E	F
7371 Computer Programming Services	138	29	12	12	1	90
7372 Prepackaged Software	109	153	6	40	8	368
7373 Computer Integrated Systems Design	165	57		13	3	78
7374 Computer Processing and Data Preparation and Processing Services	38	7	7	4		74
7375 Information Retrieval Services	28	73		9	1	15
7376 Computer Facilities Management Services	2	1				
7377 Computer Rental and Leasing			1			
7378 Computer Maintenance and Repair	3	1	3	1		
7379 Computer Related Services, NEC	58	28	7	5		6
7381 Detective, Guard, and Armored Car Services	2	3	9			
7382 Security Systems Services	11	3	2	1	2	
7383 News Syndicates		2				
7384 Photofinishing Laboratories	9		24			
7389 Business Services, NEC	101	9	179	5		257
7320 Business services	1					1
7330 Business services				1		
7341 Business services			2			
7350 Business services			1			
7370 Business services	2		1			34
7390 Business services			1			
7399 Business services			8			

Exhibit 12.5 Sample Transaction Report from *IBA Market Database*

SIC Code:	5568

The information below is supplied in response to your request for data to be used in applying the "Market Data Approach" to business appraisal. Because of the nature of sources from which the information is obtained, we are not able to guarantee its accuracy. Neither do we make any representation as to the applicability of the information to any specific appraisal situation.

The following is an explanation of the entries in the data table:

Business Type	Principal line of business.
SIC Code	Principal Standard Industrial Classification number applicable to the business sold.
Annual Gross	Reported annual sales volume of business sold.
Discretionary Earnings	Reported annual earnings, excluding owner's compensation and before interest and taxes.
Owner's Comp.	Reported owner's compensation.
Sales Price	Total reported consideration; i.e., cash, liabilities assumed, etc., excluding real estate.
Price/Gross	Ratio of total consideration to reported annual gross.
Price/Earnings	Ratio of total consideration to reported annual earnings.
Yr/Mo of Sale	Year and month during which transaction was consummated.

Business Type	Annual Gross $000's	Annual Earnings $000's	Owner's Comp. $000's	Sale Price $000's	Price/ Gross	Price/ Earnings	Geographic	Yr/Mo of Sale
Widgets—Retail	1300			1350	1.04		FL	94/04
Widgets	1256	300		1350	1.07	4.50	FL	94/11
Widgets	1202	357		1700	1.41	4.76	FL	97/04
Widget Store	1149	208		450	0.39	2.16	CA	92/06
Widgets	960	432		860	0.90	1.99	CA	90/06
Widgets	671	105		225	0.34	2.14		98/02
Widgets	559	162		98	0.18	0.60	Texas	93/01
Widgets	550	102		85	0.15	0.83	Texas	95/01
Widgets	540	155		710	1.31	4.58		98/01
Retail Widgets	506	72		194	0.38	2.69		98/03
Widgets Store	500	150		488	0.98	3.25	NY	91/12
Widgets	460	132		1350	2.93	10.23		97/01
Widget Store	452	137		115	0.25	0.84	Texas	95/01
Widgets	441	136		190	0.43	1.40	FL	93/11
Widgets	441	81		780	1.77	9.63	IN	95/03
Widgets	437	183		500	1.14	2.73		96/05
Widgets	400	139		90	0.23	0.65	FL	01/03
Widgets	384	66		107	0.28	1.62		98/01
Retail Widgets	321	94		145	0.45	1.54		97/10
Widgets Store	306	138	45	450	1.47	3.26	New England	86/09
Widgets	301	91		266	0.88	2.92	FL	93/01
Widget Store	285	50		105	0.37	2.10	FL	
Widgets	280	79		80	0.29	1.01	FL	
Widgets	275	50		116	0.42	2.32		98/04
Retail Widgets	265	86		453	1.71	5.27	New England	87/09
Widgets Store	265			364	1.37		CA	91/07
Widgets	250	75		40	0.16	0.53	FL	01/11

Source: Data from *Market Analysis Portfolio Report of Widgets—Retail; SIC Code - 5568.*

- Sometimes may consider post–valuation date transactions (especially if already announced at the valuation date) if only evidence of value and *not* transactions that affected value (e.g., just another potentially comparable guideline sale, but not something regarded as an event that had any impact on the value of the subject).
- Unless acquired company was public, no legal requirement that transaction data be reported.

SELECTION OF GUIDELINE M&A COMPANIES

Search Mechanisms for Guideline M&A Companies

- No single search directory; usually need to use multiple sources.
- Both print and electronic sources available (see Chapter 21).

Criteria for Selection

- Similar to publicly traded guideline company criteria.
- May have to loosen criteria because fewer transactions are available.

Comprehensiveness of Selection

- Define selection criteria.
- As with public companies, define population considered.
- Select all transactions that meet the criteria.
- Explain reasons for any later elimination.
- Number of guideline companies usually is limited by available transactions on arm's-length basis with adequate data available.

Selection of Guideline M&A Companies References

Market pp. 55–71, 269–271
VAB4 pp. 266–277

VALUATION METHODOLOGY

- Value multiple concepts and definitions same as for public companies.
- Need to identify whether asset or stock sale.

- Need to compare what was included (e.g., working capital) with what is being valued for subject company and adjust indicated values for any differences.
- Financial statement analysis and adjustments generally same as for guideline public companies.
- Because M&A transactions are not on the same date as effective valuation date for subject company, may need to make some adjustments for time differences.
- Most common adjustment is for differences in industry valuation multiples (e.g., price/earnings multiples that were prevalent in the market for the particular industry) between guideline transaction date and subject effective valuation date.

ADJUSTMENTS FROM INDICATED VALUE

- Mergers and acquisitions usually represent control transactions.
- Sales of entire companies do not have the liquidity characteristics of public stock transactions.
- If valuing a controlling interest:
  - No control or minority adjustment in most cases.
  - Discount for lack of marketability may be considered on a case-by-case basis and may be controversial.
- If valuing a minority interest, usually would need a minority interest discount *and* a discount for lack of marketability.
- Consider the possibility that prices may reflect elements of investment value rather than strictly fair market value.

   Note: See Chapter 7 for relative advantages and disadvantages of guideline M&A method.

Market Approach: Guideline Merger and Acquisition Method References

   BV201 p. 39
   BV203 Ch. 6, 7
   BV204 Module 1
   D&P pp. 31–32, Ch. 5, 9
   FBVII Ch. 2 pp. 58–71
   IBA3
   Lawyer Ch. 9
   Market all chapters
   VAB4 Ch. 12, pp. 374, 806
   VSB3 Ch. 18, 21

Prior Transactions, Offers, and Buy-Sell Agreements

Types of Subject Company Transactions
Factors to Analyze Regarding Prior Transactions
    Were They Arm's Length?
    Proximity in Time
    Size of Transaction
    Was the Transaction Pursuant to a Buy-Sell or Other Contractual Agreement?
Prior Offers
Buy-Sell Agreements

It is important not to overlook prior transactions involving the subject company as part of the market approach. They may provide some of the best evidence of value.

TYPES OF SUBJECT COMPANY TRANSACTIONS

- Transfer of ownership of the entire company controlling interest or a minority interest.
- Purchases or sales of minority interests.
- Acquisitions by the subject company.

FACTORS TO ANALYZE REGARDING PRIOR TRANSACTIONS

Were They Arm's Length?

If prior transactions were not on an arm's-length basis (i.e., either between unrelated parties or clearly a negotiated transaction) they may provide only weak (or no) evidence of value.

Proximity in Time

Value may require adjustments for:

- Internal company conditions.
- External market conditions.

Size of Transaction

Was the size of the transaction relevant to the size currently being valued? (i.e., was it a somewhat similar size of ownership block?)

Was the Transaction Pursuant to a Buy-Sell or Other Contractual Agreement?

- If so, does same agreement apply to subject interest?
- If not, how was prior transaction value determined?

Factors to Analyze Regarding Prior Transactions References

BV202 "Other Considerations," pp. 74–82
Guide Section 708
Lawyer pp. 162–163
Market Ch. 4
RR59-60
VAB4 pp. 84, 272–274
VT Lesson 7

PRIOR OFFERS

- Were they bona fide?
- Did offeror have the financial capability to consummate the transaction?
- Was the offer on an arm's-length basis?
- Are enough details available to compute or estimate a cash-equivalent price and value multiples?

BUY-SELL AGREEMENTS

- Is the interest subject to a buy-sell, redemption, or any other contractual agreement?
- If so, is it an arm's-length agreement?
- Is it enforceable?
- Has it been used in past transactions?
- Is it controlling for this particular transaction?

- How does it affect marketability?
  - Helps provide liquidity or
  - Restricts marketability.
- Was it representative of what unrelated parties reasonably could have agreed to at the time it was executed?

Note: A buy-sell agreement might not be determinative of value for gift and estate tax purposes, even though it is legally enforceable. Consequently, it is possible that an estate could be liable for a greater amount of estate tax on stock than the amount the estate would be able to realize on the forced sale of the stock pursuant to the buy-sell agreement (see Chapter 23).

Buy-Sell Agreements References

Lawyer pp. 162–163
Market Ch. 4
NACVA-BV Ch. 1
VAB4 pp. 72, 386, 590, 595–596, 610–611, Ch. 29, pp. 824, 845–846
VSB3 pp. 52–54, 58, 439, Ch. 28, 38
VT Lesson 10

Chapter 14

Adjusted (Net) Asset Method

THEORY OF THE ADJUSTED NET ASSET METHOD

- The theory of the adjusted net asset method (also called the *asset accumulation method*) is that a buyer would not pay more than it would cost to create an entity of equivalent utility (economic principle of substitution).

- The concept is to adjust all assets and liabilities, tangible and intangible, whether recorded on the balance sheet or not, to fair market value (FMV); the net of the adjusted asset minus liability values is the indicated value of the equity.
- Adjustment to asset values should reflect appropriate premise of value:
  - *Going concern:* If valuing on a going-concern basis, adjust all assets and liabilities to FMV on a going-concern basis.
  - *Liquidation:* If valuing on a liquidation basis, adjust all assets and liabilities to FMV on a liquidation basis.
    - Orderly liquidation
    - Forced liquidation
- Business appraisers are not expected to be expert appraisers of tangible assets.
- However, because asset appraisals come into play, the business appraiser using them should know the basics of how appraisals in other disciplines (e.g., machinery and equipment, real estate) are conducted; all appraisal disciplines recognize the three basic valuation approaches:
  1. Income.
  2. Market (in real estate, called "*sales comparison*").
  3. Cost.

Exhibit 14.1 presents a sample balance sheet summary based on adjusted net assets.

Exhibit 14.1   Sample Balance Sheet Adjustments XYZ Company

	6/30/94 ($)	Adjustment ($)	As Adjusted ($)
Assets			
Current assets			
Cash and equivalents	740,000		740,000
Accounts receivable	2,155,409		2,155,409
Inventory	1,029,866	200,300[a]	1,230,166
Prepaid expenses	2,500		2,500
Total current assets	3,927,775	200,300	4,128,075
Fixed assets			
Land and buildings	302,865	(49,760)[b]	253,105
Furniture and fixtures	155,347	(113,120)[b]	42,227
Automotive equipment	478,912	(391,981)[b]	86,931
Machinery and equipment	759,888	(343,622)[b]	416,266
Total fixed assets, cost	1,697,012	(898,483)	798,529
Accumulated depreciation	(1,298,325)	1,298,325[c]	0

Exhibit 14.1   (Continued)

	6/30/94 ($)	Adjustment ($)	As Adjusted ($)
Total fixed assets, net	398,687	399,842	798,529
Real estate—nonoperating	90,879	43,121[d]	134,000
Other assets			
Goodwill, net	95,383	(95,383)[e]	0
Organization costs, net	257	(257)[e]	0
Investments	150,000	20,000[d]	170,000
Patents	0	100,000[e]	100,000
Total other assets	245,640	24,360	270,000
Total assets	4,662,981	667,623	5,330,604
Liabilities and equity			
Current liabilities			
Accounts payable	1,935,230		1,935,230
Bank note, current	50,000		50,000
Accrued expenses	107,872		107,872
Additional tax liability	0	267,049[f]	267,049
Total current liabilities	2,093,102	267,049	2,360,151
Long-term debt	350,000		350,000
Total liabilities	2,443,102	267,049	2,710,151
Equity			
Common stock	2,500		2,500
Paid-in capital	500,000		500,000
Retained earnings	1,717,379	400,574[g]	2,117,953
Total equity	2,219,879	400,574	2,620,453
Total liabilities and equity	4,662,981	667,623	5,330,604

Source: American Society of Appraisers, BV201 course, v.1.2 (9/02), Exhibit 21.
[a] Add back LIFO reserve.
[b] Deduct economic depreciation.
[c] Remove accounting depreciation.
[d] Add appreciation of value, per real estate appraisal.
[e] Remove historical goodwill. Value identifiable intangibles and put on books.
[f] Add tax liability of total adjustment at 40 percent tax rate.
[g] Summation of adjustments.

REAL ESTATE APPRAISALS

Distinction between Real Estate and Real Property

- *Real estate:* Subset of the broader term *real property,* with *real estate* representing the tangible elements of real property (e.g., land, land improvements, buildings, and building improvements).

- *Real property:* Includes real estate as well as the intangible legal rights associated with real property (e.g., a leasehold estate, mineral rights).

Real Estate Appraisal Methods and Terminology

Cost Approach

- Several cost approach methods.
- One of most common methods is the depreciated reproduction cost method:

Reproduction Cost (New) of Buildings and Improvements

Less:	Allowance for incurable functional obsolescence
Equals:	Replacement cost
Less:	Allowance for physical deterioration
Equals:	Depreciated replacement cost
Less:	Allowance for economic or external obsolescence
Less:	Allowance for curable functional obsolescence
Equals:	Market value of buildings and improvements

To complete the cost approach, the value of the land is added to the value of the buildings and improvements. The sum of these two values estimates the market value of the subject real estate.

Income Capitalization Approach

As with business appraisal, there are two methods with slightly different terminology and definitions of variables.

- *Direct capitalization method:* Capitalizes normalized economic income; most common economic income variable used is *pretax net operating income (NOI)*, defined as normalized rental income less operating expenses, including normal repairs and maintenance.
- *Yield capitalization method:* Analogous to the business valuation discounting method, usually involving a discrete projection period and a residual (terminal) value; generally uses pretax net operating income as economic income variable to be discounted.

Sales Comparison Approach

Appraiser seeks sales of other properties as comparable as possible to the subject property and as close in time to the effective valuation date as reasonably possible. Factors to consider in making quantitative adjustments between comparables and subject include:

- Age of each transaction (i.e., elapsed time from the valuation date).
- Land-to-building ratio of each property.

- Absolute location and relative location of each property compared with population centers, highways, and so forth.
- Age of each property.
- Physical condition of each property.
- Municipal and other services available to each property.
- Frontage and access of each property.
- Topography of land and soil type of each comparable property.
- Environmental aspects of each property.
- Special financing or other terms regarding each sales transaction.

Market Value

Real estate terminology typically uses the phrase *market value* rather than *fair market value*. The *Uniform Standards of Professional Appraisal Practice* (USPAP)[1] defines *market value* as:

> The major focus of most real property appraisal assignments. Both economic and legal definitions of market value have been developed and refined. A current economic definition agreed upon by agencies that regulate federal financial institutions in the United States of America is:
>
> The most probable price which a property should bring in a competitive and open market under all conditions requisite to a fair sale, the buyer and seller each acting prudently and knowledgeably, and assuming the price is not affected by undue stimulus. Implicit in this definition is the consummation of a sale as of a specified date and the passing of title from seller to buyer under conditions whereby:
>
> 1. buyer and seller are typically motivated;
> 2. both parties are well informed or well advised and acting in what they consider their best interests;
> 3. a reasonable time is allowed for exposure in the open market;
> 4. payment is made in terms of cash in United States dollars or in terms of financial arrangements comparable thereto; and
> 5. the price represents the normal considerations for the property sold unaffected by special or creative financing or sales concessions granted by anyone associated with the sale.
>
> Substitution of another currency for United States dollars in the fourth condition is appropriate in other countries or in reports addressed to clients from other countries.
>
> Persons performing appraisal services that may be subject to litigation are cautioned to seek the exact legal definition of market value in the jurisdiction in which the services are being performed.

Real Estate Appraisal on a Fee Simple Interest Basis

- Unlike the business valuation situation, in which the appraisal may represent either entire invested capital or equity, there is no comparable method to directly appraise only the equity value of a real estate holding.

- Most estate appraisal methods value the fee simple interest (entire ownership interest in the subject property), without regard to how the ownership or debt interests may be divided.

Real Property Appraisals References

FBVII Ch. 1 p. 14
VAB4 pp. 317–320
VSB3 pp. 408–409

MACHINERY AND EQUIPMENT APPRAISALS

Machinery and Equipment Appraisal Definitions

- *Reproduction cost new:* Current cost of reproducing an exact replica.
- *Replacement cost new:* Current cost of buying a similar item with the *nearest equivalent utility* to the item being appraised.
- *Fair market value:*
  - *Basic definition:* Same as definition of FMV used in business valuation.
  - *Fair market value in continued use:* The amount that reasonably may be expected to be paid between a willing buyer and a willing seller, with equity to both, neither under compulsion to buy or sell and both fully aware of all relevant facts and *including freight, tax, and installation.*
- *Liquidation Value:*
  - *Orderly liquidation value:* The amount of gross proceeds that could be expected from the sale of the appraised assets, held under *orderly sales conditions,* given a reasonable period of time to find a purchaser, considering a complete sale of all of the assets *as is, where is,* with the buyer assuming all cost of removal, with all sales made free and clear of all liens and encumbrances.
  - *Forced liquidation (e.g., one-week liquidation):* Same as orderly liquidation value but with a very limited time to sell the assets.

Machinery and Equipment Depreciation Methods

Use one of the following:

- Age and useful economic life analysis.
- Estimate of FMV of assets by used equipment market; difference between used FMV and replacement cost represents measure of depreciation.

Exhibit 14.2 shows the ASA's Machinery and Equipment Committee value definitions.

Exhibit 14.2   American Society of Appraisers' Machinery and Equipment Valuation Definitions

---

Reproduction cost new is the cost of reproducing a new replica of the property on the basis of current prices with same or similar materials, as of a specific date. *(Reproducing an exact machine, part by part, bolt by bolt, rather than replacing its utility, as you might with a newer model. Replacing its utility, as you might with a newer model, is "replacement cost new," as described above.)*

Replacement cost new is the current cost of a similar property having the nearest equivalent utility as the property being appraised, as of a specific date.

a. Replaces the utility of an asset, does not necessarily "reproduce" the asset exactly.

b. Is the amount to replace item with a *new* one.

c. Definition sometimes applicable for insurance purposes.

d. Fails to recognize loss of value of existing item as result of deterioration (age, wear and tear, etc.).

e. Not generally applicable to business appraisals.

Depreciated replacement cost new (or replacement cost, present age/condition or used) is "replacement cost new" less physical depreciation, functional obsolescence, and economic obsolescence.

a. Takes account of loss of value of existing item as result of age, deterioration (wear and tear), and/or obsolescence.

b. May or may not include make-ready costs such as delivery, installation, tooling, debugging, etc.

c. "Depreciation" here is the loss in value from *all causes*, including such factors as physical deterioration, functional obsolescence, and economic obsolescence.

   (1) Physical depreciation is a loss in value caused by wear and tear, etc. Physical conditions that affect value are deterioration from age, wear and tear from use, fatigue and stress, exposure to the elements, and lack of maintenance.

   (2) Functional obsolescence is a loss in value caused by conditions *within* the property. Causes of functional obsolescence are lack of utility, excess capacity, changes in design, and efficiency.

   (3) Economic obsolescence is the loss in value caused by conditions *external* to the property. Causes of economic obsolescence are government regulation, availability of raw materials, availability of labor supply, market accessibility, earning power, and management concepts.

Fair market value in continued use (value in use) is the fair market value of an item, including installation and the contribution of the item to the operating facility. This value presupposes the continued utilization of the item in conjunction with all other installed items.

a. In theory, measure of "economic contribution" of asset being valued.

b. In practice, is usually "Depreciated Replacement Cost New" plus delivery, installation, and other make-ready costs.

c. Is the definition generally used for "Going Concern" asset appraisals and purchase price allocation.

Source: American Society of Appraisers (ASA), definitions approved by ASA's Machinery & Equipment Committee. BV201 course, v.l.2 (9/02), pp. 88–91.

Machinery and Equipment Appraisals References

FBVII Ch. 1 p. 15

VAB4 pp. 321–324

VSB3 pp. 106–108, 385–386

INVENTORY APPRAISALS

Types of Inventory

- Service firms (e.g., accounting and law firms): Work in process (essentially, un-filled receivables, sometimes for contingency fee work) usually is primary inventory item of significant value.
- Manufacturing firms:
  - Raw materials.
  - Work in process.
  - Finished goods.
- Merchandising firms (e.g., retailers and wholesalers): Generally inventory held for sale.

Inventory Valuation Methods

- For tangible inventory, three common methods of valuation:
  1. Cost of reproduction.
  2. Comparative sales methods.
  3. Income method.
- Revenue Procedure 77-12 concisely summarizes the previously mentioned methods.

INTANGIBLE ASSET APPRAISALS

Types of Intangible Assets

- Generally, all intangible assets can be grouped conveniently into 10 categories:
  1. Customer related (e.g., customer lists).
  2. Contract related (e.g., favorable supplier contracts).
  3. Location related (e.g., certificates of need).
  4. Marketing related (e.g., trademarks and trade names).
  5. Data processing related (e.g., computer software).

6. Technology related (e.g., engineering drawings and technical documentation).
7. Employee related (e.g., employment agreements).
8. Goodwill related (e.g., going-concern value).
9. Engineering related (e.g., patents and trade secrets).
10. Literary related (e.g., literary and musical composition copyrights).

- In addition (related to points 4, 5, 9, and 10), there is a special subgroup of intangible assets called intellectual properties; all intellectual properties (which are themselves part of the 10 categories of intangible assets) can be grouped conveniently into two categories:
  1. Creative (e.g., copyrights).
  2. Innovative (e.g., patents).

Intangible Asset Valuation Methods

As with other assets, intangible assets are valued by these generally accepted appraisal approaches:

- *Income approach:* Present value of expected benefits; approach used most often in valuing intangibles, partly because it addresses directly what creates value in the intangible and partly because of difficulty in obtaining reliable data for other approaches.
- *Market approach:* Uses guideline market sales of license transactions; good for those instances in which reliable guideline sales or license transaction data are available.
- *Cost approach:* Cost to replace or reproduce the intangible asset or costs avoided (e.g., royalty payments) as a result of having or using the intangible asset. (If using this approach, be careful to verify that there is or will be a related income stream that justifies this cost.)
- *Rules of thumb:* Sometimes used, but their reliability is open to question; generally should not be used as only method.

WHEN ASSET APPRAISALS MAY BE NEEDED

If the asset valuations are important to the assignment, and appraisals of certain assets are beyond the scope of the business appraiser's qualifications, then a separate asset appraisal by a qualified party may be appropriate. Examples of such situations can include:

- If asset liquidations are a consideration.
- If purchase price allocations are required.

- If company value primarily or heavily depends on asset values (e.g., holding companies).
- If nonoperating assets are a factor.

When Asset Appraisals May Be Needed References

Guide 701.7–701.10
VSB3 Ch. 23

SELECTING AND EVALUATING ASSET APPRAISERS

If the business appraiser is using an asset appraisal, it is often important to understand and evaluate that appraisal:

- Several organizations offer certification in various appraisal disciplines (e.g., American Society of Appraisers is multidisciplinary; Appraisal Institute offers real estate certification).
- USPAP applies to appraisals of all kinds of assets and allows for:
  - Complete appraisals.
  - Limited appraisals (invoking certain departure provisions).
- Look for same factors as in a business appraisal:
  - Appraiser certification.
  - Appraiser's qualifications (including state certification, such as state-licensed real estate appraiser, state-certified real estate appraiser, and state-certified general appraiser as well as professional associations designations).
  - Statement of contingent and limiting conditions.
  - No errors.
  - Comprehensiveness, full documentation, reasonableness, and persuasiveness.

TAX-AFFECTING ASSET WRITE-UPS

- Tax-affecting is clearly appropriate if sale of assets is imminent (e.g., inventory, other assets intended to be sold).
- Tax-affecting is controversial if asset sale is not imminent or is speculative:
  - Internal Revenue Service (IRS) objects to tax-affecting if sale is not contemplated.
  - Family law courts often take similar position.
  - But since Tax Reform Act of 1986 (repeal of General Utilities Doctrine), cannot liquidate corporation or assets to avoid capital gains tax.

- Thus, if sale of assets not being imminent is the argument given for not tax-affecting asset value adjustments, why put *any* weight on asset value method?
- As a practical matter, it seems reasonable that a willing buyer would pay less for stock with a large trapped-in capital gain, and a willing seller would be willing to take less to get rid of the overhanging liability.

TYPE OF VALUE FROM ADJUSTED NET ASSET METHOD

Control versus Minority Value

Generally, asset-based methods produce a control value; consequently, in valuing a minority interest, asset value usually must be discounted for minority status.

Control versus Minority Value References

D&P pp. 32–33
Guide 702.21
VAB4 pp. 379–383

Discount for Lack of Marketability

- Confusing and controversial in both terminology and application.
- Some say asset value is control marketable, but no company or its assets is fully marketable in the sense of a publicly traded stock; companies usually take months to sell and usually both timing and price of sale are somewhat speculative.
- Courts are inconsistent about allowing discounts for lack of marketability for controlling interests.

---

[1]The definition of market value on page 167 is extracted from *The Uniform Standards of Professional Appraisal Practice* (USAP). Copyright © 2002 by The Appraisal Foundation. Additional copies of USPAP (including Advisory Opinions and Statements) are availabe for purchase from The Appraisal Foundation, 1029 Vermont Avenue N.W., Suite 900, Washington, DC 20005-3517, (202) 347-7722.

Chapter 15

Excess Earnings Method

BACKGROUND AND THEORY OF THE EXCESS EARNINGS METHOD

- First promulgated in 1920 Internal Revenue Service (IRS) Appeals and Review Memorandum 34 (ARM 34).
- Purpose was to develop value of intangibles to compensate brewers and distillers for the loss of their business as a result of Prohibition.
- The method is now embodied in RR68-609, which superseded ARM 34.
- The basic concept is to estimate intangible value by capitalizing the amount of earnings over and above a reasonable return on tangible assets (thus called the *excess earnings method*).
- Although the method was designed only for the purpose of estimating the value of a company's intangible assets, many people value a company by using the excess earnings method to estimate the value of intangible assets and adding that amount to the value of tangible assets.
- In effect the method values a company at its tangible asset value plus what could be thought of as a "bonus" for goodwill and other intangible assets.
- IRS position (RR68-609): The method should be used *only* when no better method exists; most appraisers probably would agree.

- However, since 1996 the IRS has used the method for valuation of health care entities.
- Despite the IRS position, the excess earnings method remains one of the most popular methods to value small businesses and professional practices.

BACKGROUND AND THEORY OF THE EXCESS EARNINGS METHOD

> BV202 "Excess Earnings," pp. 62–71
> CoC2 Ch. 17
> FBVII Ch. 1 p. 22
> Guide 203.21, 205.9, Section 705, 1002.32, 1103.18, VAL-12
> IBA1 A.3, B.6
> IBA2 Ch. 9
> IBA3 Ch. K
> Lawyer pp. 174–176
> NACVA-CA Sect. 6
> RR59-60; RR68-609
> VAB4 Ch. 13, pp. 282–283
> VSB3 Ch. 23
> VT Lesson 7

HOW THE EXCESS EARNINGS METHOD WORKS

Steps in Applying the Excess Earnings Method

1. Estimate net tangible asset value (usually at market values).
2. Estimate a normalized level income.
3. Estimate a required rate of return to support the net tangible assets.
4. Multiply the required rate of return to support the tangible assets (from step 3) by the net tangible asset value (from step 1).
5. Subtract the required amount of return on tangibles (from step 3) from the normalized amount of returns (from step 2); this is the amount of excess earnings. (If the results are negative, there is no intangible value and this method is no longer an appropriate indicator of value. Such a result indicates that the company would be worth more on a liquidation basis than on a going-concern basis.)
6. Estimate an appropriate capitalization rate to apply to the excess economic earnings. (This rate normally would be higher than the rate for tangible assets and higher than the overall capitalization rate; persistence of the customer base usually is a major factor to consider in estimating this rate.)

7. Divide the amount of excess earnings (from step 5) by a capitalization rate applicable to excess earnings (from step 6); this is the estimated value of the intangibles.

8. Add the value of the intangibles (from step 7) to the net tangible asset value (from step 1); this is the estimated value of the company.

9. Reasonableness check: Does the blended capitalization rate approximate a capitalization rate derived by weighted average cost of capital (WACC).

10. Determine an appropriate value for any excess or nonoperating assets that were adjusted for in step 1. If applicable, add the value of those assets to the value determined in step 8. If asset shortages were identified in step 1, determine whether the value estimate should be reduced to reflect the value of such shortages. If the normalized income statement was adjusted for identified asset shortages, it is not necessary to further reduce the value estimate.

11. Determine whether the value of the company computed in step 8 should be adjusted for minority interest discounts or other discounts.

Example of the Excess Earnings Method

Assumptions:

1. Net tangible asset value	$100,000
2. Normalized annual economic income	$ 30,000
3. Required return to support tangible assets	10%
4. Capitalization rate for excess earnings	25%

Calculations:

Net tangible asset value		$100,000
Required return on tangible assets	$0.10 \times \$100,000 =$	$ 10,000
Excess earnings	$\$30,000 - \$10,000 =$	$ 20,000
Value of excess earnings	$20,000/0.25 =$	$ 80,000
Indicated value of company		$180,000

Reasonableness Check for the Excess Earnings Method

$$\frac{\text{Normalized income } \$30,000}{\text{Indicated value of company } \$180,000} = 0.167$$

If 16.7% is a realistic WACC for this company, then the indicated value of the invested capital meets this reasonableness test. If not (see Chapter 8), then the values should be reconciled. More often than not, the problem lies with the value indicated by the excess earnings method rather than with the WACC.

PROBLEMS WITH THE EXCESS EARNINGS METHOD

Tangible Assets Not Well Defined

- RR68-609 does not specify standard of value for tangible assets (e.g., fair market value [FMV] on going-concern basis or replacement cost); although some type of FMV seems to be implied, some analysts simply use book value due to lack of existing asset appraisals.
- It is not clear whether clearly identifiable intangible assets (e.g., leasehold interests) should be valued separately or simply left to be included in all intangible assets in the aggregate.
- RR68-609 does not address when or whether asset write-ups should be tax-affected; practice on this issue is mixed, but most appraisers probably lean toward tax-affecting, at least if there is any prospect of near-term sale of assets, while they may not tax-affect long-term assets such as equipment.

Definition of Income Not Specified

- RR68-609 does not specify what definition of earnings should be utilized.
- Trend is toward preference for net cash flow, but many use net income, pretax income, or some other measure.
- Since some debt usually is contemplated in estimating required return on tangible assets, returns should be amounts available to all invested capital.
- If no debt is contemplated, then returns would be those available to equity.
- The implication of the preceding two bullet points is that the method can be conducted on either an invested capital basis or a 100% equity basis.

Capitalization Rates Not Well Defined

- RR68-609 recommends using rates prevalent in the industry at the time of valuation.
- Required return on tangibles is controversial but usually a blend of:
  - Borrowing rate times percentage of tangible assets that can be financed by debt.
  - Company's cost of equity capital.
- No empirical basis has been developed for estimating a required capitalization rate for excess earnings.

The result of these ambiguities is highly inconsistent implementation of the excess earnings method.

TYPE OF VALUE PRODUCED BY THE EXCESS EARNINGS METHOD

The Excess Earnings Method Produces Control Value

- There is virtually unanimous agreement that the value estimated by the excess earnings method is control value.
- Therefore, if minority value is sought, a discount for lack of control may be applicable.

Issue of Marketability

- Some say the value is marketable.
- However, unlike a public stock, a company cannot be readily sold at an assured price with proceeds in the seller's pocket in three business days.
- Therefore, many would consider applying a discount for lack of marketability.
- If a discount for lack of marketability is applied to a controlling interest, it is generally much less than a discount for lack of marketability for a minority interest.

WHEN THE EXCESS EARNINGS METHOD IS APPLICABLE

- Since it produces a control value, the excess earnings method is more readily applicable to control-basis valuations than to minority-basis valuations.
- Like almost everything about the excess earnings method, considerable controversy exists about the types of companies for which the method is suitable:
  - Used primarily for smaller companies rather than larger companies.
  - Widely used for valuation of professional practices (although some say that it is less appropriate for entities with small capital asset bases).
- Widely used in family law courts in many states but not accepted in others.
- Most practitioners would not consider using it as the only method of valuation.
- Generally not appropriate for a company whose earnings stream is expected to be variable.

The Excess Earnings Method References

D&P pp. 32–33
FBVII Ch. 1 p. 22
Guide Section 705
Lawyer Ch. 11
RR59-60; RR68-609
VAB4 Ch. 13
VSB3 Ch. 23
VT Lesson 7

Discounts and Premiums

Trapped-In Capital Gains
Voting versus Nonvoting Stock

OVERVIEW OF DISCOUNTS AND PREMIUMS

- Discounts and premiums are usually expressed as a percentage of some base amount, and the dollar amount of the discount or premium is subtracted from or added to that base amount.
- Therefore, the obvious (but sometimes neglected) cardinal rule is that discounts and premiums are meaningless until the base to which they are to be applied is clearly defined. (Exhibit 16.1 schematically diagrams the bases to which discounts and premiums are most commonly applied.)
- As discussed in earlier chapters, different valuation methods, and different assumptions embraced within a method, will produce different types of value (e.g., control, marketable minority, and nonmarketable minority); the result of each indication of value should be understood and labeled as to the type of value it represents; only then is it possible to address the critical question of what discount(s) and/or premium(s) should be applied to each respective indication of value.
- Controversies over discounts and premiums frequently impact the value conclusion more than controversies over the base values to which discounts or premiums are applied.
- Two primary discount or premium subjects:
  - Discount for lack of control or premium for control.
  - Discount for lack of marketability.
- When addressing the preceding discounts or premiums, it is important to *first* address the minority-control issue, because discounts for lack of marketability are much less for control interests, if applicable at all.
- Other areas of discounts:
  - Key person.
  - Blockage (normally in the context of public stock valuation).
  - Portfolio (group of nonhomogeneous holdings of subsidiaries, operations, or assets that may be less attractive as a group than the sum of the individual values).
  - Trapped-in capital gains.
  - Lack of access to or reliability of information (important, but because it defies separate quantification, it is usually lumped in with discount for lack of marketability).
  - Voting versus nonvoting stock.

Exhibit 16.1 "Levels of Value" in Terms of Characteristics of Ownership

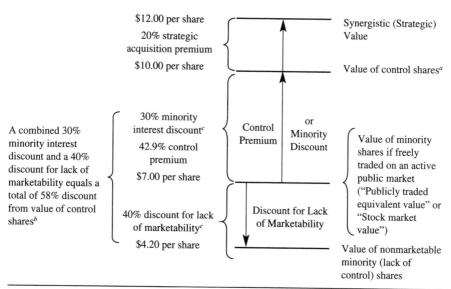

[a] Control shares in a privately held company may also be subject to some discount for lack of marketability, but usually not nearly as much as minority shares.

[b] Minority and marketability discounts normally are multiplicative rather than additive. That is, they are taken in sequence:

$	10.00	Control Value
−	3.00	Less: Minority interest discount (.30 × $10.00)
$	7.00	Marketable minority value
−	2.80	Less lack of marketability discount (.40 × $7.00)
$	4.20	Per share value of nonmarketable minority shares

[c] Note that neither the minority/control nor the marketability issue is an all-or-nothing matter. Each covers a spectrum of degrees as discussed in the accompanying text.

- Many of the discounts and premiums reflect additional risk not captured in discount and capitalization rates, pricing multiples, cash flow projections, or other variables already reflected in the various valuation methods:
  - A control owner might feel less risk than a minority owner.
  - Lack of marketability reflects a risk as to when the interest can be sold and for how much.
- Minority and marketability are distinctly different concepts, and the trend is for courts to prefer or even demand separate treatment for them:

- Minority deals with shareholder rights.
- Marketability deals with ability to liquidate position quickly, at low cost, and for a relatively certain price.

Are Publicly Traded Stock Values Minority or Control?

- They trade as minority interests, by definition.
- In spite of that, some trade at control prices.
- The public stock market and the merger and acquisition (M&A) markets are separate (but related). See Exhibit 16.2 for a schematic relationship of the stock market and the M&A market.
- In the four-year period from 1998 to 2001, over 15% of public company takeovers were at less than their prior public trading prices (see Exhibit 16.3).

Overview of Discounts and Premiums References

BV202 "Market Approach," VI. D. 7, p. 41
BV203 Ch. 5, pp. 2–13
BV204 Module 4
D&P Ch. 1
FBVII Ch. 3 p. 2
Guide Sect. 803
IBA5
Lawyer Ch. 13
NACVA Sect. 3
NACVA-BV Ch. 7
QMD Ch. 1–3
RR59-60; RR77-287; RR83-120; RR93-12
VAB4 Ch. 15–18
VSB3 pp. 247, 265, 448–449, Ch. 24, 40
VT Lesson 9

MINORITY VERSUS CONTROL

Elements of Ownership Control

Some of the more common prerogatives of ownership control include:

1. Appoint or change operational management.
2. Appoint or change members of the board of directors.
3. Determine management compensation and perquisites.

Exhibit 16.2 Schematic Relationship of Stock Market and M&A Market

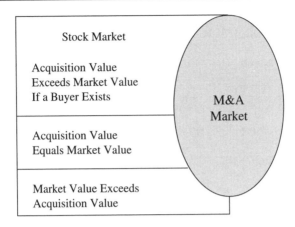

1. The oval in the chart above is the M&A market. The box is the stock market. (The sizes of the two are not proportionate.)

2. If a potential acquirer believes that it can create sufficient added economic benefits, the acquisition value of the company will exceed its market value. The additional economic benefit can pay for the cost of the acquisition premium. These are the transactions reported in the *Control Premium Study* and similar publications.

3. Most publicly traded companies are not taken over in a given year. Generally, there is no market available that can create benefits large enough to justify payment of the premium required for the acquisition of these companies in view of other alternatives.

   If there is no M&A market available to sell a company at a premium to its stock market value, then there is little or no acquisition premium, much less a "theoretical" premium based on an average of acquisitions of dissimilar companies.

4. In emerging industries, such as the Internet in 1998 and 1999, the value of the common stock of a corporation as a whole often is worth less than the aggregate market value of common stock trading as minority interests. While the new industry is viewed as very attractive for investment, individual corporations are perceived as too risky. As a result, individual and institutional investors will pay more for minority interests as part of a diversified industry portfolio than individual acquirers will pay for the entire company.

5. Similarly, many companies spin off units or sell them in an IPO rather than sell the units in the M&A market because a higher price can be obtained in the market than in an M&A transaction.

Source: Mark Lee of Sutter Securities, Incorporated, "Control Premiums and Minority Discounts: The Need for Specific Economic Analysis," *Shannon Pratt's Business Valuation Update* (August 2001), p. 1. Reprinted in Shannon P. Pratt, *Business Valuation Discounts and Premiums* (New York: John Wiley & Sons, Inc., 2001), p. 41. This material is used by permission of John Wiley & Sons, Inc.

Exhibit 16.3   Quarterly Summary Statistics from Mergerstat/Shannon Pratt's Control Premium Study™

EXHIBIT 1: ONLY DOMESTIC TRANSACTIONS

Quarter	Mean Premium w/o Negatives	Mean Premium w/ Negatives	Median Premium w/o Negatives	Median Premium w/ Negatives	Total Count	Total Negatives	Percent Negative	Median TIC/EBITDA
1Q1998	35%	29%	33%	29%	75	9	12%	15.10
2Q1998	35%	33%	31%	27%	59	3	5%	10.10
3Q1998	27%	10%	17%	11%	58	20	34%	12.30
4Q1998	42%	25%	31%	16%	105	29	28%	11.50
1Q1999	52%	45%	33%	29%	109	12	11%	11.03
2Q1999	52%	44%	36%	29%	115	14	12%	10.36
3Q1999	45%	40%	32%	30%	141	10	7%	10.18
4Q1999	45%	39%	32%	28%	168	19	11%	11.07
1Q2000	59%	52%	34%	32%	103	10	10%	13.01
2Q2000	52%	30%	43%	29%	139	37	27%	10.84
3Q2000	51%	41%	42%	37%	137	17	12%	11.15
4Q2000	50%	34%	45%	32%	148	30	20%	9.18
1Q2001	56%	38%	35%	26%	121	24	20%	8.75
2Q2001	64%	50%	51%	38%	107	17	16%	8.86
3Q2001	51%	36%	39%	32%	112	18	16%	11.62
4Q2001	54%	37%	33%	27%	106	22	21%	9.36
				Total	1,803	291	16%	

EXHIBIT 2: ONLY FOREIGN TRANSACTIONS

Quarter	Mean Premium w/o Negatives	Mean Premium w/ Negatives	Median Premium w/o Negatives	Median Premium w/ Negatives	Total Count	Total Negatives	Percent Negative	Median TIC/EBITDA
1Q1998	37%	32%	29%	29%	18	1	6%	NMF
2Q1998	37%	31%	28%	25%	20	2	10%	NMF
3Q1998	27%	25%	23%	19%	35	2	6%	8.75
4Q1998	45%	36%	35%	33%	36	5	14%	8.68
1Q1999	35%	31%	24%	24%	29	2	7%	6.56
2Q1999	37%	30%	25%	23%	35	7	20%	NMF
3Q1999	32%	29%	26%	21%	35	3	9%	11.33
4Q1999	48%	38%	38%	34%	46	6	13%	9.86
1Q2000	47%	40%	37%	34%	62	6	10%	10.74
2Q2000	47%	37%	32%	27%	129	19	15%	10.17
3Q2000	42%	28%	32%	26%	107	22	21%	9.10
4Q2000	38%	25%	24%	17%	100	24	24%	7.86
1Q2001	50%	36%	37%	28%	107	19	18%	6.74
2Q2001	51%	33%	36%	27%	96	21	22%	6.48
3Q2001	45%	24%	31%	18%	111	35	32%	7.56
4Q2001	38%	13%	25%	15%	80	27	34%	6.81
				Total	1,046	201	19%	

Exhibit 16.3 (Continued)

EXHIBIT 3: ALL FOREIGN AND DOMESTIC TRANSACTIONS

	Mean Premium		Median Premium		Total			
Quarter	w/o Negatives	w/ Negatives	w/o Negatives	w/ Negatives	Count	Negatives	Percent Negative	Median TIC/EBITDA
1Q1998	35%	30%	32%	29%	93	10	11%	14.90
2Q1998	35%	32%	30%	26%	79	5	6%	10.10
3Q1998	27%	16%	19%	15%	93	22	24%	11.85
4Q1998	43%	27%	33%	21%	141	34	24%	10.72
1Q1999	49%	42%	33%	29%	138	14	10%	9.43
2Q1999	49%	41%	33%	27%	150	21	14%	9.86
3Q1999	42%	38%	31%	30%	176	13	7%	10.12
4Q1999	46%	39%	34%	29%	214	25	12%	10.78
1Q2000	55%	48%	36%	32%	165	16	10%	11.92
2Q2000	50%	33%	38%	28%	268	56	21%	16.67
3Q2000	47%	35%	37%	31%	244	39	16%	10.14
4Q2000	45%	30%	36%	23%	248	54	22%	8.88
1Q2001	53%	37%	37%	27%	228	43	19%	7.75
2Q2001	58%	42%	42%	33%	203	38	19%	7.59
3Q2001	49%	30%	35%	23%	223	53	24%	8.35
4Q2001	48%	26%	30%	22%	186	49	26%	8.11
				Total	2,849	492	17%	

Source: Mergerstat LP: *www.mergerstat.com.*

4. Set operational and strategic policy and change the course of the business.
5. Acquire, lease, or liquidate business assets, including plant, property, and equipment.
6. Select suppliers, vendors, and subcontractors with whom to do business and award contracts.
7. Negotiate and consummate mergers and acquisitions.
8. Liquidate, dissolve, sell out, or recapitalize the company.
9. Sell or acquire Treasury shares.
10. Register the company's equity securities for an initial or secondary public offering.
11. Register the company's debt securities for an initial or secondary public offering.
12. Declare and pay cash and/or stock dividends.
13. Change the articles of incorporation or bylaws.
14. Set one's own compensation (and perquisites) and the compensation (and perquisites) of related-party employees.
15. Select joint venturers and enter into joint venture and partnership agreements.

16. Decide what products and/or services to offer and how to price those products/services.
17. Decide what markets and locations to serve, to enter into, and to discontinue serving.
18. Decide which customer categories to market to and which not to market to.
19. Enter into inbound and outbound license or sharing agreements regarding intellectual properties.
20. Block any or all of the above actions.

The value of these rights varies greatly from one situation to another, depending on the benefit a control owner can realize by exercising such rights, and must be analyzed on a case-by-case basis.

Elements of Ownership Control References

D&P p. 20
FBVII Ch. 3 p. 13
Guide 803.6–803.7
IBA15 at 14
Lawyer p. 199
Market, pp. 137–138
NACVA p. 17
NACVA-BV Ch. 9
NACVA-CA Sect. 7
VAB4 pp. 347–349, 365–367
VSB3 pp. 26–28, 46, 313–314, Ch. 24

Minority Control Is a Spectrum, Often Not Black and White

- The issue of control or minority is often a question of degree.
- Usually, anything at or above 50% plus one share is defined as operating *control,* and in some states may be complete control.
- However, minority interests might have some degree of control (e.g., ability to elect a director, swing vote).
- 80% or more desirable for some companies because it allows consolidation of accounting.
- Control holder might not have absolute control (e.g., might not be able to effect all corporate actions unilaterally).
- If stock is extremely widely scattered, as in many public companies, a small percentage might be sufficient for day-to-day operating control.

Minority Control Is a Spectrum, Often Not Black and White References

D&P pp. 5–10
FBVII Ch. 3 p. 16
Guide 803.4–803.6
Lawyer pp. 199–200
Market p. 143
VAB4 pp. 346–347, 367–368
VSB3 pp. 27, 275, 428–430

Factors Affecting Degree of Control

Distribution of Ownership

The possibility to align with one or a few owners to have collective control might have some value:

- A 49% block might have little or no control value if there is one 51% block.
- A 49% block might have effective control if all other ownership is highly fragmented.
- A 20% owner is in a much better position with four other 20% owners than with one 80% owner.
- Relative distribution of shares amongst the number of shareholders (few versus many) might be one of the largest determinants of degree of control.

Swing Vote

- A 2% block would have some value as a swing vote block if there were two 49% interests.
- The potential value of a swing vote increases with disharmony.
- Internal Revenue Service (IRS) has recognized (and perhaps overstated) the value of the swing vote in TAM9436005.

State Supermajority Statutes: Blocking Control

- About half of the states require a supermajority (most often two-thirds) to effect certain corporate actions (e.g., merger, liquidation).
- In those states, a block large enough to veto a corporate action is said to have blocking control.

State Minority Dissolution Statutes

- Some states have statutes allowing minority interests of certain sizes (percentage varies from state to state) to take action to dissolve an entity under certain conditions (required conditions vary but generally involve some form of minority oppression).

- Blocks that qualify for such power might have less of a minority interest discount than blocks that do not have such power.
- No empirical data are available to help quantify this factor.

Articles of Incorporation and Bylaws

- Some company articles and bylaws require supermajorities for certain actions, even if state statutes do not.
- Effect usually is the same as if a supermajority were required by state statutes.
- Some articles and bylaws confer certain rights on minority owners under certain conditions, which must be analyzed on a case-by-case basis.

Factors Affecting Degree of Control References

CoC2 Ch. 15
D&P pp. 21–29
FBVII Ch. 3 p. 14
Guide 803.7–803.17
IBA5 at 18
Lawyer pp. 199–200
NACVA Sect. 3
NACVA-BV Ch. 8
RR59-60; RR77-287; RR83-120; RR93-12
VSB3 pp. 247, 463–469, 551–552, Ch. 40

Three Basic Methods for Valuing Minority Interests

Top Down: Proportionate Share of Enterprise Value Less a Discount

- Steps in top-down method:
  1. Estimate the value of the subject overall business enterprise (value of 100%).
  2. Calculate the minority owner's pro rata allocation of the overall enterprise value.
  3. Estimate the amount of the valuation adjustment—that is, discount (if any) applicable to the pro rata allocation of the overall business enterprise value to properly reflect the value of the subject minority (or less than 100%) ownership interest.
- Sources of minority discount data:
  - *Mergerstat/Shannon Pratt's Control Premium Study*™: The idea of using the control premium data is that the difference between the acquisition price and

the previous publicly traded minority price, computed as a percentage of the acquisition price, is the implied minority discount; consider this example:

Public stock selling at $20 gets merged or acquired at $25

Difference: $25 − $20 = $5
Implied minority discount: $5/$25 = 20%

Caution: The difference between the acquisition price and prior trading price might represent an *acquisition premium,* which might include some value due to synergies and thus might represent value for more than just the elements of control.

- Coolidge study (base is book value, and discount combines minority and marketability; see VAB4, pp. 382–383).

Parallel: Direct Comparison with Other Minority Interests

- Compare with transactions of other minority interests.
- Usually use value multiples, or the prices of transactions relative to company fundamentals.
- If based on publicly traded stock, discount for lack of marketability usually needed.
- Best bet usually is prior transactions in the subject company's stock.

Bottom Up: Start with Nothing and Find Benefits of Value to the Interest Holder

- Capitalization of dividends or withdrawals usually first step.
- Check to see whether holder is receiving excess compensation.
- Then may estimate a time and price to sell and discount to a present value. (Method is similar to the discounting method; as value by this method approaches zero, could value by other methods be overstated?)

DISCOUNTS FOR LACK OF MARKETABILITY

Concept of Marketability

- Marketability is the ability to quickly convert the interest to cash, with minimum costs and maximum certainty about the price that will be received.
- Investors prefer liquidity and exact a very high discount for lack of it compared with otherwise comparable securities with high liquidity.
- Active publicly traded stocks and bonds can be sold in seconds, at or very close to the last sale, with very low transaction costs, and proceeds delivered to the seller in three business days; this is the benchmark against which many investors measure marketability or lack thereof.

Concept of Marketability References

BV203 Ch. 5, pp. 6–11
BV204 Module 4
CoC2 Ch. 16, App. D
D&P pp. 10, 166–167
FBVII Ch. 3 p. 27
Guide 803.26–803.27
IBA1 Ch. 2
IBA2 Ch. 10
IBA3 Ch. M, 6
IBA5 at 21
Lawyer pp. 204–205
NACVA Sect. 3
NACVA-BV Ch. 7
QMD Ch. 1, 5–8, 11–14
RR59-60; RR77-287; RR83-120
VAB4 pp. 49–50, 392–395
VSB3 Ch. 25, 34
VT Lesson 9

Two Types of Empirical Sources for Discount for Lack of Marketability Data for Minority Interests

Private Placements of Restricted Shares of Public Stocks

- Many public companies have unregistered or restricted shares that are otherwise identical to their unrestricted public shares.
- The restricted shares may be sold in private placements but not on the public market.
- Many studies have compared private placement prices with public market prices on the same day to estimate the discount for lack of marketability:
  - Securities and Exchange Commission (SEC) Institutional Investor Study covered late 1960s; published 1971 average discount of about 26%; discount for smaller over-the-counter stocks about 33%; still the largest of all of the studies.
  - Gelman Study.
  - Trout Study.
  - Moroney Study.
  - Maher Study.
  - Standard Research Consultants Study.
  - Willamette Management Associates Study.
  - Silber Study.
  - The FMV *Restricted Stock Study*™ by FMV Opinions, Inc.

- Management Planning Study.
- Johnson Study.
- Columbia Financial Advisors Study.
- The most comprehensive of the restricted stock studies is the FMV study.
  - 243 transactions.
  - 44 data points for each transaction.
  - Available online at *BVMarketData.com*^{sm}.
  - Exhibit 16.4 is a sample transaction report from *The FMV Restricted Stock Study*™.
- Many independent studies (thousands of transactions over almost 30 years) continue to show very similar results.
- RR77-287 references private placement studies as empirical evidence to help quantify discounts for lack of marketability.

Private Transactions Compared with Subsequent Initial Public Offerings (IPOs)

- Companies that register public offerings are required to report transactions in their stock as a private company during the three years before registering public offerings.
- Three sets of studies have compared private transaction prices with subsequent IPO prices:
  - John Emory (formerly Baird & Co.) Studies: Compare transaction prices up to five months before IPO with IPO prices.
  - Willamette Management Associates Studies: Compare transaction prices up to three years before IPO with IPO prices, adjusting for changes in company earnings and industry price/earnings ratios.
  - The *Valuation Advisors' Lack of Marketability Discount Study*™: Compare transaction prices up to two years before the IPO with the IPO prices, with no adjustments.
    - By far the most extensive of the pre-IPO studies, with over 2,000 transactions as of mid-2002.
    - Available online at *BVMarketData.com*^{sm}.
    - Exhibit 16.5 is a sample printout from *Valuation Advisors' Lack of Marketability Discount Study*™.
- Pre-IPO studies show average discounts about 10 percentage points higher than private placement studies.
- The three series of pre-IPO studies now cover more than 25 years and well over 3,000 transactions.
- Not referenced in RR77-287 because they had not been published in 1977 but recognized by U.S. Tax Court (e.g., *Estate of Mandelbaum v. Commissioner, Davis v. Commissioner*).

Exhibit 16.4   FMV Restricted Stock Study™ Transaction Report

Company

SIC	3559 Special Industry Machinery, NEC
NAICS	– No description –
Name	Genus, Inc.
Company Description	
City	
State	
Country	
Ticker	GGNS
Exchange	OTC

Transaction Data		**Financial Data ($000s)**	
Transaction Date	2/1/95	Market Value	110,581.88
Registration Rights	N	Book Value	36,986.00
Discount	20.09%	MTB Ratio	2.99
Offering Price	$6.89	Intangible Assets	2,816.00
Prior Month High	$9.38	Total Assets	54,997.00
Prior Month Low	$7.50	Debt	5,528.00
Prior Month High-Low Average	$8.44	Total Revenues	63,616.00
Prior Month Volume	3,723,900	Depreciation Expense	2,622.00
Shares placed to Volume Ratio	0.7x	Interest Expense	0.00
Shares Outstanding	13,106,000	Pretax Income	4,390.00
Shares Placed	2,539,018	Net Income	4,177.00
Placement Amount	17,500,000	Prior Year Dividend ($)	0.00
Shares Placed/Shares After	0.16	EBITDA	7,012.00
Transaction Month High	$9.38	Operating Profit Margin	0.07
Transaction Month Low	$7.88	Net Profit Margin	0.07
Transaction Month High - Low Average	$8.63		
Transaction Month Close	$8.38		
Transaction Month Volume	3,249,100		

Source: FMV Opinion, Inc. © 2002.

N/A = Not available

Discounts and Premiums, Two Types of Sources for Empirical Discount for Lack of Marketability Data for Minority Interests References

   BV203 Ch. 5 pp. 7–11
   BV204 Module 4
   D&P Ch. 5, 6, 7
   FBVII Ch. 3 p. 28
   Guide 803.29–803.35

Exhibit 16.5 Valuation Advisors' Lack of Marketability Discount Study™
Transaction Report

Company	
Company	Plumtree Software
Product, Service, or Business	Corporate Portal Software
SIC	7371 Computer Programming Services
NAICS	5112 Software Publishers

Transaction Data		Financial Data	
Pre-IPO Timeframe	6 mth(s)	Net Sales	$81,473,000
Transaction Date	12/6/01	Percent Discount	1.882%
Transaction Price per Share	$8.34	Total Assets	$54,268,000
CPS. S. or O	O	Operating Income	($7,132,000)
IPO Date	6/4/02	Operating Profit Margin	– 8.754%
IPO Price per Share	$8.50		

N/A = Not available
Source: "Valuation Advisors' Lack of Marketability Discount Study." Used with permission.
All rights reserved. Available at *www.BVMarketData.com*. (888) BUS-VALU, (503) 291-7963

Lawyer pp. 208–214
NACVA Sect. 3, pp. 113–169
QMD pp. 33–36, 185–201, 257–259, 364–370, Ch. 9, 10, App. A, App. B
VAB4 pp. 395–411
VSB3 Ch. 25
VT Lesson 9

Factors Influencing Discounts for Lack of Marketability

Dividends or Withdrawals

The greater the dividend or withdrawal amount, the less the discount for lack of marketability, because investors rely less on being able to sell the investment to realize their return.

Put Rights

- An option to sell can greatly reduce or even eliminate a discount for lack of marketability.
- Since 1986 all new employee stock ownership plans (ESOPs) are required to have put rights for withdrawing stockholders.

Potential Pool of Buyers

The wider the pool of realistic potential buyers, the less the discount for lack of marketability (DLOM).

Size of Block

- Empirical studies of transactions in private companies that subsequently had initial public offerings (specifically, the Willamette Management Associates Studies) have shown that the largest blocks, *as a percentage of the stock outstanding,* tend to sell at slightly greater-than-average DLOMs.
- The absolute size of the block does not seem to be a factor.

Prospect of IPO or Buyout

The more imminent a prospective transaction that will provide liquidity, the less the DLOM. However, one reason that discounts from subsequent IPO prices are substituted is the risk that the IPO might not be completed.

Information Access and Reliability

The more difficult it is to get information about the company and the less reliable the information, the greater the DLOM.

Restrictive Transfer Provisions

Restrictions that limit the ability to transfer the interest usually cause a higher DLOM.

Other Factors Listed in Mandelbaum *Case*

In *Estate of Mandelbaum v. Commissioner,* the only issue was the DLOM. In addition to most of the factors already mentioned, the court also listed:

- Financial statement analysis.
- Nature of the company, its history, its position in the industry, and its economic outlook.
- Management.

In most valuations, these three factors usually would already be fully reflected in the base value to which the DLOM was applied, so they would not be counted again.

The court also listed costs associated with a public offering. Such costs normally would not be considered in quantifying the DLOM for a minority interest, because only a control stockholder can authorize a public offering.

Discounts for Lack of Marketability References

BV204 Module 4
D&P Ch. 5–11
FBVII Ch. 3 pp. 27–51
Guide 803.26–803.42
IBA5 at 15
Lawyer pp. 204–217

NACVA Sect. 3, pp. 106–185
NACVA-BV Ch. 7
VAB4 Ch. 17
VSB3 pp. 27–28, 275–276, 314, 429–430, Ch. 25

Restrictive Transfer Provisions References

Guide 803.28
RR59-60; RR77-287; RR83-120
VT Lesson 10

OTHER DISCOUNTS

Key Person Discount

- Death of a key person may result in a loss to the company warranting a specific discount for that factor (e.g., *Estate of Paul Mitchell v. Commissioner:* Paul Mitchell Hair Products; $15 million discount for death of Paul Mitchell).
- Discount could be ameliorated or even eliminated by life insurance proceeds to the company.
- Estimating the impact on earnings of the loss of the key person may help quantify the discount.

Key Person Discount References

BV203 Ch. 5, p. 12
BV204 Module 4
D&P Ch. 13
FBVII Ch. 3 p. 54
Guide 803.48
IBA2 Ch. 10
Lawyer p. 220
NACVA Sect. 3, pp. 201–223
RR59-60
VAB4 pp. 431, 433–434, 601–602, 615
VSB3 p. 58
VT Lesson 9

Blockage

- Concept of blockage (generally considered in the context of public companies) is that a large block of stock may take considerable time for the market to absorb without depressing price.
- Average trading volume by day and acceptable absorption rate into the market usually are analyzed to help quantify discount.

- Stock volatility during absorption period is likely.
- Discussions with block traders may assist in quantifying a blockage discount.

Blockage References

BV204 Module 4
D&P Ch. 15
FBVII Ch. 3 p. 68
Guide 803.48
IBA2 Ch. 10
Lawyer p. 225
NACVA Sect. 3
QMD pp. 383–385
RR59-60
VAB4 pp. 428–430, 432–433, 613–615

Portfolio Discount

- Investors generally prefer a single operation or group of similar operations over a conglomerate group.
- Demonstrated in public market by conglomerate shares that typically sell at discounts from company's breakup value; some conglomerate companies have spun off dissimilar operations, with the result that the combined market prices of the separate independent companies exceeded the market value of the conglomerate.

Portfolio Discount References

BV204 Module 4
D&P Ch. 16
Lawyer pp. 220–221

Trapped-In Capital Gains

- Concept is that investors would pay less for a stock with appreciated assets subject to capital gains taxes on sale than they would to buy the assets directly:
- The trapped-in gains adjustment usually is taken from the adjusted asset value.
- Amount (or even recognition) of discount tends to be influenced heavily by imminence of the sale of the property subject to the gains tax (courts have often said trapped-in gains are recognizable only if sale is imminent).

Trapped-In Capital Gains References

BV204 Module 4
D&P Ch. 14
Lawyer pp. 221–223

Voting versus Nonvoting Stock

• If a company has both a nonvoting and a voting class of stock outstanding, with other rights being equal, the nonvoting stock may be valued at a discount relative to the voting stock.

• When valuing very small minority interests, and large amounts of both voting and nonvoting stock are outstanding, there may be little or no appreciable difference between voting and nonvoting stock values, and thus no additional discount for the nonvoting stock may be warranted.

• In instances in which a tiny portion of all of the stock has voting control, analysis of the value of voting control must be on a case-by-case basis, depending on what factors might give the control extra value.

Voting versus Nonvoting Stock References

BV204 Module 4
D&P Ch. 12

Environmental, Litigation, and other Contingent Liabilities

• Can arise from a number of different sources, such as lawsuits, environmental liability, and product liability.

• When value must be determined before actual cost of liability is determined, dollar amount of impact must be estimated.

• U.S. Tax Court recognizes discounts for contingent liabilities when appropriate.

• Financial Accounting Standard No. 5 deals with contingent liabilities for purposes of financial statement reporting; may provide guidance in quantifying contingent liabilities for valuation purposes.

Discounts and Premiums References

BV204 Module 4
D&P all chapters
FBVI Ch. 1 p. 37
FBVII Ch. 3
Guide Section 803
Lawyer Ch. 13
NACVA-CA App.
QMD pp. 33–36, 70–76, 80–84, 92
VAB4 Ch. 15–18
VSB3 p. 26, Ch. 24, 25, App. A

Chapter 17

Reconciliation and Value Conclusion

Reconciliation Process
Criteria for Selection and Weighting of Methods
    Legal or Contractual Requirements
        Statutory or Contractual Requirements
        Regulatory Guidance and Precedential Case Law
    Conceptual Conformance to Definition of Value
    Quantity and Quality of Available Data
    Type of Company
Mathematical versus Subjective Weighting

RECONCILIATION PROCESS

- The process of reconciliation is the analysis of alternative indications of value to arrive at a final value estimate.
- All work should be reviewed for appropriateness and accuracy:
  - Was the right property appraised? Are all rights and restrictions reflected?
  - Does each appraisal method comport to the definition of value sought?
  - Have all computations been checked and input verified against original sources?
- Assess relative strengths and weaknesses of each method relative to:
  - Appraisal objective.
  - Adequacy of data.
- Decide which to use and not use and relative weight of each.

CRITERIA FOR SELECTION AND WEIGHTING OF METHODS

Legal or Contractual Requirements

Statutory or Contractual Requirements

Consider whether the methods used conform to the legally mandated requirements.

Regulatory Guidance and Precedential Case Law

- Regulations that are NOT legally binding (including IRS Revenue Rulings):
  - Always safest to comply.
  - If departing, should so recognize and make a strong case for noncompliance.
- Binding case precedent:
  - Almost always should follow case precedent of a binding nature.
  - May need to consult with attorney about whether certain precedent is binding.
  - If departing from what could be interpreted as binding precedent, provide strong explanation of the rationale and perhaps distinguishing facts and circumstances of case at bar from case that may appear to create binding precedent.
  - Recognize that you are the expert and there is some bad case law, often created by bad (and often distinguishable) facts and poor evidence and testimony presented to the court.
- Nonbinding case precedent:
  - Valuation procedures have been accepted by courts without establishing binding precedent in many cases; consult lawyer for guidance.
  - If it makes sense to rely entirely or primarily on previously accepted procedures in the value reconciliation, doing so is usually the safest course.
  - If using procedures not previously found in the relevant case history, a strong explanation of the rationale for the procedures used is warranted.
  - Recognize that every case is unique.
- No case precedent:
  - Use your best judgment and the best approaches in the circumstances, conceptually and in light of available data.
  - May consider precedent from other jurisdictions.
  - If other jurisdictions' precedents are conflicting (which is common), may need strong rationale for procedures chosen.
  - May give court alternatives depending on what legal precedent court might choose to rely on.

Conceptual Conformance to Definition of Value

- If valuing on control basis, may prefer methods that reach control value without having to start with minority value and estimate control premium.
- If valuing on minority basis, may prefer methods that reach minority value directly without having to start with control value and estimate minority discount.

Quantity and Quality of Available Data

The quantity and quality of available data often greatly affect the methods selected or the relative weight accorded the methods:

- The more reliable the projections, the more weight can be accorded to the discounting method. (Although the appraiser usually does not prepare the projections, he or she usually would discuss the underlying assumptions with the preparer to assess their reasonableness.)
- The more similar the guideline companies' risk characteristics and growth expectations (either public companies or merger and acquisition transactions), the more weight can be accorded to the market approach.
- The more likely for the subject company to either have a successful initial public offering (IPO) or participate in a consolidation IPO or be acquired by a public company, the more weight can be accorded to the guideline public company method (with thorough analysis of the discount for lack of marketability issue).
- The more confidence in the adequacy of adjusted asset values (including intangible assets and items not reflected on the balance sheet), the more weight can be accorded to the adjusted asset method, especially in a control valuation.
- Within the market approach, the most weight generally should be accorded to value multiples that have the least dispersion among the guideline companies (as measured by the coefficient of variation).

Type of Company

Some valuation methods lend themselves well to certain types of companies and not to others.

- Holding versus operating companies:
  - Relatively more emphasis on asset values for holding companies (e.g., adjusted net asset method, price/book or price/adjusted book multiples within market approach).
  - Relatively more emphasis on income variables for operating companies.
  - Many companies are part operating company and part holding company; sometimes it is best to value the operating and nonoperating segments separately.
  - Preceding concepts articulated in RR59-60.
- Relative importance of asset values in operations:
  - For distribution companies and financial institutions, asset values are important and usually fairly readily obtainable, so some weight usually should be accorded to asset value method or price/book or price/adjusted book multiples within market method.

- For service businesses and professional practices, asset values usually play only a very minor role.
- For manufacturing companies, most or all of the emphasis is on income; accounting policies and equipment age vary widely, asset values are difficult to estimate, and liquidation values are often less than 10% of replacement cost.

MATHEMATICAL VERSUS SUBJECTIVE WEIGHTING

- Either mathematical or subjective weighting is acceptable.
- In either case, the reasoning for the relative weights (and sometimes reasons for *not* giving one or more methods weight) should be clearly explained.
- RR59-60 correctly points out that there is no empirical basis for arriving at relative mathematical weights and notes that using a formula could lead to omission of relevant factors.
- But the client (and sometimes the court) asks *how much* weight was accorded a method and why.
- Mathematical weighting is appropriate, with a disclaimer that there is no empirical basis for assigning mathematical weights and that the weights are presented only to help clarify the thought process of the analyst; it should be clearly demonstrated that all relevant facts were considered.
- The "Delaware Block Method" uses mathematical weightings in the context of dissenting stockholder actions and can still be used as long as it is demonstrated that all relevant factors have been considered and reflected, if appropriate.

References

Guide Section 801
Lawyer Ch. 14
Market pp. 239–240
VAB4 Ch. 19
VSB3 pp. 283–292

PART IV

Analysis of the Company

Chapter 18

Financial Statement Analysis

ADJUSTMENTS TO FINANCIAL STATEMENTS

Financial statement adjustments generally can be assigned to three categories:

1. Normalizing adjustments, including normalized accounting adjustments and elimination of nonrecurring items.
2. Control adjustments.
3. Separation of operating and nonoperating items.

It is important to note that if a market approach is used for valuation, statements of the guideline companies, if available, also should be considered for possible adjustments.

Normalizing Adjustments

The general idea of normalizing adjustments is to present data using generally accepted accounting principles (GAAP) and industry accounting standards and to eliminate nonrecurring items, so that the information will be presented on a basis comparable to that of other companies and will provide a foundation for developing future expectations about the subject company.

Examples of Normalizing Adjustments

- Adequacy of allowance and reserve accounts:
  - Allowance for doubtful accounts.
  - Pension liabilities.
- Inventory accounting methods:
  - First in first out (FIFO), last in first out (LIFO), and other methods (all *usually* assumed to be lower of cost or market).
  - Write-down and write-off policies.
- Depreciation methods and schedules.
- Depletion methods and schedules (adjustments to industry reporting norms often appropriate).
- Treatment of intangible assets:
  - Leasehold interests.
  - Other intangible assets.
- Policies regarding capitalization or expensing of various costs.
- Timing of recognition of revenues and expenses:
  - Contract work (including work in progress; e.g., percentage of completion or completed contract).
  - Installment sales.
  - Sales involving actual or contingent liabilities (e.g., guarantees, warranties).
  - Prior period adjustments (e.g., for changes in accounting policy or items overlooked).
- Net operating losses carried forward.
- Treatment of interests in affiliates.
- Adequacy or deficiency of assets:
  - Excess or deficient net working capital.
  - Deferred maintenance.
- Adequacy or deficiency of liabilities:
  - Pension termination liabilities.
  - Deferred income taxes.
  - Unrecorded payables.

Note: Except as discussed in the asset approach to valuation (and lower of cost or market inventory), financial statement adjustments usually are not intended to bring assets and/or liabilities to their respective fair market values.

Examples of Nonrecurring Item Adjustments

- Unusual gains or losses on sale of assets.

Note: It does not have to be extraordinary in a GAAP sense to be nonrecurring in a financial analysis sense. This factor is a matter of the analyst's judgment (e.g., rental income).

- Nonrecurring gains or losses:
  - Fire, flood, or other casualty, both physical damage and business interruption to extent not covered by insurance.
  - Strikes (unless common in the industry and considered probable to recur).
  - Litigation costs, payments, or recoveries.
  - Gain or loss on sale of business assets.
- Discontinued operations.

Control Adjustments

A control owner or potential owner might make control adjustments, but a minority owner could not force the same changes. Therefore, control adjustments normally would be made only in the case of a control interest valuation, unless there was reason to believe that the changes were imminent:

- Excess or deficient compensation and perquisites.
- Gains, losses, or cash realization from sale of excess assets.
- Elimination of operational inefficiencies and excess costs.
- Changes in transactions involving company insiders (e.g., employment, nonmarket rate leases).
- Changes in capital structure.

Separation of Operating and Nonoperating Items

Valuation procedures sometimes involve valuing a company's operations and then adding back all or some part of the value of nonoperating assets to the value of the company's operations. This procedure is more common for controlling interest valuations than for minority valuations, because the minority owner cannot force the liquidation of nonoperating assets or the realization of proceeds therefrom. If this procedure is followed, any income or expense produced by the nonoperating assets separated on the balance sheet must be removed from the income statement.

Examples of typical nonoperating assets include:

- Securities.
- Real estate.
- Planes, automobiles, and sporting facilities (e.g., duck hunting preserve, skybox).

Some companies also have underutilized assets that may require adjustment.

References for Adjustments to Financial Statements

FBVI Ch. 4 p. 5
IBA8
Lawyer Ch. 15
VAB4 Ch. 7

COMPARABLE TREND AND RATIO ANALYSIS

Bases for Comparison

Company data can be compared with:

- Company data over time.
- Industry averages.
- Specific guideline company data:
  - Publicly traded companies.
  - Merged or acquired companies for which financial statement information is available.

Types of Comparative Analysis

Common Size Statements

- *Common size income statements:* Each line item expressed as a percentage of sales.
- *Common size balance sheets:* Each line item expressed as a percentage of total assets.

Trend Analysis

- Annually compounded rates of change in financial statement variables.

  Note: Five years of statements (e.g., 19X1 through 19X5) equal only four years of compound change, since 19X1 is the base year.

- Linear or log-linear regression rates of change in variables.

Ratio Analysis

- *Activity ratios* (sometimes also called *asset utilization ratios):* Activity ratios relate an income statement variable to a balance sheet variable. Ideally, the balance sheet variable would represent the average of the line item for the year, or at least the average of the beginning and ending values for the line item. However, many sources of comparative industry ratios are based only on year-end data. *For the ratios to have comparative meaning, it is imperative that they be computed for the subject company on the same basis as the average or individual company ratios with which they are being compared.* It also should be noted that many ratios can be distorted significantly by seasonality, so it may be important to match comparative time periods.

- Accounts receivable turnover:

$$\frac{\text{sales}}{\text{accounts receivable}}$$

- Inventory turnover:

$$\frac{\text{cost of goods sold}}{\text{inventory}}$$

Note: Some people use sales instead of cost of goods sold in this ratio. This method inflates the ratio, since it does not really reflect the physical turnover of the goods.

- Sales to net working capital:

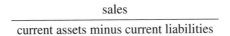

$$\frac{\text{sales}}{\text{current assets minus current liabilities}}$$

- Sales to net fixed assets:

$$\frac{\text{sales}}{\text{net fixed assets}}$$

- Sales to total assets:

$$\frac{\text{sales}}{\text{total assets}}$$

Generally speaking, activity ratios are a measure of how efficiently a company is utilizing various balance sheet components.

- *Performance ratios (income statement):* The four most common measures of operating performance are:
  1. Gross profit as a percentage of sales.

2. Operating profit (earnings before interest and taxes [EBIT]) as a percentage of sales.

3. Pretax income as a percentage of sales.

4. Net profit as a percentage of sales.

All four measures can be read directly from the common size income statements.

- *Return on investment ratios:* Like activity ratios, return on investment ratios relate an income statement variable to a balance sheet variable. Ideally, the balance sheet variable would represent the average of the line item for the year or at least the average of the beginning and ending values for the line item. Unlike activity ratios, return on investment ratios sometimes are computed on the basis of the balance sheet line item at the *beginning* of the year. However, many sources of comparative ratios are based only on year-end data. For the ratios to have comparative meaning, it is imperative that they be computed for the subject company on the same basis as the average or individual company ratios with which they are being compared.

- Return on equity:

$$\frac{\text{net income}}{\text{equity}}$$

Note: The preceding ratio normally is computed based on book value of equity. It also may be enlightening to compute it based on market value of equity.

- Return on investment:

$$\frac{\text{net income} + [(\text{interest})(1 - \text{tax rate})]}{\text{equity} + \text{long-term debt}}$$

- Return on total assets:

$$\frac{\text{net income} + [(\text{interest})(1 - \text{tax rate})]}{\text{total assets}}$$

Each measure of investment returns provides a different perspective on financial performance. In valuation, return on equity influences the price-to-book-value measure, and return on investment influences the market-value-of-invested-capital (MVIC)-to-EBIT ratio.

- *Leverage ratios:* The general purpose of balance sheet leverage ratios (capital structure ratios) is to aid in quantifiable assessment of the long-term solvency of the business and its ability to deal with financial problems and opportunities as they arise. Balance sheet leverage ratios are important in assessing the risk of the individual components of the capital structure. Above-average levels of debt may increase both the cost of debt and the company-specific equity risk factor in a build-up model for estimating a discount or capitalization rate, or the levered beta in the Capital Asset Pricing Model (CAPM).

- Total debt to total assets:

$$\frac{\text{total liabilities}}{\text{total assets}}$$

- Equity to total assets:

$$\frac{\text{total equity}}{\text{total assets}}$$

- Long-term debt to total capital:

$$\frac{\text{long-term debt}}{\text{long-term debt} + \text{equity}}$$

- Equity to total capital:

$$\frac{\text{total equity}}{\text{long-term debt} + \text{equity}}$$

- Fixed assets to equity:

$$\frac{\text{net fixed assets}}{\text{total equity}}$$

- Debt to tangible equity:

$$\frac{\text{total liabilities}}{\text{total equity}}$$

Note: The preceding ratio sometimes is computed using total equity minus intangible assets in the denominator.

- *Liquidity ratios:* Liquidity ratios are indications of a company's ability to meet its obligations as they come due—in this sense, they are factors that may be considered in assessing the company-specific risk.

- Current ratio:

$$\frac{\text{current assets}}{\text{current liabilities}}$$

- Quick ("acid test") ratio:

$$\frac{\text{cash + cash equivalents + short-term investments + receivables}}{\text{current liabilities}}$$

- Times interest earned:

a. $$\frac{EBIT}{\text{interest expense}}$$

or

b. $$\frac{\text{earnings before depreciation, interest, and taxes } (EBDIT)}{\text{interest expense}}$$

Note: Depreciation in the preceding formula is usually construed to include amortization and other noncash charges, sometimes expressed by the acronym EBITDA (earnings before interest, taxes, depreciation, and amortization).

- Coverage of fixed charges:

$$\frac{\text{earnings before interest, taxes, and lease payments}}{\text{interest + current portion of long-term debt + lease payments}}$$

- *Other risk analysis ratios:*
  - Business risk (variability of return over time):

$$\frac{\text{standard deviation of net income}}{\text{mean of net income}}$$

Note: This measure is called the *coefficient of variation*. It can be applied to any measure of income, including sales, EBITDA, EBIT, gross profit, pretax profit, or net cash flow.

  - Degree of operating leverage:

$$\frac{\text{percentage change in operating earnings}}{\text{percentage change in sales}}$$

Note: This is really another measure of business risk. The numerator could be any of the measures of income listed earlier.

- Financial risk (degree of financial leverage):

$$\frac{\text{percentage change in income to common equity}}{\text{percentage change in } EBIT}$$

Ratio Analysis References

BV201 "Beta Analysis," V.G, pp 35–36
CoC2 pp. 225–226
FBVI Ch. 4 p. 14
Guide 405.4–405.5
IBA1 B.16
Lawyer Ch. 15, 16
NACVA Sect. 1 pp. 15–16
NACVA-BV Ch. 3
NACVA-CA Sect. 7
RR59-60; RR68-609; RR77-287
VAB4 Ch. 8
VT Lesson 6

IMPORTANCE OF FINANCIAL STATEMENT RATIO AND TREND ANALYSIS TO VALUATION

1. *Cost of capital:* In the income approach, ratios and trends for the subject company can help to estimate the risk and thus appropriate discount and capitalization rates relative to broad sources of cost of capital used as a starting point. The analysis also may help to quantify prospective growth to subtract from the cost of capital to develop a capitalization rate.

2. *Valuation multiples:* In the market approach, ratios and trends for the subject company as compared with the guideline companies can help to estimate appropriate valuation multiples for the subject company relative to valuation multiples observed for the guideline companies.

3. *Excess assets or asset deficiencies:* Ratios can help to identify the extent to which a company may have excess assets or asset deficiencies for which valuation adjustments may be appropriate.

Financial Statement Analysis References

BV201 p. 33
BV203 Ch. 3
FBVI Ch. 4

Guide Sections 404, 405
IBA1 A.11, A.12, B.3, B.4
IBA2 Ch. 5, 16, 18
IBA3 Ch. F, I
IBA8
Lawyer Ch. 15, 16
NACVA Sect. 4, 5, 7
RR59-60
VAB4 Ch. 7, 8
VSB3 Ch. 7, 8, 10, 11, 28, 31
VT Lesson 8

Chapter 19

Using Economic and Industry Data

OVERVIEW OF ECONOMIC AND INDUSTRY DATA

- No company operates in a vacuum; economic and industry conditions are influential, with different conditions affecting different companies.

- The key word is *relevant* economic and industry factors that impact the particular company.

- Economic and industry data should be utilized to understand the direct impact of the value drivers for the subject company.

- In discussing economic and industry factors, an analyst should point out *how* they impact the subject company.

- Comparative industry performance data, showing how a company is performing relative to its peers, provides guidance for selecting multiples in the market approach and for selecting discount and capitalization rates in the income approach.

ECONOMIC DATA

National Economic Information

- Pinpoint national economic factors that impact the subject and explain why and how the subject is affected (e.g., cost and availability of home financing will impact a home developer).
- There are many sources of economic data (see Chapter 21), including:
  - *Federal Reserve Bulletin*
  - *Survey of Current Business*
  - *Statistical Abstract of the United States*
  - *Economic Report of the President*
  - *The Economic Outlook Update*™, published quarterly by Business Valuation Resources as a supplement to *Shannon Pratt's Business Valuation Update*®
- Many banks and national statistical periodicals and data services produce helpful national economic historical and outlook data.

Regional Economic Data

- Some companies (e.g., banks, many types of service providers) are influenced much more by regional and local economic factors than by national factors.
- Primary sources of regional economic data:
  - Bank economics departments
  - State departments of commerce and economic development
  - Chambers of commerce
  - Public utilities
  - Some universities
- National sources that provide data by region:
  - *Regional Economics and Markets* (Economic and Business Environment Program of the Conference Board)
  - *The Complete Economic and Demographic Data Source* (Wilson & Poole Economics)
  - *Metro Insights* (DRI/McGraw-Hill)
  - *Survey of Buying Power* (published annually in two monthly editions of *Sales and Marketing Management* magazine)
- Many new and amazingly comprehensive sources are rapidly becoming available; the trend is toward electronic access.

Regional Economic Data References

BV201 "Data Gathering"
Guide 403.15
IBA2 Ch. 16
Lawyer p. 294
NACVA-BV Ch. 9, App. 1
NACVA-CA Sect. 3, 7, App.
RR59-60; RR83-120
VAB4 pp. 91, 101
VSB3 Ch. 17, App. A, pp. 151–154, 534–535

INDUSTRY OUTLOOK INFORMATION

Standard Industry Sources

- *U.S. Industry and Trade Outlook*
- *Standard & Poor's Industry Surveys*
- *Moody's Investor's Industry Review*
- *First Research Industry Profiles* (over 120 industry profiles available online at *www.1stresearch.com*)
- *Integra Information* (customized industry research in narrative format available online at *www.integrainfo.com*)

Other Industry Sources

- Brokerage house industry reports
- Trade association publications
- Trade magazines

Indexes

Many indexes of industry information are available in print and online. See references for sources of listings.

Indexes References

BV201 "Data Gathering," IV.C–E, p. 21–24
Guide 403.11
IBA2 Ch. 16

NACVA-BV App. BV
NACVA-CA Sec. 3, App.
VAB4 pp. 98–99, 105–106
VSB3 pp. 135–144, Ch. 17, App. A

INDUSTRY COMPOSITE INFORMATION

Industry composite information falls largely into three categories:

1. Compilations from tax returns.
2. General industry sources.
3. Trade association or trade magazine compilations.

Composite Data from Tax Returns

The Statistics of Income (SOI) division of the Department of Commerce compiles composite data from a stratified sample of tax returns (data lagging three to four years). The data are available from the Government Printing Office and commercial sources.

Government Composite Income Publications

- *Corporation Source Book*
- *Partnership Source Book*
- *Sole Proprietorship Source Book*

Commercial Publications Based on Tax Return Data

- *Almanac of Business and Industrial Financial Ratios* (Prentice-Hall)
- *IRS Corporate Financial Ratios* (Schonfeld & Associates)
- *Financial Ratio Analyst* (Warren, Gorham & Lamont)
- *IRS Corporate Ratios* (electronic only) (John Wiley & Sons)

Note: All of the preceding sources based on tax return data are published with about a four-year lag from the dates of the tax returns.

General Industry Composite Data Sources

- *Standard & Poor's Analysts' Handbook* (covers primarily large companies)
- Risk Management Association's (RMA) (formerly Robert Morris Associates) *An-*

~~nual Statement Studies~~ (compiled from bank loan departments, not a statistically valid sampling of all companies in an industry)

- Financial Research Associates' *Financial Studies of the Small Business* (companies with less than $1 million in sales or assets, compiled from data submitted by certified public accountant [CPA] firms)
- *Integra Information*

Note: An example of a company comparison with composite industry averages based on RMA's *Annual Statement Studies* is included in the sample case.

Caution: Various industry composite data sources compute ratios differently. When comparing the subject with ratios from any source, the source's ratio definitions should be used for comparability.

Trade Association or Trade Publication Industry Composite Compilations

Many trade associations and publications compile industry composite statistics annually or less frequently.

Industry Composite Information References

Guide 403.16–403.19
IBA1 A. 12
IBA2 Ch. 16
Lawyer pp. 291–294
NACVA-CA Sect. 3, 7, App.
NACVA-CV Ch. 9
RR59-60; RR68-609; RR77-287
VAB4 pp. 91–97, 101–103
VSB3 pp. 155–159, 535

COMPARING THE SUBJECT WITH GUIDELINE PEER COMPANIES

If using guideline public companies or merger and acquisition transactions, subject company financial statement ratios and performance also can be compared with the averages for the peer companies.

Note: An example of comparing subject company performance data with guideline public company performance data is shown in the sample case.

Comparing the Subject with Guideline Peer Companies References

BV201 p. 33
BV204 Module 1
FBVII Ch. 2 p. 46
Guide 403.23
IBA1 B.4
IBA2 Ch. 16, 18
NACVA-BV Ch. 3
NACVA-CA Sect. 7, App.
RR59-60
VAB4 pp. 238–240, 266–271
VSB3 Ch. 6, 9, 30
VT Lessons 7, 8

COMPARATIVE COMPENSATION DATA

* The most frequent income statement adjustment found in valuations on a controlling interest basis is for owners' compensation.
* There are many sources for comparative compensation data, some of which are general and some of which are specific to certain industries or professions.
* In addition to publications providing compensation data, proxy statements of public guideline companies are good sources of compensation data.

Industry Comparative Analysis References

BV201 p. 33
FBVII Ch. 2
Guide 403.20
IBA1 B4
IBA2 Ch. 16, 18
NACVA-BV Ch. 3
NACVA-CA Sect. 3, 7, App.
RR59-60; RR83-120
VAB4 pp. 97, 103–104
VSB3 Ch. 6, 9, 30
VT Lesson 8

Chapter 20

Site Visits and Interviews

Objective of Site Visits and Interviews
When to Do Site Visits and Interviews
Site Visit and Interview Topics

OBJECTIVE OF SITE VISITS AND INTERVIEWS

The general objective of site visits and interviews is to gain a better understanding of the company, where it fits in its industry, and its strengths and weaknesses to assess its risks and analyze it with greater insight.

- Seeing the facilities helps provide an understanding of the physical operation:
  - A better understanding of the business operations.
  - Layout and flow of product or data.
  - Physical efficiency of operations.
  - Cleanliness.
  - State-of-the-art facilities, deferred maintenance, or obsolete equipment.
  - Capacity constraints.
  - Possible environmental problems.
  - Obsolete inventory.
- Interviewing management provides insights to the people, their objectives, their capabilities, and the history of the enterprise:
  - Philosophy of company objectives.
  - Quality of management. (Can management fully explain work flow and impact on expected results?)
  - Factors affecting company outlook.
  - Strengths, weaknesses, opportunities, and threats.
- Overall, seeking to understand how the company's future will relate to its past is important:
  - Continue historical trends. (Extrapolation of historical trends is rarely an accurate projection of a company's future.)
  - What will make the company's future different from an extrapolation of its past?

- How will the factors causing change impact the company's results?
- What is the level of certainty (risk) of the company's expected future results?
- Growth assessment: How fast will the company grow, both on an absolute basis and relative to its industry?
  - In sales.
  - In return variables (e.g., net income, net cash flow).

  What additional investment, if any, will be required to support projected operations? (We are valuing returns only to the *current* level of investment.)
- Risk assessment:
  - What is the level of confidence in the company's expected future performance?
  - What is the level of certainty (risk) of the company's expected future results?

WHEN TO DO SITE VISITS AND INTERVIEWS

- Generally best to do site visits and interviews after at least a preliminary financial statement analysis, comparative industry analysis, and study of industry outlook.
- Study of company and industry data will prepare the analyst for a meaningful visit and interview and raise questions the analyst might not otherwise think of.
- Regardless of the amount of preparation, the on-site visit and interactive discussion with management almost always raises additional questions.
- Leave the door open for follow-up questions on matters that may come up after the visit and initial interview.
- If any significant time elapses between the visit and the effective valuation date, a good policy is to ask management whether anything that could materially affect value has changed.

　　Note: The preceding relates to time *up to the effective date* of the valuation. Subsequent events that affect value between the effective date and the date the report is issued normally would not be considered, but the analyst may wish to consult the client's attorney regarding possible exceptions to the general rule.

- Even if the analyst has visited and interviewed during an earlier valuation, it is desirable to visit again for the contemporaneous valuation or at least consider a telephone interview to discuss changes since the initial visit and interviews.

SITE VISIT AND INTERVIEW TOPICS

　　Most valuation texts provide fairly extensive discussions of areas of inquiry and checklists of questions. Analysts typically use such checklists and often emphasize:

- How developing economic and industry forces are likely to affect the company.

- How markets for the company's products or services are changing and how the company is reacting.
- Channels of distribution.
- Competition—current and prospective.
- Technological changes.
- Sources of industry information to complement the analyst's information.
- Possible public guideline companies, guideline merger and acquisition transactions, and details of past transactions in company ownership, especially the extent to which they are conducted on an arm's-length basis.
- Impact of present regulations and potential changes in regulatory environment. (This single factor can have a major impact on both risk and value multiples in an industry.)
- Research and development and changes in product or service lines.
- Strength and importance of patents, copyrights, and trademarks.
- Supplier relationships.
- Customer relationships.
- Depth and quality of management.
- Employee relations and continuity.
- Adequacy of accounting and operating controls.
- Special risk factors.
- Plans for future financing.
- Dividend and withdrawal policy.
- Expected capital expenditures.
- Existing or prospective litigation.
- Catch-all question (e.g., "Are you aware of anything we have not discussed that could materially affect value?").

Site Visits and Interviews References

Guide 402.25– 402.30
Lawyer pp. 52–55, 74–75, 243, 307
Market pp. 29, 255–256
VAB4 Ch. 5
VSB3 pp. 528, 787–789

PART V

Supporting Data

Chapter 21

Sources of Supporting Data

APPRAISERS NEED TO BE ABLE TO FIND DATA

A critical part of the business valuation practitioner's body of knowledge is knowing what data exists and where to find it to develop all of the facts and figures relevant to a business valuation opinion. Sources listed in this chapter are by no means comprehensive but do include most of those widely used by business appraisers. The sources for types of data needed are listed more or less in the order discussed in this book up to this point. Some are listed under more than one classification because they contain more than one type of data.

More detailed descriptions of each source, current costs, and ordering information are found in the *Business Valuation Data Directory, Publications & Internet* published each year as a supplement to *Shannon Pratt's Business Valuation Update®*.

COST OF CAPITAL DATA

Ibbotson Associates Data

- *Beta Book:* Published semiannually in January and July.

    Description: Several different measures of beta for each of more than 5,000 companies.

- Cost of Capital Center Web site: Available at *http://www.ibbotson.com.*

    Description: Cost of Capital Yearbook information available on a page-by-page basis and can be searched by SIC code or industry description.

- *Cost of Capital Yearbook:* Published annually in June; plus three quarterly updates.

    Description: Provides several measures of cost of equity capital, capital structures, and weighted average costs of capital (WACCs) for more than 300 industries based on two-, three-, or four-digit Standard Industrial Classification (SIC) code.

- *Stocks, Bonds, Bills, and Inflation—Valuation Edition 2002 Yearbook:* Published annually in March.

    Description: Provides information used for equity risk premium and size premium data in developing cost of equity capital.

Sources of Beta Data

- *COMPUSTAT* (Standard & Poor's Corp.): Available online at *www.compustat.com.*

    Description: Financial data on publicly held companies.

* ~~*Standard & Poor's Stock Reports*~~ (Standard & Poor's Corp.): Available in print and on CD-ROM.

  Description: Provides data on more than 4,700 public companies. (Also see Ibbotson data listed earlier.)

* *Tradeline* (IDD Information Services).

  Description: Provides beta data.

* *Value Line Investment Survey* (Value Line Publishing, Inc.): Published weekly in print.

  Description: Earnings estimates, stock prices, rankings, betas, and other data for close to 1,700 stocks.

Earnings Forecasts and Related Data

* *First Call Real Time Earnings Estimates* (The Thomson Corporation).

  Description: Provides more than 200 data items on more than 17,500 companies.

* *I/B/E/S United States Database* (The Thomson Corporation: Now integrated with the First Call database online (*www.firstcall.com*).

  Description: Source for earnings forecasts for comparable companies.

* *Value Line Investment Survey—Expanded Edition* (Value Line Publishing, Inc.): Published weekly.

  Description: Stock prices, betas, and other data for more than 1,800 companies.

* *Zacks Earnings Forecaster* (Zacks Investment Research, Inc.): Published quarterly in print.

  Description: Provides earnings per share (EPS), valuation multiples, income and balance sheet, and more information on Wall Street's top 1,500 companies.

* *Zacks EPS Calendar* (Zacks Investment Research, Inc.): Published quarterly in print.

  Description: Provides EPS report dates and estimates for 6,100 companies.

* *Zacks Profit Guide* (Zacks Investment Research, Inc.): Published quarterly in print.

  Description: Provides total returns and profit projections for 6,100 companies.

Source of Arbitrage Pricing Theory Data

* *BIRR Risk and Return Analyzer* (BIRR Portfolio Analysis, Inc.).

  Description: Information for developing arbitrage pricing theory cost of capital estimates.

GUIDELINE PUBLIC COMPANY DATA

Sources of Company Lists

- Directory of Companies Required to File Annual Reports with the SEC (U.S. Government Printing Office): Published annually in March.

  Description: Lists companies alphabetically and classified by industry group according to the *Standard Industrial Classification Manual.*
- *Moody's Manuals* (Moody's Investors Services): Published annually in print.

  Description: A master index identifies the industry volume in which each of the more than 15,000 public companies is included.

Public Company Data Sources

- *Compact D/SEC* (Disclosure, Inc.): Available on CD-ROM and in laser and microfiche formats; published monthly.

  Description: SEC filings data encompassing all public companies in the United States.
- *COMPUSTAT* (Standard and Poor's Corp.): Online database with real-time, daily, and weekly updates; available at *www.compustat.com.*

  Description: Financial data on publicly held corporations.
- *EDGAR* (Electronic Data Gathering and Retrieval system): Available online; enhanced SEC EDGAR available at *www.freedgar.com.*

  Description: Online database provides access to all Securities and Exchange Commission (SEC) filings information.
- *Global Access* (Disclosure, Inc.): Available online at *www.disclosure.com.*

  Description: The world's largest comprehensive company database.
- *Moody's Company Data* (Moody's Investor Service): Published monthly and available on CD-ROM.

  Description: A comprehensive, accurate business and operating descriptions database.
- *Moody's Company Data Direct* (Moody's Investor Service): Published online at *www.moodys.com/fisonline.*

  Description: An enhanced version of Moody's Company Data.
- *Moody's Industrial Manual* (Moody's Investor Service): Published annually in August.

  Description: Individual manuals present detailed company descriptions and data for nearly 2,000 companies listed on the major exchanges.
- *Moody's Industry Review* (Moody's Investor Service): Published annually, with bimonthly updates.

  Description: A 3,000-company database broken down and ranked in 137 industry categories.

- *Moody's OTC Industrial Manual* (Moody's Investor Service). Published annually in September; weekly supplements in *Moody's Industrial News Reports.*

  Description: Individual manuals present nearly 2,000 companies whose stock is traded over the counter.

- *Moody's OTC Unlisted Manual* (Moody's Investor Service): Published annually in October; weekly supplements in *Moody's OTC Unlisted News Reports.*

  Description: Individual manuals present detailed information on more than 2,000 companies not listed on regional or national exchanges.

- *Peerscape* (Deloitte & Touche): Available online at *www.peerscape.com.*

  Description: Allows user to compare subject company with information on more than 7,000 companies that are grouped into 46 different industry categories.

- *Standard & Poor's Corporation Records* (Standard & Poor's Corp.): Published annually, daily, or monthly updates available in print and on CD-ROM.

  Description: Detailed information on both public and closely held companies.

GUIDELINE MERGER AND ACQUISITION DATA

Merged or Acquired Public Companies

- *Business Valuation by Industry Review Series* (NVST, Inc.®): Published annually. Available in print and CD-ROM.

  Description: Presents the valuations of hundreds of businesses recently sold and is organized by industry.

- *Done Deals®* (NVST, Inc.®): Available in CD-ROM (updated quarterly) and on-line (updated weekly).

  Description: Allows the user to search by SIC code, key words, location, closing date, price, and seller and buyer name.

- *Econometria*™ (NVST, Inc.®): Available online at *www.econometria.com.*

  Description: Database of over 5,000 transactions for companies that sold between $1 million and $250 million.

- *The Merger & Acquisition Sourcebook* (NVST, Inc.®): Published annually. Available in print and CD-ROM.

  Description: A reference manual that contains analysis of over 3,000 transactions in public, private, and foreign markets.

- *The Merger Yearbook* (Thomson Financial): Published annually in March. Available in print.

  Description: Provides essential information on tens of thousands of announced and completed deals.

- *Mergerstat eMonthly Update* (Mergerstat LP): Published monthly. Distributed via e-mail.

Description: Features a graphical, top-down overview of the latest trends in the mergers and acquisitions market, as well as bottom-up analysis of the key industry statistics driving today's private and public deals.

- *Mergerstat Online Transaction Roster 2001–2002* (Mergerstat LP): Available online.

  Description: Search and print from up to three years of deal profiles via the Internet.

- *Mergerstat Review 2002* (Mergerstat LP): Published annually. Available in print.

  Description: In-depth research and analysis of mergers and acquisitions activity and multi-year trend analysis.

- *Mergerstat/Shannon Pratt's Control Premium Study*™ (Mergerstat LP): Published quarterly. Available online at *www.BVMarketData.com*^{sm} back to 1998.

  Description: Study tracks acquisition premiums for completed transactions involving publicly traded target companies where a controlling interest was acquired.

- *Public Stats*™ (Business Valuation Resources, LLC): Available online at *www.BVMarketData.com*^{sm}.

  Description: Detailed information on the sales of public businesses.

- *The Weekly Corporate Growth Report* (NVST, Inc.®): Published weekly. Available in print and online.

  Description: A complete weekly newsletter on corporate growth in the U.S. with fast-breaking news of the M&A market.

Merged or Acquired Private Companies

- *BIZCOMPS® 2000 Special Food Service Edition* (BIZCOMPS®): Published every three years. Available in print.

  Description: Includes 795 transactions drawn from overall BIZCOMPS® database.

- *BIZCOMPS® 2001* (BIZCOMPS®): Published annually in four editions. Available in print.

  Description: Data for each sale includes SIC code, type of business, ask price, sale price, annual sales, seller's discretionary cash flow, percent down, terms, inventory, fixtures and equipment, rent percent of sales, general location, ratio of sale price to gross sales, and sale price to seller's discretionary cash flow.

- *BIZCOMPS® 2001 on Disk* (BIZCOMPS®): Available on disk.

  Description: Windows-driven program cataloging over 5,000 transactions.

- *BIZCOMPS® Online* (BIZCOMPS®): Available online at *www.BVMarketData .com*^{sm}.

  Description: Annual subscription with unlimited searches.

- *Business Valuation by Industry Review Series* (NVST, Inc.®): Published annually. Available in print and CD-ROM.

  Description: Presents the valuations of hundreds of businesses recently sold and is organized by industry.

- *Done Deals®* (NVST, Inc.®): Available in CD-ROM (updated quarterly) and on-line (updated weekly).

  Description: Allows the user to search by SIC code, key words, location, closing date, price, and seller and buyer name.

- *Econometria*™ (NVST, Inc.®): Available online at *www.econometria.com*.

  Description: Database of over 5,000 transactions for companies that sold between $1 million and $250 million.

- *IBA Market Data Base* (Institute of Business Appraisers): Published regularly with updates from brokers.

  Description: Data on one or more transactions over the last 10 years or so in over 400 SIC code.

- *The Merger & Acquisition Sourcebook* (NVST, Inc.®): Published annually. Available in print and CD-ROM.

  Description: A reference manual that contains analysis of over 3,000 transactions in public, private, and foreign markets.

- *The Merger Yearbook* (Thomson Financial): Published annually in March. Available in print.

  Description: Provides essential information on tens of thousands of announced and completed deals.

- *Mergerstat eMonthly Update* (Mergerstat LP): Published monthly. Distributed via e-mail.

  Description: Features a graphical, top-down overview of the latest trends in the mergers and acquisitions market, as well as bottom-up analysis of the key industry statistics driving today's private and public deals.

- *Mergerstat Online Transaction Roster 2001–2002* (Mergerstat LP): Available online.

  Description: Search and print from up to three years of deal profiles via the Internet.

- *Mergerstat Review 2002* (Mergerstat LP): Published annually. Available in print.

  Description: In-depth research and analysis of mergers and acquisitions activity and multi-year trend analysis.

- *Pratt's Stats*™ (Business Valuation Resources, LLC): Available online at *www.BVMarketData.com*[sm].

  Description: Detailed information on the sales of private and closely held businesses.

- *The Purchase & Sale of Privately-Held Businesses* (Calcap Corporate Finance Limited): Available in print.

Description: Examines the topics of the buying and selling process, transaction planning, valuation and pricing, and transaction-specific topics.

- *Valuation for M&A: Building Value in Private Companies* (John Wiley & Sons, Inc.): Available in print.

  Description: Emphasizes strategic value, the value to the party to whom the business is most valuable.

- *The Weekly Corporate Growth Report* (NVST, Inc.®): Published weekly. Available in print and online.

  Description: A complete weekly newsletter on corporate growth in the U.S. with fast-breaking news of the M&A market.

Miscellaneous Merged or Acquired Companies

- *Alcar* (The Alcar Group): Available in CD-ROM.

  Description: A complete financial planning system to facilitate all aspects of financial planning.

- *The Arcane World of Buying and Selling A Small Business, and How to Deal With it* (iUniverse): Available in CD-ROM.

  Description: Shows buyers and sellers how to manage their deals from start to finish.

- *The Art of M&A Due Diligence: Navigating Critical Steps and Uncovering Crucial Data* (McGraw-Hill Professional Book Group): Available in print.

  Description: A question-and-answer resource that focuses on the most critical steps in the M&A process.

- *The Art of M&A Financing and Refinancing: Sources and Instruments for Growth* (McGraw-Hill Professional Book Group): Available in print.

  Description: Concentrates especially on the act of obtaining money order to finance a merger or acquisition.

- *The Art of M&A: A Merger Acquisition Buyout Guide, Third Edition* (McGraw-Hill Professional Book Group): Available in print.

  Description: A question-and-answer format, comprehensive guide to all aspects of corporate mergers and acquisitions.

- *Buying & Selling Businesses: Including Forms, Formulas, and Industry Secrets* (John Wiley & Sons, Inc.): Available in print.

  Description: Resource for CPAs, business brokers, and appraisers who need to market services on valuing, buying, and selling businesses.

- *Capital Growth* (Capital Growth Interactive): Available in print, online, and PDF format.

  Description: Monthly newsletter on private capital deals and resources.

- *Directory of Buyout Financing Sources 2002* (Thomson Financial): Published annually in November. Available in print.

Description: Provides descriptions of 1000 financing sources in three separate sections: U.S. senior lenders, U.S. equity and mezzanine providers, and foreign financing sources.

- *Directory of M&A Intermediaries* (Thomson Financial): Published annually in November. Available in print.

  Description: Quick access to the most experienced and effective deal makers, with profiles of over 850 major players, including commercial, merchant, and investment banks, business brokers, plus other M&A intermediaries and service providers to the M&A industry.

- *Mergers and Acquisitions Business Strategies for Accountants* (John Wiley & Sons, Inc.): Available in print.

  Description: A guide in deciding whether a merger or acquisition should take place and what to do once that decision is made.

- *Mergers and Acquisitions Handbook for Small and Midsize Companies* (John Wiley & Sons, Inc.): Available in print.

  Description: a step-by-step guide to buying and selling a business for anyone who is selling a business or hoping to buy one.

- *Mergers, Acquisitions and Corporate Restructuring, Third Edition* (John Wiley & Sons, Inc.): Available in print.

  Description: Explains many types of corporate restructuring.

- *Mergers & Acquisitions of CPA Firms: A Guide to Practical Valuation* (American Institute of Certified Public Accountants): Available in print.

  Description: Explains the advantages and disadvantages of mergers and acquisitions, and contains the entire merger and acquisition process including practical valuation.

- *Selling Your Business Successfully* (John Wiley & Sons, Inc.): Available in print.

  Description: Provides steps to help the business owner or financial advisor to sell a business.

- *SNL Bank Mergers & Acquisitions Yearbook* (SNL Financial): Available in print.

  Description: Source for data on M&A activity in the banking industry.

- *SNL Specialty Lender Directory Mergers & Acquisitions Yearbook 2001* (SNL Financial): Available in print.

  Description: Private and public 2000 data for specialty lender deals.

- *Structuring Venture Capital, Private Equity, and Entrepreneurial Transactions, 2001 Edition* (Aspen Publishers, Inc.): Available in print and CD-ROM.

  Description: One-step-at-a-time, start-to-finish structural guidance for several common business transactions.

- *Super Searchers on Mergers & Acquisitions: The Online Secrets of Top Corporate Researchers and M&A Pros* (Cyberage Books): Available in print.

  Description: Essential keys to using the Internet and online services to research potential M&A opportunities.

- *The Upstart Guide to Buying, Valuing, and Selling Your Business* (Upstart Publishing company): Available in print.

  Description: Looks at the three most critical issues all business owners face: the buying, valuing, and selling of their business.

DISCOUNT AND PREMIUM DATA

Minority Discount and Control Premium Data

- *Mergerstat/Shannon Pratt's Control Premium Study*™ (Mergerstat LP): Published quarterly. Available online at *www.BVMarketDat.com*ˢᵐ back to 1998.

  Description: Study tracks acquisition premiums for completed transactions involving publicly traded target companies where a controlling interest was acquired.

- *Minority Interest Discount Database* (Partnership Profiles, Inc.): Available online at *www.partnershipprofiles.com.*

  Description: Software database for business valuation professionals, real estate appraisers, and CPAs who need empirical data to support minority interest discounts when valuing family limited partnerships and other fractional interests involving real estate.

Discounts for Lack of Marketability

Restricted Stock Transaction Data

- *An Economist-Financial Analyst's Approach to Valuing Stock of a Closely-Held Company,* by Milton Gelman (*Journal of Taxation,* June 1972).
- *Discounts for Lack of Marketability for Closely Held Business Interests,* by J. Michael Maher (*Taxes—The Tax Magazine,* September 1976). Available to subscribers to *BVLibrary.com.*
- *Discounts on Restricted Stock: The Impact of Illiquidity on Stock Prices,* by William L. Silber (*Financial Analysts Journal,* July—August 1991). Available to subscribers to *www.BVLibrary.com.*
- *Discounts Seen in Private Placements of Restricted Stock: The Management Planning, Inc. Long-Term Study (1980–1996),* by Robert P. Oliver and Roy H. Meyers (Chapter 5 of *Handbook of Advanced Business Valuation,* McGraw-Hill, 2000).
- *Estimation of the Discount Associated with the Transfer of Restricted Securities,* by Robert R. Trout (*Taxes—The Tax Magazine,* June 1977). Available to subscribers to *www.BVLibrary.com.*
- *The FMV Restricted Stock Study*™ (FMV Opinions, Inc.) Available online at *www.BVMarketData.com.*

- *Institutional Investor Study Reports of the Securities and Exchange Commission* (H.R.Doc.N.64, part 55, 92nd Cong., 1st Session, 1971, pp. 2444–2456). Available to subscribers to *www.BVLibrary.com.*
- *Most Courts Overvalue Closely Held Stocks,* by Robert E. Moroney (*Taxes—The Tax Magazine,* March 1973). Available to subscribers to *www.BVLibrary.com.*
- *Quantitative Support for Discounts for Lack of Marketability,* by Bruce Johnson (*Business Valuation Review,* December 1999). Available to subscribers to *www.BVLibrary.com.*
- *Restricted stock discounts decline as result of 1-year holding period,* by Kathryn F. Aschwald (*Shannon Pratt's Business Valuation Update,* May 2000).
- *Revenue Ruling 77-287 Revisited,* by William F. Pittock and Charles H. Stryker (*SRC Quarterly Reports,* Spring 1983). Available to subscribers to *www.BVLibrary.com.*

Pre-IPO Transaction Data

- *Emory Pre-IPO Studies* (formerly Robert M. Baird & Company Studies) (*Business Valuation Review,* multiple issues).

  Description: Series of studies, starting in 1980, that describe the results of IPO prices relative to transactions while companies are still private up to five months before IPO. Underlying data available to subscribers to *www.BVLibrary.com.*

- *Valuation Advisors Lack of Marketability Discount Study,* developed by Brian Pearson (Valuation Advisors, LLC).

  Description: Includes pre-IPO transactions from 1995 to the present, based upon filed prospectuses. Subscription to the study database is available at *www.BVMarketData.com.*

- *Willamette Management Associates Studies:* Series of studies starting in 1975.

  Description: Analyzed transactions in privately held company stocks before IPO. Not available for public use.

General Marketability Discount Sources

- *Marketability in the Courts, 1991–1st Q 2002,* by Janet Hamilton, Linda Kruschke, Tanya Hanson, and Jill Johnson (Business Valuation Resources, LLC, 2002). Available in PDF format on disk.

  Description: Summarizes 186 federal and state court cases regarding discounts for marketability, and includes a table highlighting the marketability discount positions of the parties and the conclusion of the court for all cases included in the report.

- *Quantifying Marketability Discounts,* by Z. Christopher Mercer, published by Peabody Publishing, LP (2001). Available in print.

  Description: Presents the Quantitative Marketability Discount Model (QMDM) as a tool to assist business appraisers in developing, quantifying, and defending marketability discounts used in valuation reports based upon the specific facts and circumstances of each case.

Miscellaneous Discount and Premium Data

- *Business Valuation Discounts and Premiums,* by Shannon Pratt (John Wiley & Sons, 2001). Available in print.

  Description: The "whats," the "how-tos," and the "applications" of the various discounts and premiums.
- *Discount Tools*™ (National Association of Certified Valuation Analysts). Available on CD-ROM.

  Description: Includes over 300 federal court cases involving discounts for marketability, minority interest, key person, and more.
- *The Partnership Spectrum* (Partnership Profiles, Inc.). Available in print.

  Description: Bimonthly publication that tracks the partnership industry, especially focusing on but not limited to publicly traded real estate partnerships.
- *Quantitative Business Valuation: A Mathematical Approach for Today's Professionals,* by Jay Abrams (McGraw-Hill, 2000). Available in print.

  Description: Guides professionals through the business valuation process with a quantitative—as opposed to qualitative—focus.

INDUSTRY DATA

Outlook Data

- *Standard & Poor's Industry Survey* (Standard & Poor's Corp.): Published weekly and annually in print.

  Description: Provides information on industry structure, trends, and outlook.
- *U.S. Industry and Trade Outlook* (NTIS): Published annually in print.

  Description: Provides information on the global and U.S. economies, U.S. industries, growth forecasts, and economic and trade trends.

Performance Data

- *The Almanac of Business and Industrial Financial Ratios* (Prentice-Hall): Published annually in April.

  Description: Source for 22 financial ratios for different types and sizes of businesses; information derived from corporate tax returns and Internal Revenue Service (IRS) files.
- *Annual Statement Studies* (Risk Management Association): Published annually in October in print and on disk.

Description: Information taken from financial statements and separated by asset size and sales volume; data provided by bank commercial lending departments.

- *Dun's Direct Access* (Dun & Bradstreet Corp.): Available online at *http://dnb.com.*
  Description: Covers specific information on more than 10 million U.S. businesses.

- *Industry Norms and Key Business Ratios* (Dun & Bradstreet Corp.): Published annually in the spring in print and on disk.
  Description: Covers 800 lines of business, broken down into three size ranges by net worth for each SIC.

- *Moody's Industry Review* (Moody's Investor Service): Published annually, with bimonthly updates, in print.
  Description: Provides ranked and unranked data on companies in 137 industry categories.

- *Standard & Poor's Industry Reports* (Standard & Poor's Corp.): Published monthly in print.
  Description: Provides both outlook and performance data for 50 industries.

COMPENSATION DATA

Medical or Dental Practitioner Compensation Data

- *AAHSA Assisted Living Salary and Benefits Report 2000–2001* (Hospital & Healthcare Compensation Service): Available in print.
  Description: Covers salary and bonus data on 14 management and 23 nursing, dietary, and clerical positions.

- *AAHSA Continuing Care Retirement Community Salary and Benefits Report 2001–2002* (Hospital & Healthcare Compensation Service): Available in print.
  Description: Covers salary and bonus data on 39 management and 40 nursing, therapy, dietary, and clerical positions.

- *AAHSA Nursing Home Salary and Benefits Report 2001–2002* (Hospital & Healthcare Compensation Service): Available in print.
  Description: Covers salary and bonus data on 39 management and 40 nursing, therapy, dietary, and clerical positions.

- *Cost Survey 2001* (Medical Group Management Association): Published annually in September. Available in print and CD-ROM.
  Description: Data on the financial performance and productivity of medical practices.

- *Home Care Salary and Benefits Report 2001–2002* (Hospital & Healthcare Compensation Service): Available in print.

Description: Covers salary and bonus data on 69 management, nursing, therapy, and clerical jobs according to five auspices, five revenue sizes, states, geographical regions, principal cities, and nationally.

- *Hospice Salary and Benefits Report 2001–2002* (Hospital & Healthcare Compensation Service): Available in print.

  Description: Covers salary and bonus data on 72 management, nursing, therapy, and clerical jobs according to auspices, revenue size, states, geographical region, and nationally.

- *Hospital Salary and Benefits Report 2000–2002* (Hospital & Healthcare Compensation Service): Available in print.

  Description: Covers salaries and bonuses for 140 hospital positions.

- *Management Company Compensation Report on Management Employees in Hospital, Long Term Care, and Home Care Management Companies 2001–2002* (Hospital & Healthcare Compensation Service): Available in print.

  Description: Covers salary and bonus payments for exempt management positions nationally.

- *Management Compensation Survey* (Medical Group Management Association): Published annually in August. Available in print.

  Description: Helps plan compensation, conduct comparative analysis against other practices, structure equitable salaries across multiple management levels, and determine appropriate benefits packages.

- *Medical Economics Magazine/Earnings Survey* (Thomson Medical Economics): Published annually. Free on-line at *http://m-be-prod.bmsecs.com*.

  Description: Annual earnings survey for doctors classified by specialty, region, size of practice, years in practice, age, managed-care participation, and gender.

- *MGMA Cost Survey Interactive Report 2001* (John Wiley & Sons, Inc.): Available in CD-ROM.

  Description: Includes data on medical practice charges, revenues, costs, assets, liabilities, staffing, and production.

- *MGMA Physician Compensation and Production Survey Interactive Report 2001* (John Wiley & Sons, Inc.): Available in CD-ROM.

  Description: Includes the ability to search for data, conduct analysis, graph, and download information compiled by MGMA.

- *Nursing Department Report 2000–01* (Hospital & Healthcare Compensation Service): Available in print.

  Description: Covers salary data on nursing and aide positions in hospitals, home care, hospice, and nursing homes.

- *Physician Compensation and Production Survey* (Medical Group Management Association): Published annually in August. Available in print.

  Description: Contains data on more than 60 physician specialties.

- *Physician Socioeconomic Statistics, 2000–2002* (American Medical Association): Available in print.

Description: Provides detailed statistics on physician practice characteristics such as physician compensation, distribution of physician income by payor, fees for physician services, and professional expenses of self-employed physicians.

- *Physician Salary Survey Report 2001* (Hospital & Healthcare Compensation Service): Available in print.

  Description: Covers salary and bonus data on 42 physician specialties, Chief of Staff/Medical Director, interns and residents.

- *Physician Starting Salary Survey* (The Health Care Group): Published annually in September. Available in print.

  Description: Data on salaries, benefits, malpractice coverage, restrictive covenants, perquisites, and more.

- *Staff Salary Survey* (The Health Care Group): Published annually in December. Available in print.

  Description: Provides salary and fringe benefit information for 25 different non-physician medical practice administrative, clerical, and clinical job categories.

- *The Survey of Dental Practice: Income from the Private Practice of Dentistry* (American Dental Association): Published annually. Available in print.

  Description: Analyzes the net income of independent dentists by factors including age, source of income, geographic region, hours worked, and employment status.

Professional and Executive Compensation Data

- *Employee Compensation Report 2000* (The National Association of Wholesaler-Distributors): Available online.

  Description: Compiled from survey responses by thousands of wholesale distribution companies.

- *Executive Compensation Assessor* (Economic Research Institute): Available in CD-ROM.

  Description: Reports competitive salaries and bonuses for more than 300 top management position titles.

- *Executive Compensation: Annual Survey Results 2001* (National Institute of Business Management): Published annually. Available in print.

  Description: Results of surveys conducted by National Institute of Business Management.

- *The Hay Report: Compensation and Benefits Strategies for 2001 & Beyond* (The Hay Group): Published annually in December. Available in print and online.

  Description: Details the practices of thousands of companies and compensation activity by industry, job level, and function.

- *Law Department Compensation Benchmarking Survey* (Altman Weil, Inc.): Available in print.

Description: Provides information by job title, industry group, size of law department, geographic location, centralized or decentralized organization, use of Hay salary plan, area of specialization, and year first admitted to the bar.

- *Management Compensation Study for Loss Prevention Positions 1997–1998* (Food Marketing Institute): Available in print.

    Description: Supplemental report on security/loss prevention positions geared to the food distribution industry.

- *Management Compensation Study for Wholesalers and Large Retailers 2001* (Food Marketing Institute): Published annually in Fall. Available in print.

    Description: Industry's survey of management compensation data, covering more than 60 key positions ranging from CEO to meat department manager.

- *Management Compensation Survey* (American Apparel and Footwear Association): Available in print.

    Description: Provides information on each of the 42 management positions surveyed.

- *Metal Treating Institute Wage and Benefit Survey 2001* (Metal Treating Institute): Published annually. Available in print.

    Description: Analyzes labor wage scale, management weekly salaries, fringe benefits, and includes a profile of survey participants.

- *NOPA Compensation & Benefits Survey 2000* (The Independent Office Products and Furniture Dealers Association): Available in print.

    Description: Analyzes the compensation practices and policies supplies dealers use to pay outside salespeople, inside salespeople, telemarketing, and various management and administrative employees.

- *NRF 2001 Annual Specialty Store Compensation & Benefit Survey* (National Retail Federation): Available in print.

    Description: Information is gathered from over 75 full- and part-time positions.

- *Officer Compensation Report 2002i* (Aspen Publishers, Inc.): Available in print.

    Description: Provides data on salaries, bonuses, pay increases, ownership levels, and incentives.

- *Radio Station Salaries* (National Association of Broadcasters): Published annually. Available in print.

    Description: Data on median and average compensation for management and staff positions.

- *Salary Assessor* (Economic Research Institute): Available in CD-ROM.

    Description: Provides detailed median and mean pay range information for over 4,500 positions in 298 U.S. and Canadian metro areas.

- *Standard & Poor's Execucomp* (Standard & Poor's): Published quarterly. Available in CD-ROM.

    Description: Comprehensive database that covers S&P 500, S&P mid-cap 400, and S&P small-cap companies, with data on over 12,500 executives.

- *Wage and Benefit Survey* (National Paperbox Association). Published annually. Available in print.

  Description: Provides data on cost of sales, gross profit, direct expenses, and more.

ECONOMIC DATA

National Economic Data

- *ASAE Member Associations Online* (American Society of Association Executives). Available at *http://info.asaenet.org/gateway/OnlineAssocSlist.html*.

  Description: Dedicated to enhancing the professionalism and competency of association management, and increasing the effectiveness of associations to better serve members and society.
- *Bloomberg Data License* (Bloomberg). Available at *www.Bloomberg.com*.

  Description: Provides access to all of Bloomberg's financial databases for custom applications.
- *The Center for Economic and Industry Research Industry Reports* (National Association of Certified Valuation Analysts). Available at *www.bvri.com*.

  Description: Provides information for a particular area and length of time.
- *The Complete Economic and Demographic Data Source* (Woods & Poole Economics). Available in print and CD-ROM.

  Description: Presents financial data and projections for U.S. states, counties, MSAs, and regions through 2025 and includes over four million U.S. statistics.
- *Economic Forecasts Reports* (Economy.com, Inc.). Available at *www.economy.com/research*.

  Description: Reports available by country, state, or metropolitan area.
- *Economic Outlook Update* (Business Valuation Resources, LLC). Available in print and PDF format.

  Description: Quarterly supplement to *Shannon Pratt's Business Valuation Update,* reports general economic conditions for a specified quarter, with citation to supporting data sources.
- *Financial Times* (Financial Times). Available in print.

  Description: Source for international news and analysis, emerging markets, industry sectors, business and economic developments, and much more.
- *Global Access* (Primark). Available at *www.primark.com*.

  Description: Direct access to real-time, value-added EDGAR filings, institutional ownership, earnings estimates, investment research reports, economic data, company news articles and summaries, and more.
- *The Livingston Survey* (Federal Reserve Bank of Philadelphia). Published biannually. Available online.

Description: Provides information on treasury securities, federal reserve news and views, economic forecasts, and links to other Web sites providing economic and financial information.

- *National Economic Review* (Mercer Capital). Published quarterly. Available in print and on disk.

  Description: Provides an overview of the major factors affecting the economy and a discussion of current and expected performance of the economy.

- *The National Economic Review 2001* (John Wiley & Sons, Inc.). Available in CD-ROM.

  Description: An overview of the major factors affecting the national economy.

- *Newslink* (Newslink Associates). Available at *www.newslink.org/news.html.*

  Description: Comprehensive starting point for searching local newspapers on the Internet.

- *Statistical Abstract of the U.S. 2001* (U.S. Government Printing Office). Available in print and CD-ROM.

  Description: A collection of statistics on social and economic conditions in the United States.

- *U.S. Financial Data* (Federal Reserve Bank of St. Louis). Published weekly. Available in print.

  Description: Charts and tables relating to weekly monetary data and selected interest rate data with a brief analysis of current conditions.

- *U.S. Industry and Trade Outlook 2000* (National Technical Information Service). Published annually. Available in print and in CD-ROM.

  Description: Provides information on the global and U.S. economies, U.S. industries, growth forecasts, and economic and trade trends.

Regional and Local Economic Data

- *City and County Databook 2000* (U.S. Government Printing Office): Available in print.

  Description: Includes the latest statistics for all U.S. counties, cities with 25,000 or more inhabitants, and places of 2,500 or more inhabitants.

- *The Complete Economic and Demographic Data Source* (Woods & Poole Economics): Available in print and CD-ROM.

  Description: Presents financial data and projections for U.S. states, counties, MSAs, and regions through 2025 and includes over four million U.S. statistics.

- *Economic Forecasts Reports* (Economy.com, Inc.): Available at *www.economy.com/research.*

  Description: Reports available by country, state, or metropolitan area.

- *Newslink* (Newslink Associates): Available at *www.newslink.org/news.html.* *Description:* Comprehensive starting point for searching local newspapers on the Internet.

Source for Updated Data

- *2002 Business Valuation Data, Publications & Internet Directory,* published annually by Business Valuation Resources, LLC. Available for purchase individually or included as supplement to *Shannon Pratt's Business Valuation Update®*.

PART VI

Sample Case

Sample Case: Shannon's Bull Market

Selection of Guideline Company Multiples
Weights Assigned to Guideline Public Company Valuation Multiples
Guideline Merger and Acquisition Method
Guideline Merger and Acquisition Company Data Presentation
Criteria for Selection of Guideline Merged and Acquired Companies
Descriptions of Selected Guideline Merged and Acquired Companies
Selection of Merged and Acquired Company Multiples
Weights Assigned to Guideline Merger and Acquisition Valuation Multiples
Reconciliation of Valuation Methods
Reconciliation of Controlling Interest Methods
Discount for Lack of Marketability for Controlling Interest
Reconciliation of Minority Interest Methods
Discount for Lack of Marketability for Minority Interests
Epilogue to the Sample Case

INTRODUCTION TO THE SAMPLE CASE

This case has been designed primarily to illustrate some of the approaches and methods most commonly used in valuing a business or an interest in a business. However, resemblance to actual institutions or characters may be casually intentional.

Much of the material normally found in a written valuation work product has been omitted for brevity. Some of the items omitted include:

- Statement of contingencies and limiting conditions (see Chapter 3).
- Appraiser's certification.
- List of documents and sources, including site visits and management interviews.
- Qualifications of appraisers.
- Discussion of relevant economic and industry factors, including how they impact the subject company at the effective valuation date.

The income and market approaches will be used to value the restaurant chain and stock interest in it. Within the income approach, the discounted cash flow and capitalized cash flow methods will be used. Within the market approach, the guideline public company and the comparative merger and acquisition methods will be used. Controlling and minority interest valuations as well as valuation of invested capital and equity methods will be illustrated.

DESCRIPTION OF SHANNON'S BULL MARKET

Shannon's Bull Market, Inc., an Oregon corporation, is an established chain of 12 steak and seafood restaurants located in the Pacific Northwest. These upscale (business casual) restaurants have enjoyed tremendous success since the first one opened 10 years ago. Shannon prides himself on ensuring that his customers receive high-quality food and service at reasonable prices. The restaurants have a wine collection from more than 200 Pacific Northwest wineries and more than 50 Pacific Northwest microbrews on tap; they claim to have the country's best selection of Irish whiskey. They also sell market memorabilia, including attractive drinking glasses and mugs with the Shannon's Bull Market logo.

Although it still appears on the menu (probably for nostalgic reasons), the restaurants report being out of stock on one of their most popular items, Logger's Soup, otherwise known as Cream of Spotted Owl.

One restaurant reviewer characterized the decor as "Wall Street West." The decor prominently displays stock certificates of dozens of defunct railroads and pictures of prominent transcontinental rail barons. One glass case in each restaurant contains an unusual collection of dining car glassware featuring logos of railroads from around the world. One part of the bar area in each restaurant features booths along a wall with a table-height G-scale model train with flatcars that deliver drinks and snack foods to the booths.

The restaurants are located in or near financial districts or affluent suburbs and enjoy an enthusiastic clientele among stock brokers, security traders, and money managers, starting about 1 P.M., when the market closes on the West Coast.

The company had $30 million in sales last year. The restaurants averaged $2.5 million per location. Shannon has been expanding his operation at a pace of one new restaurant per year. However, because of the restaurants' success, he would like to expand at a faster pace. He is considering going public now or making a private placement, with the idea of going public in a few years to raise the necessary funds.

Shannon wants to value his restaurant chain, as well as the minority interest in it, before he decides what he will do. He also plans to issue stock or stock options to key employees and gifts of shares of stock to his family.

The company leases all of the spaces that the restaurants use. Shannon personally owns two of the buildings that the company leases. The lease payments for the restaurants that Shannon owns are above market rates. The company owns all of its equipment and leasehold improvements, which it depreciates on a five-year cycle, the industry average. Shannon's salary is well above the industry average for his position. The company has never paid dividends.

The company currently has 1,000,000 shares authorized; of those, 100,000 are issued and outstanding. There are currently no options outstanding. The general manager of Shannon's Bull Market, Gary Gormay, owns a 15% interest in the business. There have been no transactions in the company stock in the last five years.

THE VALUATION ASSIGNMENT

Client and Appraiser

- Client: Shannon's Bull Market, Inc. (SBM).
- Appraiser: Olympic Valuation Advisors, L.L.C. (OVA).

Interests to Be Appraised

- Controlling (100%) interest in the company stock.
- Minority shares of stock (interests of 15% or less).

Effective Date of Appraisal

The effective date of appraisal is December 31, 19X1.

Purpose of the Appraisal

- Possible sale of company.
- Possible sale or repurchase of minority stock.
- Possible initial public offering (IPO).
- Gifts of stock to family members and estate planning.
- Possible stock options to employees and directors.

Standard (Definition) of Value

The standard of value is fair market value (see Chapter 3).

Premise of Value

The premise of value is as a going concern.

Ownership Characteristics

Control or Minority

Both control and minority values are sought, as noted previously.

Marketability

The company is privately held, with no restrictions on transferability.

Form and Extent of Work Product

This appraisal is strictly advisory and requires only schedules and minimal explanations. It does *not* need to conform to the *Uniform Standards of Professional Appraisal Practice* (USPAP).

Contingencies and Limiting Conditions

Use of this report is limited to existing owners, directors, and managers and their professional advisors (see Chapter 3 for more complete contingent and limiting conditions.)

Schedule

Tabular presentation and preliminary indications of value must be presented to the board 90 days following receipt of materials on documents request list, subject to timely availability of management for site visits and interviews.

Fees

Fees are strictly hourly, based on professional and support staff individual hourly rates, which range from $50 to $500 per hour. Estimated range of $15,000 to $25,000 plus out-of-pocket expenses, based on estimated 100 hours at estimated blended rate of $150 per hour. Retainer $7,500, with progress billing semimonthly; retainer applied to final billing. Fees not to exceed $25,000 without client's written permission.

VALUATION APPROACHES AND METHODS

Controlling Interest

- Discounted cash flow (DCF), using adjusted statements (adjusted for owner's excess compensation and rent; see subsequent adjusted statement exhibits):
  - DCF available to invested capital.
  - DCF available to equity.
- Capitalization of cash flow, using adjusted statements:
  - Capitalized cash flow available to invested capital.
  - Capitalized cash flow available to equity.
- Guideline public company method, using adjusted statements.
- Guideline merger and acquisition method, using adjusted statements.

Minority Interest

- DCF, using statements as reported:
  - DCF available to invested capital.
  - DCF available to equity.
- Capitalized cash flow using statements as reported:

- Capitalized cash flow available to invested capital.
- Capitalized cash flow available to equity.
- Guideline public company method, using statements as reported

SAMPLE CASE PROBLEMS

The following questions based on the case information exhibits that follow are provided for those who would like to practice actually working out calculations. I suggest that people check out the answers and make corrections to each set of problems before going on to the next set.

First Set of Case Problems (Ratio Analysis)

Based on year-end data only and using the adjusted (control basis) income statement, balance sheet as of December 31, 19X1, and 19X1 statements, compute each of the following ratios. (Refer to Exhibits 22.1, balance sheet, and 22.7, adjusted income statement):

Current ratio
Quick (acid test) ratio
Accounts receivable turnover
Inventory turnover
Sales to net working capital
Sales to fixed assets
Sales to total assets
Times interest earned

Based on using *both* the 19X0 and 19X1 adjusted control basis statements (using averages of 19X0 and 19X1 balance sheet data where appropriate), compute each of the following ratios (refer to Exhibits 22.1 and 22.7):

Degree of operating leverage
Degree of financial leverage (percentage change in income to common stockholders divided by percentage change in earnings before interest and taxes [EBIT])
Return on equity
Return on investment (tax affected)

Based on the adjusted income statements (control basis) for Shannon's Bull Market, Inc. (SBM), from 19X2 through 19X6. (Refer to Exhibit 22.7.)

Exhibit 22.1 Shannon's Bull Market Historical Balance Sheets
Years Ending December 31 ($000)

	1992	1993	1994	1995	1996
Assets					
Current Assets					
Cash and equivalents	507	587	672	819	1,034
Accounts receivable	110	128	146	165	186
Inventory	617	715	818	927	1,040
Other current assets (including prepaid expenses)	374	434	497	563	632
Total Current Assets	1,608	1,864	2,133	2,474	2,892
Property and Equipment	4,514	5,468	6,521	7,676	8,939
Less accumulated depreciation	(1,716)	(2,227)	(2,811)	(3,473)	(4,217)
Net Property and Equipment	2,798	3,241	3,710	4,203	4,722
Total Assets	4,406	5,105	5,843	6,677	7,617
Liabilities and Equity					
Current Liabilities					
Current portion long-term debt	176	204	234	265	297
Other current payables	863	1,000	1,145	1,297	1,458
Accrued expenses	264	306	351	397	446
Other liabilities[a]	0	0	0	0	0
Total Current Liabilities	1,303	1,510	1,730	1,959	2,201
Long-term Liabilities					
Long-term debt (net of current portion)	1,587	1,585	1,527	1,450	1,350
Other long-term liabilities	0	0	0	·0	0
Total Long-term Liabilities	1,587	1,585	1,527	1,450	1,350
Stockholders' Equity					
Common stock[b]	300	300	300	300	300
Preferred stock	0	0	0	0	0
Retained earnings	1,216	1,710	2,286	2,968	3,763
Total Stockholders' Equity	1,516	2,010	2,586	3,268	4,063
Total Liabilities and Equity	4,406	5,105	5,843	6,677	7,614
Book Value per Share (not $000)	15.16	20.10	25.86	32.68	40.63

[a] Includes short-term notes payable, trade payables, and taxes payable.

[b] Includes capital surplus and net of treasury stock; authorized 1,000,000 shares; issued and outstanding 100,000 shares.

What was the annually compounded percentage rate of growth in net income for that period?

What was the "business risk"? (the covariance of net income, defined as the standard deviation of net income divided by the mean of net income)

Second Set of Case Problems (Computation of Net Cash Flows)

Using the adjusted (control basis) projected income statements and projected statements of cash flows for SBM (refer to Exhibits 22.13 and 22.18) and assuming that required additions to working capital will be 2.79% of projected incremental sales, compute each of the following:

The net cash flow to equity as projected for 1997

The net cash flow to invested capital as projected for 1997

For more practice with this exercise, compute the net cash flows to equity and invested capital for the minority basis projections. The answers to this exercise are found in the 1997 columns of Exhibits 22.25 and 22.26.

Third Set of Case Problems (Valuation by DCF Method)

Exhibit 22.27 presents cost of capital statistics for Standard Industrial Classification Code 5812, Eating and Drinking Places. After carefully studying the information and considering current (somewhat bullish) conditions for the restaurant industry, we have decided to use an equity discount rate halfway between the industry median three-stage DCF equity cost of capital estimate, 13.93% and the Sharpe-Lintner median small-cap equity rate, 14.93%, for an average of 14.4%, less a 1% company-specific adjustment, resulting in 13.4%.

Using an equity discount rate of 13.4%, the control basis projected cash flow available to equity from Exhibit 22.25 (page 285) and an estimated long-term growth rate of 7% beyond the year 2001, compute the indicated present value of Shannon's Bull Market's equity by the DCF method.

For additional practice with this method, compute the minority basis DCF value using the minority basis projected cash flows to equity from Exhibit 22.26 and the same 7% terminal growth rate projection. The solutions to this exercise are found in Exhibits 22.28 and 22.29.

Fourth Set of Case Problems (Weighted Average Cost of Capital)

Using the 13.4% cost of equity, a 9.4% pretax cost of debt, a 40.6% tax rate, and an estimated capital structure (at market value of 90% equity and 10% debt), compute the weighted average cost of capital (WACC).

The solution to this problem is shown in Exhibit 22.30. For additional practice with applying the DCF method, you may compute the present market value of invested capital on control and minority bases, using the net cash flows to invested capital from Exhibits 22.25 and 22.26. The solutions to the present market value of invested capital are shown in Exhibit 22.31 for the control basis and Exhibit 22.32 for the equity basis.

Fifth Set of Case Problems (Computation of Company Fundamentals)

Compute the following company fundamentals as of December 31, 1996 (refer to Exhibits 22.1, 22.3, and 22.7):

	Control Value	Source	Minority Value	Source
Net income		Adjusted income statement		Income statement as reported
Gross cash flow		Adjusted income statement		Income statement as reported
Earnings before taxes		Adjusted income statement		Income statement as reported
Net sales		Income statement as reported		Income statement as reported
Net tangible asset value		Balance sheet		Balance sheet
Earnings before interest, taxes, depreciation, and amortization		Adjusted income statement		Income statement as reported
Earnings before interest and taxes		Adjusted income statement		Income statement as reported
Debt in capital structure		Balance sheet		Balance sheet

Exhibit 22.33 shows the solution to this problem set.

HISTORICAL FINANCIAL STATEMENTS

Five-year summary historical financial statements are presented as follows:

- Exhibit 22.1, historical balance sheets.
- Exhibit 22.2, common size balance sheets (unadjusted).
- Exhibit 22.3, historical income statements (as reported).
- Exhibit 22.4, common size income statements (as reported).
- Exhibit 22.5, historical statements of cash flows (as reported).

Exhibit 22.2 Shannon's Bull Market Common Size Balance Sheets (Unadjusted)
Years Ending December 31

	1992	1993	1994	1995	1996
Assets					
Current Assets					
Cash and equivalents	11.5%	11.5%	11.5%	12.3%	13.6%
Accounts receivable	2.5%	2.5%	2.5%	2.5%	2.4%
Inventory	14.0%	14.0%	14.0%	13.9%	13.7%
Other current assets (including prepaid expenses)	8.5%	8.5%	8.5%	8.4%	8.3%
Total Current Assets	36.5%	36.5%	36.5%	37.1%	38.0%
Property and Equipment	102.5%	107.1%	111.6%	116.0%	120.2%
Less accumulated depreciation	(39.0%)	(43.6%)	(48.1%)	(52.5%)	(56.7%)
Net Property and Equipment	63.5%	63.5%	63.5%	62.9%	62.0%
Total Assets	100.0%	100.0%	100.0%	100.0%	100.0%
Liabilities and Equity					
Current Liabilities					
Current portion long-term debt	4.0%	4.0%	4.0%	4.0%	3.9%
Other current payables	19.6%	19.6%	19.6%	19.4%	19.1%
Accrued expenses	6.0%	6.0%	6.0%	6.0%	5.9%
Other liabilities[a]	0.0%	0.0%	0.0%	0.0%	0.0%
Total Current Liabilities	29.6%	29.6%	29.6%	29.4%	28.9%
Long-term Liabilities					
Long-term debt (net of current portion)	36.0%	31.0%	26.1%	21.7%	17.7%
Other long-term liabilities	0.0%	0.0%	0.0%	0.0%	0.0%
Total Long-term Liabilities	36.0%	31.0%	26.1%	21.7%	17.7%
Stockholders' Equity					
Common stock[b]	19.2%	14.9%	11.6%	9.2%	7.4%
Preferred stock	0.0%	0.0%	0.0%	0.0%	0.0%
Retained earnings	80.2%	85.1%	88.4%	90.8%	92.6%
Total Stockholders' Equity	34.4%	39.4%	44.3%	48.9%	53.4%
Total Liabilities and Equity	100.0%	100.0%	100.0%	100.0%	100.0%

[a] Includes short-term notes payable, trade payables, and taxes payable.
[b] Includes capital surplus / net of treasury stock.

Exhibit 22.3   Shannon's Bull Market Historical Income Statements (as Reported)
Years Ending December 31 ($000)

	1992	1993	1994	1995	1996
Sales					
Food	13,392	15,316	17,292	19,328	21,419
Beverage (alcoholic)	4,229	5,105	6,076	7,149	8,329
Net Sales	17,621	20,421	23,368	26,477	29,748
Cost of Sales					
Food	5,029	5,770	6,534	7,327	8,144
Beverage	1,226	1,481	1,762	2,073	2,416
Total Cost of Sales	6,255	7,251	8,295	9,400	10,560
Gross Profit	11,366	13,170	15,072	17,077	19,188
Operating Expenses					
Officer's compensation	264	306	351	397	446
Salaries and wages	4,405	5,105	5,842	6,619	7,437
Employee benefits	722	837	958	1,086	1,220
Direct operating expenses	1,022	1,184	1,355	1,536	1,725
Marketing	493	572	654	741	833
Utilities	441	511	584	662	744
Occupancy	1,507	1,722	1,949	2,189	2,441
Repairs and maintenance	300	347	397	450	506
Depreciation	441	511	584	662	744
General and administrative	899	1,039	1,195	1,350	1,516
Total Operating Expenses	10,493	12,134	13,870	15,692	17,611
Income from Operations	872	1,036	1,202	1,385	1,577
Other Income (Expense)					
Interest expense	(194)	(204)	(234)	(238)	(238)
Other income (expense)	0	0	0	0	0
Total Other Income (Expense)	(194)	(204)	(234)	(239)	(238)
Income before Income Taxes	678	832	968	1,147	1,339
Income taxes (40.6% tax bracket)	(275)	(338)	(393)	(466)	(544)
Net Income	403	494	575	681	795
Net Income per Share	4.03	4.94	5.75	6.81	7.95

Exhibit 22.4 Shannon's Bull Market Common Size Income Statements (as Reported) Years Ending December 31

	1992	1993	1994	1995	1996
Sales					
Food	76.0%	75.0%	74.0%	73.0%	72.0%
Beverage (alcoholic)	24.0%	25.0%	26.0%	27.0%	28.0%
Net Sales	100.0%	100.0%	100.0%	100.0%	100.0%
Cost of Sales					
Food	28.5%	28.3%	28.0%	27.7%	27.4%
Beverage	7.0%	7.3%	7.5%	7.8%	8.1%
Total Cost of Sales	35.5%	35.5%	35.5%	35.5%	35.5%
Gross Profit	64.5%	64.5%	64.5%	64.5%	64.5%
Operating Expenses					
Officer's compensation	1.5%	1.5%	1.5%	1.5%	1.5%
Salaries and wages	25.0%	25.0%	25.0%	25.0%	25.0%
Employee benefits	4.1%	4.1%	4.1%	4.1%	4.1%
Direct operating expenses	5.8%	5.8%	5.8%	5.8%	5.8%
Marketing	2.8%	2.8%	2.8%	2.8%	2.8%
Utilities	2.5%	2.5%	2.5%	2.5%	2.5%
Occupancy	8.6%	8.4%	8.3%	8.3%	8.2%
Repairs and maintenance	1.7%	1.7%	1.7%	1.7%	1.7%
Depreciation	2.5%	2.5%	2.5%	2.5%	2.5%
General and administrative	5.1%	5.1%	5.1%	5.1%	5.1%
Total Operating Expenses	59.6%	59.4%	59.4%	59.3%	59.2%
Income from Operations	4.9%	5.1%	5.1%	5.2%	5.3%
Other Income (Expense)					
Interest expense	(1.1%)	(1.0%)	(1.0%)	(0.9%)	(0.8%)
Other income (expense)	0.0%	0.0%	0.0%	0.0%	0.0%
Total Other Income (Expense)	(1.1%)	(1.0%)	(1.0%)	(0.9%)	(0.8%)
Income before Income Taxes	3.8%	4.1%	4.1%	4.3%	4.5%
Income taxes (40.6% tax bracket)	(1.6%)	(1.7%)	(1.7%)	(1.8%)	(1.8%)
Net Income	2.3%	2.4%	2.5%	2.6%	2.7%

Exhibit 22.5 Shannon's Bull Market Historical Statements of Cash Flows Years Ending December 31 ($000)

	1992	1993	1994	1995	1996
Sales					
Cash Flow from Operating Activities:					
Net income	403	494	575	681	795
Adjustments to Reconcile Net Income					
to Net Cash Provided from Operating					
ActivitiesDepreciation	441	510	584	662	744

Exhibit 22.5   (Continued)

	1992	1993	1994	1995	1996
Net Change in Operating Assets and Liabilities					
Receivables	(16)	(18)	(18)	(19)	(21)
Inventories	(92)	(98)	(103)	(109)	(113)
Other current assets	(57)	(60)	(63)	(66)	(69)
Other current payables	130	137	145	152	161
Accrued expenses	40	43	45	46	49
Net Cash Provided from Operating Activities	849	1,008	1,166	1,348	1,546
Cash Flow from Investing Activities:					
Payments for property and equipment[a]	(861)	(954)	(1,053)	(1,155)	(1,263)
Cash Flow from Financing Activities:					
Increase (decrease) in long-term debt	90	26	(28)	(46)	(68)
Net change in cash and cash equivalents	78	80	85	147	215
Cash and equivalents at January 1	429	507	587	672	819
Cash and equivalents at December 31	507	587	672	819	1,034

[a] Includes property and equipment for one new location per year plus replacement equipment equal to annual depreciation expense.

FINANCIAL STATEMENT ANALYSIS AND ADJUSTMENTS

No adjustments were made to the historical balance sheets, statements of retained earnings, or statements of cash flows. The following tables of adjustments and analysis are presented:

• Exhibit 22.6, income statement adjustments.

Note: For brevity of exposition, only control adjustments have been made in this example.

However, in a complete analysis, adjustments to the minority basis statements would be appropriate, if applicable, for items such as:

• Accounting adjustments to conform to generally accepted accounting practices (GAAP) or comparable company accounting practices.

• Adjustments for nonrecurring items, such as discontinued operations, lawsuit settlements, disaster losses, unusual gains or losses on sale of assets, and so on.

• Exhibit 22.7, adjusted income statements.

• Exhibit 22.8, adjusted common size income statements.

• Exhibit 22.9, common size balance sheet, with comparison to Robert Morris Associates' *Annual Statement Studies*.

Exhibit 22.6 Shannon's Bull Market Income Statement Adjustments
Years Ending December 31 ($000)

	1992	1993	1994	1995	1996
Net income per historical income statements (after tax)	403	494	575	681	795
Add pretax excess compensation (see table below)	192	222	255	288	324
Add pretax excess lease payment on two locations owned by officer (see table below)	150	150	150	150	150
Net income plus pretax adjustments	745	866	980	1,119	1,269
Provision for income taxes on addbacks	(139)	(151)	(165)	(178)	(192)
Adjusted Net Income	606	715	815	941	1,077

Adjustments to Officer's Compensation

Year	Sales	Normalized Compensation at .41% of Sales[a]	Historical Compensation	Excess Compensation
1992	17,621	72	264	192
1993	20,421	84	306	222
1994	23,368	96	351	255
1995	26,477	109	397	288
1996	29,748	122	446	324

Adjustments to Occupancy Expense

Year	Sales	Adjusted Occupancy at 7.7% of Sales[a]	Historical Occupancy Expense	Excess Occupancy[b]
1992	17,621	1,357	1,507	150
1993	20,421	1,572	1,722	150
1994	23,368	1,799	1,949	150
1995	26,477	2,039	2,189	150
1996	29,748	2,291	2,441	150

[a] Based on the high end of the range for chief executive officers' compensation from comparable companies on a percentage of sales basis.

[b] The majority stockholder leased two units to SBM, Inc., at $75,000 each over market lease rate.

Exhibit 22.7 Shannon's Bull Market Adjusted Income Statements Years Ending December 31 ($000)

	1992	1993	1994	1995	1996
Sales					
Food	13,392	15,316	17,292	19,328	21,419
Beverage (alcoholic)	4,229	5,105	6,076	7,149	8,329
Net Sales	17,621	20,421	23,368	26,477	29,748
Cost of Sales					
Food	5,029	5,770	6,534	7,327	8,144
Beverage	1,226	1,481	1,762	2,073	2,416
Total Cost of Sales	6,255	7,251	8,296	9,400	10,560
Gross Profit	11,366	13,170	15,072	17,077	19,188
Operating Expenses					
Officer's compensation	72	84	96	109	122
Salaries and wages	4,405	5,105	5,842	6,619	7,437
Employee benefits	722	837	958	1,086	1,220
Direct operating expenses	1,022	1,184	1,355	1,536	1,725
Marketing	493	572	654	741	833
Utilities	441	511	584	662	744
Occupancy	1,357	1,572	1,799	2,039	2,291
Repairs and maintenance	300	347	397	450	506
Depreciation	441	511	584	662	744
General and administrative	899	1,039	1,195	1,350	1,516
Total Operating Expenses	10,152	11,762	13,464	15,254	17,137
Income from Operations	1,214	1,408	1,608	1,823	2,051
Other Income (Expense)					
Interest expense	(194)	(204)	(234)	(238)	(238)
Other income (expense)	0	0	0	0	0
Total Other Income (Expense)	(194)	(204)	(234)	(238)	(238)
Income before Income Taxes	1,020	1,204	1,374	1,585	1,813
Income taxes (40.6% tax bracket)	(414)	(489)	(558)	(644)	(736)
Net Income	606	715	815	941	1,077
Net Income per Share	6.06	7.15	8.15	9.41	10.77

Exhibit 22.8 Shannon's Bull Market Adjusted Common Size Income Statements
Years Ending December 31

	1992	1993	1994	1995	1996
Sales					
Food	76.0%	75.0%	74.0%	73.0%	72.0%
Beverage (alcoholic)	24.0%	25.0%	26.0%	27.0%	28.0%
Net Sales	100.0%	100.0%	100.0%	100.0%	100.0%
Cost of Sales					
Food	28.5%	28.3%	28.0%	27.7%	27.4%
Beverage	7.0%	7.3%	7.5%	7.8%	8.1%
Total Cost of Sales	35.5%	35.5%	35.5%	35.5%	35.5%
Gross Profit	64.5%	64.5%	64.5%	64.5%	64.5%
Operating Expenses					
Officer's compensation	0.4%	0.4%	0.4%	0.4%	0.4%
Salaries and wages	25.0%	25.0%	25.0%	25.0%	25.0%
Employee benefits	4.1%	4.1%	4.1%	4.1%	4.1%
Direct operating expenses	5.8%	5.8%	5.8%	5.8%	5.8%
Marketing	2.8%	2.8%	2.8%	2.8%	2.8%
Utilities	2.5%	2.5%	2.5%	2.5%	2.5%
Occupancy	7.7%	7.7%	7.7%	7.7%	7.7%
Repairs and maintenance	1.7%	1.7%	1.7%	1.7%	1.7%
Depreciation	2.5%	2.5%	2.5%	2.5%	2.5%
General and administrative	5.1%	5.1%	5.1%	5.1%	5.1%
Total Operating Expenses	57.6%	57.6%	57.6%	57.6%	57.6%
Income from Operations	6.9%	6.9%	6.9%	6.9%	6.9%
Other Income (Expense)					
Interest expense	(1.1%)	(1.0%)	(1.0%)	(0.9%)	(0.8%)
Other income (expense)	0.0%	0.0%	0.0%	0.0%	0.0%
Total Other Income (Expense)	(1.1%)	(1.0%)	(1.0%)	(0.9%)	(0.8%)
Income before Income Taxes	5.8%	5.9%	5.9%	6.0%	6.1%
Income taxes (40.6% tax bracket)	(2.3%)	(2.4%)	(2.4%)	(2.4%)	(2.5%)
Net Income	3.4%	3.5%	3.5%	3.6%	3.6%

Exhibit 22.9   Shannon's Bull Market (SBM) Common Size Balance Sheet (Compared with RMA), December 31, 1996

	RMA[a]	SBM
Assets		
Current Assets		
Cash and equivalents	9.5%	13.6%
Accounts receivable	4.6%	2.4%
Inventory	4.6%	13.7%
Other current assets		
(including prepaid expenses)	1.5%	8.3%
Total Current Assets	20.2%	38.0%
Property and Equipment	N/A	117.4%
Less accumulated depreciation	N/A	−55.4%
Net Property and Equipment	59.8%	62.0%
Intangibles (net)	7.5%	0.0%
All other noncurrent assets	12.5%	0.0%
Total Noncurrent Assets	79.8%	62.0%
Total Assets	100.0%	100.0%
Liabilities and Equity		
Current Liabilities		
Current portion long-term debt	5.2%	3.9%
Other current payables	12.0%	19.1%
Accrued expenses	0.0%	5.9%
Other liabilities[b]	15.3%	0.0%
Total Current Liabilities	32.4%	28.9%
Long-term Liabilities		
Long-term debt		
(net of current portion)	30.6%	17.7%
Other long-term liabilities	5.5%	0.0%
Total Long-term Liabilities	36.1%	17.7%
Stockholders' Equity		
Common stock[c]	N/A	3.9%
Preferred stock	N/A	0.0%
Retained earnings	N/A	49.5%
Total Stockholders' Equity	31.6%	53.4%
Total Liabilities and Equity	100.0%	100.0%

Source: Copyright © 2002 by RMA—The Risk Management Association. All rights reserved. No part of this table may be reproduced or utilized in any form or by any means, electronic or mechanical, including photocopying, recording, or by any information storage and retrieval system without permission in writing from RMA—The Risk Management Association.

[a] Robert Morris Associates' data based on fiscal years ended April 1, 1995, to March 31, 1996, reported for SIC #5812, sorted by assets from $2.0 million to $10.0 million.

[b] Includes short-term notes payable, trade payables, and taxes payable.

[c] Includes capital surplus and net of treasury stock.

- Exhibit 22.10, common size income statement (as adjusted), with comparison to Robert Morris Associates' *Annual Statement Studies*.
- Exhibit 22.11, ratio analysis (based on adjusted statements), with comparison to Robert Morris Associates' *Annual Statement Studies* (includes answers to problem set 1).
- Exhibit 22.12, ratio analysis (based on adjusted statements), with comparison to selected publicly traded guideline companies (includes additional answers to problem set 1).

Exhibit 22.10   Shannon's Bull Market (SBM) Adjusted Common Size Income Statement (Compared with RMA), December 31, 1996

	RMA[a]	SBM
Sales		
Food	—	72.0%
Beverage (alcoholic)	—	28.0%
Net Sales[a]	100.0%	100.0%
Cost of Sales		
Food	—	27.4%
Beverage	—	8.1%
Total Cost of Sales	44.1%	35.5%
Gross Profit	55.9%	64.5%
Operating Expenses	51.9%	57.6%
Income from Operations	4.1%	6.9%
Other Income (Expenses)		
Interest expense	—	−0.8%
All other expenses (net)	1.5%	0.0%
Income before Income Taxes	2.5%	6.1%
Income taxes (40.6% tax bracket)	—	2.5%
Net Income	—	3.6%

Source: Copyright © 2002 by RMA—The Risk Management Association. All rights reserved. No part of this table may be reproduced or utilized in any form or by any means, electronic or mechanical, including photocopying, recording, or by any information storage and retrieval system without permission in writing from RMA—The Risk Management Association.

[a] Robert Morris Associates' data based on fiscal years ended April 1, 1995, to March 31, 1996, reported for SIC #5812, sorted by assets from $2.0 million to $10.0 million.

Exhibit 22.11 Shannon's Bull Market (SBM) Historical Balance Sheet and
Adjusted Income Statement Ratio Analysis (Includes Answers to Problem Set 1)

		RMA[a]	SBM
Number of observations		237	1
Average asset size ($000)		$4,654	$7,614
Average sales volume ($000)		$12,333	$29,748
Liquidity Ratios			
Current	High	1	1.3
	Median	0.6	
	Low	0.3	
Quick	High	0.8	
	Median	0.4	0.8
	Low	0.2	
Activity Ratios			
Sales/receivables	High	999.8	
	Median	309.1	159.9
	Low	63	
Cost of sales/inventory	High	50.5	
	Median	34.1	10.2
	Low	20.6	
Cost of sales/payables	High	20.5	
	Median	11.9	7.2
	Low	7	
Sales/working capital	High	573.1	
	Median	−22.1	43.1
	Low	−11.3	
Coverage/Leverage Ratios			
EBIT/interest	High	5.4	
	Median	2.9	8.6
	Low	1.3	
Net profit + depreciation, depletion,	High	3.9	
amortization/current portion	Median	2.4	6.1
of long-term debt	Low	1.4	
Fixed/worth	High	1.1	
	Median	2.3	1.2
	Low	10.2	
Debt/worth	High	1.1	
	Median	2.6	0.9
	Low	11.9	
Percentage of profit before taxes/			
tangible net worth	High	50.9%	
	Median	22.3%	44.6%
	Low	6.9%	
Percentage of profit before taxes/total assets	High	12.4%	
	Median	6.2%	23.8%
	Low	1.5%	

(Continues)

Exhibit 22.11   (Continued)

		RMA[a]	SBM
Sales/net fixed assets	High	7.2	
	Median	4.1	6.3
	Low	2.5	
Sales/total assets	High	3.5	
	Median	2.5	3.9
	Low	1.6	
Percentage of depreciation, amortization/sales	High	4.1%	
	Median	3.3%	2.5%
	Low	2.3%	
Percentages of officers', directors',	High	6.4%	
and owners' compensation/sales	Median	4.1%	0.41%
	Low	1.9%	

[a] Robert Morris Associates

PROJECTED FINANCIAL STATEMENTS

Control Basis Projections (Using 1996 Adjusted Base Year Income Statement)

- Exhibit 22.13, control basis projected income statements (adjusted).
- Exhibit 22.14, control basis projected common size income statements.
- Exhibit 22.15, control basis projected balance sheets.
- Exhibit 22.16, control basis projected common size balance sheets.
- Exhibit 22.17, control basis projected statements of retained earnings.
- Exhibit 22.18, control basis projected statements of cash flows.

Minority Basis Projections (Using 1996 Actual Base Year Income Statement)

- Exhibit 22.19, minority basis projected income statements.
- Exhibit 22.20, minority basis projected common size income statements.
- Exhibit 22.21, minority basis projected balance sheets.

Exhibit 22.12 Ratios of Comparable Public Companies, 1996 (Includes Answers to Problem Sets 2 and 3)

	Ark Restaurants Corp.	J Alexanders Corp.	Max & Erma's Restaurants, Inc.	Morton's Restaurant Group	Timber Lodge Steakhouse, Inc.	Range	Median	Mean	Shannon's Bull Market	Comments
Activity Ratios										
Sales/receivables	52.81	757.33	151.33	91.38	151.1	52.81–757.33	151.1	287.79	159.94	Average
Days in receivables	6.91	0.48	2.41	3.99	2.42	0.48–6.91	2.41	2.33	2.28	Average
$COGS^a$/inventory	36.31	655.53	116.26	37.99	86.99	36.31–655.53	86.99	224.19	10.15	Below average due to large wine cellar with higher margins
Days in inventory	10.05	0.58	3.14	9.6	4.2	0.56–10.05	4.2	4.38	35.98	Average in highly varied category
Working capital TO^b	—	15.86	—	96.06	—	(61.07)–96.06	15.76	55.96	57.99	
Fixed assets TO	2.55	1.93	1.52	7.84	1.89	1.52–7.84	1.93	3.30	6.30	Above average
Asset TO	2.53	6.84	25.63	7.07	1.5	1.51–25.63	5.84	10.01	3.91	Below average
Alcohol sales/sales	—	0.15	0.136	—	0.15	0.136–0.15%	0.0015	0.15	0.28	Renowned wine and Irish whiskey selection
Return Ratios										
ROE^c	0.13	0.18	0.14	0.08	0.11	0.08–0.18	0.13	0.13	29.40	Above range of group
ROI^d	0.1	0.15	0.05	0.04	0.11	0.04–0.15	0.1	0.09	24.00	Above range of group

(Continues)

Exhibit 22.12 (Continued)

	Ark Restaurants Corp.	J Alexanders Corp.	Max & Erma's Restaurants, Inc.	Morton's Restaurant Group	Timber Lodge Steakhouse, Inc.	Range	Median	Mean	Shannon's Bull Market	Comments
ROA[e]	0.04	0.12	0.69	0.02	0.08	0.02–0.69	0.08	0.23	0.10	Average in highly varied category
Leverage Ratios										
Total liability/total assets	0.37	0.39	0.69	0.73	0.27	0.27–0.73	0.39	0.52	0.47	Average
Equity/total assets	0.63	0.61	0.31	0.27	0.73	0.27–0.73	0.61	0.48	0.53	Average
LTD/total capital	0.11	0.28	0.64	0.54	—	0.11–0.64	0.41	0.49	0.25	Less debt than average
Debt to equity	0.65	0.65	2.30	6.86	—	0.65–6.86	1.47	3.27	0.41	Less debt than average
Business risk	0.34	0.25	0.23	—	0.54	0.23–0.54	0.30	0.34	0.23	Less risk position
Operating risk	12.82	13.97	0.83	10.90	1.97	0.83–13.97	10.90	6.92	1.00	Less risk position
Financial leverage	0.91	0.19	0.27	—	—	0.19–0.91	0.27	0.23	1.17	Less risk position
Liquidity Ratios										
Current ratio	0.73	1.58	0.38	1.08	0.86	0.88–1.58	0.86	0.93	1.31	Above average
Quick ratio	0.5	1.53	0.3	0.91	0.78	0.30–1.53	0.78	0.88	0.84	Average
Working capital ($M)	(2.37)	5.73	(5.07)	2.01	(0.34)	5.07–5.73	−0.34	0.58	0.69	Average in highly varied category

Coverage Ratios										
EBIT^g interest										
exp cov	3.82	6.95	1.54	0.71	40.33	0.71–40.33	3.82	12.38	5.63	Average in highly varied category
EBDIT^h interest										
exp cov	8.21	8.75	4.22	1.48	69.97	1.48–69.97	8.21	21.11	8.75	Average in highly varied category
Cash flow/Curr Mat										
LTD^i	3.55	188.26	0.24	4.05	—	0–188.26	3.55	64.18	5.18	Average in highly varied category
Fixed assets/equity	2.89	1.16	2.94	1.38	1.1	1.10–2.94	1.38	1.65	1.16	Below average
Equity/total capital	0.75	0.72	0.36	0.43	1	0.36–1.00	0.72	0.63	0.71	Average
CEO^j salary/sales	0.41%	0.20%	0.31%	0.28%	0.41%	0.20–0.41%	0.31%	0.30%	1.50%	Much higher than average
Cash Flow Ratios										
Net income/equity	0.12	0.18	0.12	0.08	0.1	0.08–0.18	0.12	0.12	0.20	Above average
Net income/assets	0.04	0.11	0.69	0.02	0.07	0.02–0.69	0.07	0.22	0.10	Average in highly varied category
Net income/sales	0.02	0.08	0.03	0.01	0.05	0.01–0.08	0.03	0.04	0.03	Average
Cash flow/equity	0.36	0.25	0.43	0.18	0.19	0.18–0.43	0.25	0.26	0.38	Above average
Cash flow/assets	0.12	0.15	2.46	0.05	0.14	0.05–2.46	0.14	0.70	0.20	Average in highly varied category
Cash flow/sales	0.05	0.11	0.1	0.02	0.09	0.02–0.69	0.09	0.08	0.05	Slightly below average

(Continues)

Exhibit 22.12 (Continued)

	Ark Restaurants Corp.	J Alexanders Corp.	Max & Erma's Restaurants, Inc.	Morton's Restaurant Group	Timber Lodge Steakhouse, Inc.	Range	Median	Mean	Shannon's Bull Market	Comments
Growth										
Sales growth annualized 1992–1995	11.76%	16.06%	19.79%	20.05%	73.00%	11.76–73.00%	20.00%	32.23%	13.99%	Below average
Net income growth annualized 1992–1995	—	36.07%	18.92%	—	—	18.92–36.07%	27.00%	27.50%	18.51%	Below range of group
Cash flow growth annualized 1992–1995	—	36.31%	23.07%	19.34%	130.03%	19.34–130.03%	21.00%	52.19%	16.20%	Below range of group

[a]Cost of goods sold
[b]Turnover
[c]Return on equity
[d]Return on investment
[e]Return on assets
[f]Long-term debt
[g]Earnings before interest and taxes
[h]Earnings before depreciation, interest, and taxes
[i]Current maturities of long-term debt
[j]Chief executive officer

Exhibit 22.13   Shannon's Bull Market Projected Income Statements (Adjusted) Years Ending December 31 ($000)

	Adjusted Historical	Projected				
	1996	1997	1998	1999	2000	2001
Sales						
Food	21,419	23,900	26,511	29,257	32,143	35,177
Beverage (alcoholic)	8,330	9,295	10,310	11,378	12,500	13,680
Net Sales	29,749	33,195	36,821	40,634	44,643	48,857
Cost of Sales						
Food	6,145	9,085	10,089	11,134	12,232	13,387
Beverage	2,416	2,689	2,982	3,291	3,616	3,957
Total Cost of Sales	10,581	11,784	13,071	14,425	15,848	17,344
Gross Profit	19,188	21,411	23,750	26,209	28,795	31,513
Operating Expenses						
Officer's compensation	122	138	151	167	183	200
Salaries and wages	7,437	8,299	9,205	10,159	11,161	12,214
Employee benefits	1,220	1,361	1,510	1,666	1,830	2,003
Direct operating expenses	1,725	1,925	2,136	2,357	2,589	2,834
Marketing	833	929	1,031	1,138	1,250	1,368
Utilities	744	830	921	1,016	1,116	1,221
Occupancy	2,291	2,556	2,835	3,129	3,438	3,762
Repairs and maintenance	506	584	626	691	759	831
Depreciation	744	830	921	1,016	1,116	1,221
General and administrative	1,516	1,693	1,878	2,072	2,277	2,492
Total Operating Expenses	17,137	19,123	21,212	23,409	25,719	28,146
Income from Operations	2,051	2,288	2,537	2,800	3,076	3,366
Other Income (Expense)						
Interest	(238)	(156)	(156)	(156)	(156)	(156)
Other income (expense)	0	0	0	0	0	0
Total Other Income (Expense)	(238)	(156)	(156)	(156)	(156)	(156)
Income before Income Taxes	1,813	2,132	2,381	2,644	2,920	3,210
Income taxes (40.6% tax bracket)	(738)	(866)	(967)	(1,073)	(1,186)	(1,303)
Net Income	1,077	1,266	1,414	1,570	1,734	1,907
Net Income per Share	10.77	12.66	14.14	15.70	17.34	19.07

Exhibit 22.14   Shannon's Bull Market Projected Common Size Income
Statements (Control Interest)Years Ending December 31

	Adjusted Historical 1996	Projected 1997	1998	1999	2000	2001
Sales						
Food	72.0%	72.0%	72.0%	72.0%	72.0%	72.0%
Beverage (alcoholic)	28.0%	28.0%	28.0%	28.0%	28.0%	28.0%
Net Sales	100.0%	100.0%	100.0%	100.0%	100.0%	100.0%
Cost of Sales						
Food	27.4%	27.4%	27.4%	27.4%	27.4%	27.4%
Beverage	8.1%	8.1%	8.1%	8.1%	8.1%	8.1%
Total Cost of Sales	35.5%	35.5%	35.5%	35.5%	35.5%	35.5%
Gross Profit	64.5%	64.5%	64.5%	64.5%	64.5%	64.5%
Operating Expenses						
Officer's compensation	0.4%	0.4%	0.5%	0.5%	0.6%	0.6%
Salaries and wages	25.0%	25.0%	25.0%	25.0%	25.0%	25.0%
Employee benefits	4.1%	4.1%	4.1%	4.1%	4.1%	4.1%
Direct operating expenses	5.8%	5.8%	5.8%	5.8%	5.8%	5.8%
Marketing	2.8%	2.8%	2.8%	2.8%	2.8%	2.8%
Utilities	2.5%	2.5%	2.5%	2.5%	2.5%	2.5%
Occupancy	7.7%	7.7%	7.7%	7.7%	7.7%	7.7%
Repairs and maintenance	1.7%	1.7%	1.7%	1.7%	1.7%	1.7%
Depreciation	2.5%	2.5%	2.5%	2.5%	2.5%	2.5%
General and administrative	5.1%	5.1%	5.1%	5.1%	5.1%	5.1%
Total Operating Expenses	57.6%	57.6%	57.7%	57.7%	57.8%	57.8%
Income from Operations	6.9%	6.9%	6.8%	6.8%	6.7%	6.7%
Other Income (Expense)						
Interest expense	(0.8%)	(0.5%)	(0.4%)	(0.4%)	(0.3%)	(0.3%)
Other income (expense)	0.0%	0.0%	0.0%	0.0%	0.0%	0.0%
Total Other Income (Expense)	(0.8%)	(0.5%)	(0.4%)	(0.4%)	(0.3%)	(0.3%)
Income before Income Taxes	6.1%	6.4%	6.4%	6.4%	6.4%	6.4%
Income taxes (40.6% tax bracket)	(2.5%)	(2.6%)	(2.6%)	(2.6%)	(2.6%)	(2.6%)
Net Income	3.6%	3.8%	3.8%	3.8%	3.8%	3.8%

Exhibit 22.15 Shannon's Bull Market Projected Balance Sheets (Control Interest) Years Ending December 31 ($000)

	Adjusted Historical 1996	Projected 1997	1998	1999	2000	2001
Assets						
Current Assets						
Cash and equivalents	1,034	1,432	1,826	2,192	2,510	2,754
Accounts receivable	186	209	231	254	279	306
Inventory	1,040	1,160	1,287	1,421	1,561	1,708
Other current assets (including prepaid expenses)	632	705	782	863	948	1,038
Total Current Assets	2,892	3,506	4,126	4,730	5,298	5,806
Property and Equipment	8,939	10,172	11,508	12,952	14,510	16,185
Less accumulated depreciation	(4,217)	(5,047)	(5,968)	(6,984)	(8,100)	(9,321)
Net Property and Equipment	4,722	5,125	5,540	5,968	6,410	6,864
Total Assets	7,614	8,631	9,666	10,698	11,708	12,670
Liabilities and Equity						
Current Liabilities						
Current portion long-term debt	297	297	297	297	297	297
Other current payables	1,458	1,627	1,805	1,991	2,188	2,394
Accrued expenses	446	498	552	609	669	732
Other liabilities[a]	0	0	0	0	0	0
Total Current Liabilities	2,201	2,422	2,654	2,897	3,154	3,423
Long-term Liabilities						
Long-term debt (net of current portion)	1,350	1,350	1,350	1,350	1,350	1,350
Other long-term liabilities	0	0	0	0	0	0
Total Long-term Liabilities	1,350	1,350	1,350	1,350	1,350	1,350
Stockholders' Equity						
Common stock[b]	300	300	300	300	300	300
Preferred stock	0	0	0	0	0	0
Retained earnings	3,763	4,559	5,362	6,151	6,904	7,597

(Continues)

Exhibit 22.15   (Continued)

	Adjusted Historical 1996	Projected				
		1997	1998	1999	2000	2001
Total Stockholders' Equity	4,063	4,859	5,662	6,451	7,204	7,897
Total Liabilities and Equity	7,614	8,631	9,666	10,698	11,708	12,670
Book Value per Share	40.63	48.59	56.62	64.51	72.04	78.97

[a] Includes short-term notes payable, trade payables, and taxes payable.
[b] Includes capital surplus and net of treasury stock; authorized 1,000,000 shares; issued and outstanding 100,000 shares.

Exhibit 22.16   Shannon's Bull Market Projected Common Size Balance Sheets (Control Interest) Years Ending December 31

	Adjusted Historical 1996	Projected				
		1997	1998	1999	2000	2001
Assets						
Current Assets						
Cash and equivalents	13.6%	16.6%	18.9%	20.5%	21.4%	21.8%
Accounts receivable	2.4%	2.4%	2.4%	2.4%	2.4%	2.4%
Inventory	13.7%	13.4%	13.3%	13.3%	13.3%	13.5%
Other current assets (including prepaid expenses)	8.3%	8.2%	8.1%	8.1%	8.1%	8.2%
Total Current Assets	38.0%	40.6%	42.7%	44.2%	45.3%	45.8%
Property and Equipment	117.4%	117.9%	119.1%	121.1%	123.9%	127.7%
Less accumulated depreciation	(55.4%)	(58.5%)	(61.7%)	(65.3%)	(69.2%)	(73.5%)
Net Property and Equipment	62.0%	59.4%	57.3%	55.8%	54.7%	54.2%
Total Assets	100.0%	100.0%	100.0%	100.0%	100.0%	100.0%
Liabilities and Equity						
Current Liabilities						
Current portion long-term debt	3.9%	3.4%	3.1%	2.8%	2.5%	2.3%

Exhibit 22.16 Shannon's Bull Market Projected Common Size Balance Sheets (Control Interest) Years Ending December 31

	Adjusted Historical 1996	Projected 1997	1998	1999	2000	2001
Other current payables	19.1%	18.9%	18.7%	18.6%	18.7%	18.9%
Accrued expenses	5.9%	5.8%	5.7%	5.7%	5.7%	5.8%
Other liabilities[a]	0.0%	0.0%	0.0%	0.0%	0.0%	0.0%
Total Current Liabilities	28.9%	28.1%	27.5%	27.1%	26.9%	27.0%
Long-term Liabilities						
Long-term debt (net of current portion)	17.7%	15.6%	14.0%	12.6%	11.5%	10.7%
Other long-term liabilities	0.0%	0.0%	0.0%	0.0%	0.0%	0.0%
Total Long-term Liabilities	17.7%	15.6%	14.0%	12.6%	11.5%	10.7%
Stockholders' Equity						
Common stock[b]	3.9%	3.5%	3.1%	2.8%	2.6%	2.4%
Preferred stock	0.0%	0.0%	0.0%	0.0%	0.0%	0.0%
Retained earnings	49.5%	52.8%	55.5%	57.5%	59.0%	60.0%
Total Stockholders' Equity	53.4%	56.3%	58.6%	60.3%	61.6%	62.3%
Total Liabilities and Equity	100.0%	100.0%	100.0%	100.0%	100.0%	100.0%

[a] Includes short-term notes payable, trade payables, and taxes payable.
[b] Includes capital surplus and net of treasury stock; authorized 1,000,000 shares; issued and outstanding 100,000 shares.

Exhibit 22.17 Shannon's Bull Market Projected Statements of Retained Earnings (Control Interest) Years Ending December 31 ($000)

	Projected 1997	1998	1999	2000	2001
Retained earnings at beginning of year	3,763	4,559	5,362	6,151	6,904
Net income	1,266	1,414	1,570	1,734	1,907
Cash dividends declared and paid	(470)	(611)	(781)	(981)	(1,214)
Retained earnings at end of year	4,559	5,362	6,151	6,904	7,597

Exhibit 22.18   Shannon's Bull Market Projected Statements of Cash Flows (Control Interest) Years Ending December 31 ($000)

	Projected				
	1997	1998	1999	2000	2001
Cash Flow from Operating Activities:					
Net income	1,266	1,414	1,570	1,734	1,907
Adjustments to Reconcile Net Income to Net Cash Provided from Operating Activities					
Depreciation	830	921	1,016	1,116	1,221
Net Change in Operating Assets and Liabilities:					
Receivables	(23)	(22)	(23)	(25)	(27)
Inventories	(120)	(127)	(134)	(140)	(147)
Other current assets	(73)	(77)	(81)	(85)	(90)
Other current payables	169	178	186	197	206
Accrued expenses	52	54	57	60	63
Net Cash Provided from Operating Activities	2,101	2,341	2,591	2,857	3,133
Cash Flow from Investing Activities:					
Payments for property and equipment[a]	(1,233)	(1,336)	(1,444)	(1,558)	(1,675)
Cash Flow from Financing Activities:					
Reduction in long-term debt	0	0	0	0	0
Cash dividends paid	(470)	(611)	(781)	(981)	(1,214)
Net cash provided (used) from financing activities	(470)	(611)	(781)	(981)	(1,214)
Net change in cash and cash equivalents	398	394	366	318	244
Cash and equivalents at January 1	1,034	1,432	1,826	2,192	2,510
Cash and equivalents at December 31	1,432	1,826	2,192	2,510	2,754

[a] Includes property and equipment for one new location per year plus replacement equipment equal to annual depreciation expense.

Exhibit 22.19   Shannon's Bull Market Projected Income Statements (Unadjusted) Years Ending December 31 ($000)

	Actual 1996	Projected				
		1997	1998	1999	2000	2001
Sales						
Food	21,419	23,900	26,511	29,257	32,143	35,177
Beverage (alcoholic)	8,330	9,295	10,310	11,377	12,500	13,680
Net Sales	29,749	33,195	38,821	40,634	44,643	48,857

Exhibit 22.19   (Continued)

	Actual 1996	Projected 1997	1998	1999	2000	2001
Cost of Sales						
Food	8,145	9,082	10,062	11,093	12,188	13,338
Beverage	2,418	2,722	3,019	3,332	3,550	4,006
Total Cost of Sales	10,561	11,784	13,071	14,425	15,848	17,344
Gross Profit	19,188	21,411	23,750	26,209	28,795	31,513
Operating Expenses						
Officer's compensation	440	488	552	610	670	733
Salaries and wages	7,437	5,299	9,205	10,159	11,181	12,214
Employee benefits	1,220	1,361	1,510	1,986	1,830	2,003
Direct operating expenses	1,725	1,925	2,136	2,367	2,589	2,834
Marketing	833	929	1,031	1,138	1,250	1,388
Utilities	744	830	921	1,018	1,118	1,221
Occupancy	2,441	2,755	3,058	3,373	3,705	4,055
Repairs and maintenance	506	584	625	891	759	831
Depreciation	744	830	921	1,016	1,118	1,221
General and administrative	1,516	1,692	1,578	2,071	2,275	2,490
Total Operating Expenses	17,611	19,651	21,797	24,057	26,429	28,923
Income from Operations	1,577	1,760	1,953	2,152	2,366	2,590
Other Income (Expense)						
Interest Expense	(238)	(156)	(156)	(156)	(156)	(156)
Other income (expense)	0	0	0	0	0	0
Total Other Income (Expense)	(238)	(156)	(156)	(156)	(156)	(156)
Income before Income Taxes	1,339	1,604	1,797	1,996	2,210	2,434
Income taxes (40.6% tax bracket)	(543)	(651)	(730)	(810)	(897)	(988)
Net Income	795	953	1,067	1,186	1,313	1,446
Net Income per Share	7.95	9.53	10.67	11.86	13.13	14.46

Exhibit 22.20 Shannon's Bull Market Projected Common Size Income
Statements (Minority Interest) Years Ending December 31

	Actual 1996	Projected				
		1997	1998	1999	2000	2001
Sales						
Food	72.0%	72.0%	72.0%	72.0%	72.0%	72.0%
Beverage (alcoholic)	28.0%	28.0%	28.0%	28.0%	28.0%	28.0%
Net Sales	100.0%	100.0%	100.0%	100.0%	100.0%	100.0%
Cost of Sales						
Food	27.4%	27.4%	27.4%	27.4%	27.4%	27.4%
Beverage	8.1%	8.1%	8.1%	8.1%	8.1%	8.1%
Total Cost of Sales	35.5%	35.5%	35.5%	35.5%	35.5%	35.5%
Gross Profit	64.5%	64.5%	64.5%	64.5%	64.5%	64.5%
Operating Expenses						
Officer's compensation	1.5%	1.5%	1.5%	1.5%	1.5%	1.5%
Salaries and wages	25.0%	25.0%	25.0%	25.0%	25.0%	25.0%
Employee benefits	4.1%	4.1%	4.1%	4.1%	4.1%	4.1%
Direct operating expenses	5.8%	5.8%	5.8%	5.8%	5.8%	5.8%
Marketing	2.8%	2.8%	2.8%	2.8%	2.8%	2.8%
Utilities	2.5%	2.5%	2.5%	2.5%	2.5%	2.5%
Occupancy	8.3%	8.3%	8.3%	8.3%	8.3%	8.3%
Repairs and maintenance	1.7%	1.7%	1.7%	1.7%	1.7%	1.7%
Depreciation	2.5%	2.5%	2.5%	2.5%	2.5%	2.5%
General and administrative	5.1%	5.1%	5.1%	5.1%	5.1%	5.1%
Total Operating Expenses	59.2%	59.2%	59.2%	59.2%	59.2%	59.2%
Income from Operations	5.3%	5.3%	5.3%	5.3%	5.3%	5.3%
Other Income (Expense)						
Interest expense	(0.8%)	(0.5%)	(0.4%)	(0.4%)	(0.3%)	(0.3%)
Other income (expense)	0.0%	0.0%	0.0%	0.0%	0.0%	0.0%
Total Other Income (Expense)	(0.8%)	(0.5%)	(0.4%)	(0.4%)	(0.3%)	(0.3%)
Income before Income Taxes	4.5%	4.8%	4.9%	4.9%	5.0%	5.0%
Income taxes (40.6% tax bracket)	(1.8%)	(1.9%)	(2.0%)	(2.0%)	(2.0%)	(2.0%)
Net Income	2.7%	2.9%	2.9%	2.9%	3.0%	3.0%

Exhibit 22.21 Shannon's Bull Market Projected Balance Sheets (Minority Interest) Years Ending December 31 ($000)

	Actual		Projected			
	1996	1997	1998	1999	2000	2001
Assets						
Current Assets						
Cash and equivalents	1,034	1,432	1,826	2,192	2,510	2,754
Accounts receivable	186	209	231	254	279	306
Inventory	1,040	1,160	1,287	1,421	1,561	1,708
Other current assets (including prepaid expenses)	632	705	782	863	948	1,038
Total Current Assets	2,892	3,506	4,126	4,730	5,298	5,806
Property and Equipment	8,939	10,172	11,508	12,952	14,510	16,185
Less accumulated depreciation	(4,217)	(5,047)	(5,968)	(6,984)	(8,100)	(9,321)
Net Property and Equipment	4,722	5,125	5,540	5,968	6,470	6,864
Total Assets	7,614	8,631	9,666	10,698	11,708	12,670
Liabilities and Equity						
Current Liabilities						
Current portion long-term debt	297	297	297	297	297	297
Other current payables	1,458	1,627	1,805	1,991	2,188	2,394
Accrued expenses	446	498	552	609	669	732
Other liabilities[a]	0	0	0	0	0	0
Total Current Liabilities	2,201	2,422	2,654	2,897	3,154	3,423
Long-term Liabilities						
Long-term debt (net of current portion)	1,350	1,350	1,350	1,350	1,350	1,350
Other long-term liabilities	0	0	0	0	0	0
Total Long-Term Liabilities	1,350	1,350	1,350	1,350	1,350	1,350
Stockholders' Equity						
Common stock[b]	300	300	300	300	300	300
Preferred stock	0	0	0	0	0	0
Retained earnings	3,763	4,559	5,362	6,151	6,904	7,597
Total Stockholders' Equity	4,063	4,859	5,662	6,451	7,204	7,897
Total Liabilities and Equity	7,614	8,631	9,666	10,698	11,708	12,670
Book Value per Share	40.63	48.59	56.62	64.51	72.04	78.97

[a]Includes short-term notes payable, trade payables, and taxes payable.

[b]Includes capital surplus and net of treasury stock; authorized 1,000,000 shares; issued and outstanding 100,000 shares.

- Exhibit 22.22, minority basis projected common size balance sheets.
- Exhibit 22.23, minority basis projected statements of retained earnings.
- Exhibit 22.24, minority basis projected statements of cash flows.

GUIDELINE PUBLIC COMPANY METHOD

Guideline Public Company Data Presentation

- Exhibit 22.34, guideline public company valuation multiples.
- Exhibit 22.35, guideline public company method value summary (controlling interest basis).
- Exhibit 22.36, guideline public company method value summary (minority interest basis).

Note: Normally, summary historical statements for each of the guideline companies and market price data would be presented, so that the reader could verify data

Exhibit 22.22   Shannon's Bull Market Projected Common Size Balance Sheets (Minority Interest) Years Ending December 31

	1996	1997	1998	1999	2000	2001
Assets						
Current Assets						
Cash and equivalents	13.6%	16.6%	18.9%	20.5%	21.4%	21.8%
Accounts receivable	2.4%	2.4%	2.4%	2.4%	2.4%	2.4%
Inventory	13.7%	13.4%	13.3%	13.3%	13.3%	13.5%
Other current assets (including prepaid expenses)	8.3%	8.2%	8.1%	8.1%	8.1%	8.2%
Total Current Assets	38.0%	40.6%	42.7%	44.2%	45.3%	45.8%
Property and Equipment	117.4%	117.9%	119.1%	121.1%	123.9%	127.7%
Less accumulated depreciation	(55.4%)	(58.5%)	(61.7%)	(65.3%)	(69.2%)	(73.5%)
Net Property and Equipment	62.0%	59.4%	57.3%	55.8%	54.7%	54.2%
Total Assets	100.0%	100.0%	100.0%	100.0%	100.0%	100.0%
Liabilities and Equity						
Current Liabilities						
Current portion long-term debt	3.9%	3.4%	3.1%	2.8%	2.5%	2.3%

Exhibit 22.22   (Continued)

	1996	1997	1998	1999	2000	2001
Other current payables	19.1%	18.9%	18.7%	18.6%	18.7%	18.9%
Accrued expenses	5.9%	5.8%	5.7%	5.7%	5.7%	5.8%
Other liabilities[a]	0.0%	0.0%	0.0%	0.0%	0.0%	0.0%
Total Current Liabilities	28.9%	28.1%	27.5%	27.1%	26.9%	27.0%
Long-term Liabilities						
Long-term debt (net of current portion)	17.7%	15.6%	14.0%	12.6%	11.5%	10.7%
Other long-term liabilities	0.0%	0.0%	0.0%	0.0%	0.0%	0.0%
Total Long-term Liabilities	17.7%	15.6%	14.0%	12.6%	11.5%	10.7%
Stockholders' Equity						
Common stock[b]	3.9%	3.5%	3.1%	2.8%	2.6%	2.4%
Preferred stock	0.0%	0.0%	0.0%	0.0%	0.0%	0.0%
Retained earnings	49.5%	52.8%	55.5%	57.5%	59.0%	60.0%
Total Stockholders' Equity	53.4%	56.3%	58.6%	60.3%	61.6%	62.3%
Total Liabilities and Equity	100.0%	100.0%	100.0%	100.0%	100.0%	100.0%

[a] Includes short-term notes payable, trade payables, and taxes payable.

[b] Includes capital surplus and net of treasury stock; authorized 1,000,000 shares; issued and outstanding 100,000 shares.

Exhibit 22.23   Shannon's Bull Market Projected Statements of Retained Earnings (Minority Interest) Years Ending December 31 ($000)

	Projected				
	1997	1998	1999	2000	2001
Retained earnings at beginning of year	3,763	4,559	5,362	6,151	6,904
Net income	953	1,067	1,186	1,313	1,446
Cash dividends declared and paid	(157)	(264)	(397)	(560)	(753)
Retained earnings at end of year	4,559	5,362	6,151	6,904	7,597

Exhibit 22.24 Shannon's Bull Market Projected Statements of Cash Flows (Minority Interest) Years Ending December 31 ($000)

	Projected				
	1997	1998	1999	2000	2001
Cash Flow from Operating Activities:					
Net income	953	1,067	1,186	1,313	1,446
Adjustments to Reconcile Net Income to Net Cash Provided from Operating Activities Depreciation	830	921	1,016	1,116	1,221
Net Change in Operating Assets and Liabilities					
Receivables	(23)	(22)	(23)	(25)	(27)
Inventories	(120)	(127)	(134)	(140)	(147)
Other current assets	(73)	(77)	(81)	(85)	(90)
Other current payables	169	178	186	197	206
Accrued expenses	52	54	57	60	63
Net Cash Provided from Operating Activities	1,788	1,994	2,207	2,436	2,672
Cash Flow from Investing Activities:					
Payments for property and equipment[a]	(1,233)	(1,336)	(1,444)	(1,558)	(1,675)
Cash Flow from Financing Activities:					
Reduction in long-term debt	0	0	0	0	0
Cash dividends paid	(157)	(264)	(397)	(560)	(753)
Net Cash Provided (Used) from Financing Activities	(157)	(264)	(397)	(560)	(753)
Net change in cash and cash equivalents	398	394	366	318	244
Cash and equivalents on January 1	1,034	1,432	1,826	2,192	2,510
Cash and equivalents on December 31	1,432	1,826	2,192	2,510	2,754

[a]Includes property and equipment for one new location per year plus replacement equipment equal to annual depreciation expense.

Exhibit 22.25   Shannon's Bull Market Projected Net Cash Flow to Equity and to Invested Capital (Control Basis) ($000) (Includes Answers to Problem Set 4)

	Actual 1996	1997	Projected 1998	1999	2000	2001
Determination of Net Cash Flow Available to Equity (Used for Control Interest Valuation)						
Adjusted net income	1,077	1,266	1,414	1,570	1,734	1,907
Add depreciation	744	830	921	1,016	1,116	1,221
Less capital expenditures[a]	(1,263)	(1,233)	(1,336)	(1,444)	(1,558)	(1,675)
Less working capital requirements	(91)	(96)	(101)	(106)	(112)	(118)
Increase (decrease in long-term debt[b])	(68)	0	0	0	0	0
Net Cash Flow Available to Equity	399	767	898	1,036	1,180	1,335
Determination of Net Cash Flow Available to Invested Capital (Used for Control Interest Valuation)						
Adjusted net income	1,077	1,266	1,414	1,570	1,734	1,907
Add depreciation	744	830	921	1,016	1,116	1,221
Less capital expenditures[a]	(1,263)	(1,233)	(1,336)	(1,444)	(1,558)	(1,675)
Less working capital requirement[d]	(91)	(96)	(101)	(106)	(112)	(118)
Add tax-affected interest expense[c]	141	93	93	93	93	93
Net Cash Flow Available to Invested Capital	608	860	991	1,129	1,273	1,428

[a] Includes the cost of property and equipment for one new location per year plus replacement equipment equal to depreciation expense (from projected statement of cash flow control basis, Exhibit 22.19).

[b] Assumed debt held at 1996 level.

[c] Interest expense X$(1 - .406)$.

[d] Assumed equal to 2.79% of incremental sales.

Exhibit 22.26 Shannon's Bull Market Projected Net Cash Flow to Equity and to Invested Capital (Minority Basis) ($000)

	Actual 1996	1997	Projected 1998	1999	2000	2001
Determination of Net Cash Flow Available to Equity (Used for Minority Interest Valuations)						
Historical net income (after tax)	795	953	1,067	1,186	1,313	1,446
Add depreciation	744	830	921	1,016	1,116	1,221
Less capital expenditures[a]	(1,263)	(1,233)	(1,336)	(1,444)	(1,558)	(1,675)
Less working capital requirements	(91)	(96)	(101)	(106)	(112)	(118)
Increase (decrease) in long-term debt[b]	(68)	0	0	0	0	0
Net Cash Flow Available to Equity	117	454	551	652	759	874
Determination of Net Cash Flow Available to Invested Capital (Used for Minority Interest Valuation)						
Historical net income	795	953	1,067	1,186	1,313	1,446
Add depreciation	744	830	921	1,016	1,116	1,221
Less capital expenditures[a]	(1,263)	(1,233)	(1,336)	(1,444)	(1,558)	(1,675)
Less working capital requirements[d]	(91)	(96)	(101)	(106)	(112)	(118)
Add tax-affected interest expense[c]	141	93	93	93	93	93
Net Cash Flow Available to Invested Capital	326	547	644	745	852	967

[a]Includes the cost of property and equipment for one new location per year plus replacement equipment equal to depreciation expense (from projected statement of cash flows minority basis, Exhibit 22.24).

[b]Assumed debt held at 1996 level.

[c]Interest expense X(1 − .406).

[d]Assumed equal to 2.79% of incremental sales.

Exhibit 22.27 Restaurant Industry Cost of Capital Statistics

Statistics for SIC Code 5812	Eating Places

This Industry Comprises 57 Companies

Industry Description

Establishments primarily engaged in the retail sale of prepared food and drinks for on-premise or immediate consumption. Caterers and industrial and institutional food service establishments are also included in this industry.

Sales ($million)

Total	25,328
Average	444.4

Three Largest Companies

MCDONALDS CORP	8,320.8
FLAGSTAR COS INC	2,666.0
HOST MARRIOTT CORP	1,501.0

Three Smallest Companies

GB FOODS CORP	6.3
SIX X HOLDINGS INC	5.8
INTL FAST FOOD CORP	4.5

Annualized Statistics for Last 10 Years (%)

	Average Return	Standard Deviation
S&P 500	15.18	16.71
Ind.[a] Composite	19.63	24.08
Lg.[b] Composite	18.76	25.06
Sm.[c] Composite	28.54	56.56

Distribution of Sales ($millions)

	Latest	5 Yr. Avg.
90th Percentile	1,036.7	850.3
75th Percentile	320.6	303.2
Median	158.7	109.4
25th Percentile	53.3	45.8
10th Percentile	17.5	15.2

Industry Sales and Income ($billions)

	Operating Sales	Net Income	Income
Current Yr.[d]	25.3	5.0	1.6
Last Yr.	25.3	4.7	–0.3
2 Yrs. Ago	30.6	4.8	1.4
3 Yrs. Ago	28.7	4.3	1.2
4 Yrs. Ago	27.4	4.1	1.2

Industry Market Capitalization ($billions)

	Equity	Debt
Current Yr.	47.2	11.6
Last Yr.	36.1	11.1
2 Yrs. Ago	34.7	11.8
3 Yrs. Ago	34.2	12.5
4 Yrs. Ago	27.2	12.9

Growth Over Last 5 Years (%)

	Operating Net Sales	Net Income	Income
75th Percentile	20.72	23.35	24.43
Median	9.17	5.50	3.31
25th Percentile	–2.56	–6.14	–32.81
Ind. Composite	–2.75	4.72	–4.63
Lg. Composite	–7.05	4.31	–2.89
Sm. Composite	19.81	–40.81	–37.27

Compound Annual Equity Return (%)   Betas (in Decimals)

5 Yrs.	10. Yrs.	Unlevered Asset Beta	Levered Equity Beta
14.10	6.25	0.84	1.25
3.13	0.03	0.53	0.72
–10.90	–6.50	0.17	0.23
22.47	17.25	0.87	1.11
22.92	16.19	0.83	1.12
39.62	17.68	0.49	0.53

(Continues)

Exhibit 22.27   (Continued)

Margins (%)

	Operating Margin		Net Margin		Return On Assets		Return On Equity	
	Latest	5 Yr. Avg.	Latest	5 Yr. Avg.	Latest	5 Yr. Avg.	Latest	5 Yr. Avg.
75th Percentile	13.44	13.43	4.92	4.96	8.56	6.52	6.49	5.20
Median	9.12	9.71	1.45	2.10	2.53	3.61	4.11	3.34
25th Percentile	5.85	7.64	−1.81	−0.55	−3.30	−1.32	−6.44	−1.63
Ind. Composite	19.71	16.65	6.40	3.70	6.12	3.75	3.89	3.10
Lg. Composite	24.63	18.78	8.59	4.19	6.65	3.69	3.97	3.17
Sm. Composite	−11.37	−9.12	−33.12	−25.59	−33.52	−24.29	−12.18	−9.93

Equity Valuation Ratios (in Decimal)   **DCF[e] Growth Rates** (%)

	Price/ Earnings		Market/Book		Price/ Sales		
	Latest	5 Yr. Avg.	Latest	5 Yr. Avg.	Latest	5 Yr. Avg.	Analysis
75th Percentile	NMF[f]	NMF	2.79	3.17	1.08	1.24	15.15
Median	25.19	29.94	1.72	2.03	0.45	0.64	15.15
25th Percentile	15.75	19.23	0.81	1.19	0.21	0.41	15.15
Ind. Composite	29.15	32.26	3.99	3.08	1.86	1.19	15.15
Lg. Composite	28.74	31.55	4.61	3.31	2.47	1.32	14.89
Sm. Composite	NMF	NMF	5.85	4.21	3.40	2.58	15.15

Cost Of Equity Capital (%)   **Cost of Debt** (%)

	CAPM[g]		3-Factor	DCF		
	S-L[h] Form	S-L Sm Cap[i]	F-F[j]	Analyses	3 Stage	
75th Percentile	16.06	18.08	27.94	17.28	15.52	9.35
Median	12.17	14.93	20.92	15.15	13.93	8.50
25th Percentile	8.55	11.58	15.06	15.15	12.14	7.80
Ind. Composite	15.09	15.56	17.83	15.83	NMF	8.70
Lg. Composite	15.14	15.32	17.05	15.50	NMF	8.68
Sm. Composite	10.80	14.38	16.46	15.15	NMF	8.33

Total Capital ($millions)

Exhibit 22.27   (Continued)

		Capital Structure Ratios (%)			
Total	58,380				
Average	1,024.2	Debt/Total Capital		Debt/MV Equity	
Three Largest Companies		Latest	5 Yr. Avg.	Latest	5 Yr. Avg.
MCDONALDS CORP	38,269.0	49.35	39.75	97.44	65.97
HOST MARRIOTT CORP	4,418.5	22.21	18.09	28.55	22.09
FLAGSTAR COS INC	2,232.3	11.95	6.38	13.57	6.82
Three Smallest Companies		19.85	26.78	24.54	36.57
SIX X HOLDINGS INC	5.8	20.27	29.41	25.32	41.66
BOSTON RESTAURANT		7.27	12.48	7.74	14.26
ASSOC INC	4.9				
CIATTIS INC	4.6				

Distribution of Total Capital ($millions)

	Latest	5 Yr. Avg.
90th Percentile	1,043.6	1,251.5
75th Percentile	304.9	277.7
Median	118.1	108.6
25th Percentile	31.5	31.4
10th Percentile	10.9	14.2

Yields (% of Price)

Dividends		Cash Flow	
Latest	5 Yr. Avg.	Latest	5 Yr. Avg.
0.00	0.08	−1.46	−1.20
0.00	0.00	−7.50	−6.56
0.00	0.00	−23.03	−11.55
0.61	0.82	−0.53	−1.74
0.54	0.80	0.29	−1.29
0.00	0.00	−12.92	−13.98

Number of Companies & Total Capital ($billions)

Large Cap	Mid Cap	Low Cap	Micro Cap	Total Cap
AAA, AA, A				
1	0	0	0	1
38.3	0.0	0.0	0.0	38.3
BBB				
0	1	0	0	1
0.0	2.0	0.0	0.0	2.0
BB, B, CCC, CC, D				
0	1	0	2	3
0.0	4.4	0.0	2.4	6.8
Not Rated				
0	3	12	37	52
0.0	3.6	5.2	2.5	11.3
Totals				
1	5	12	39	57
38.3	10.1	5.2	4.9	58.4

■ S&P[k] Rating

Weighted Average Cost of Capital (%)

CAPM		3-Factor		DCF
S-L Form	S-L Sm Cap	F-F	Analysis	3 Stage
13.17	15.02	19.74	15.14	15.03
9.45	11.30	14.29	13.22	12.81
7.55	9.29	11.43	10.40	11.39
13.30	13.67	15.50	13.89	NMF
13.29	13.43	14.81	13.57	NMF
10.41	13.73	15.67	14.45	NMF

Source: Reprinted from Ibbotson Associates, Cost of Capital Quarterly: 1996 Yearbook.
Used with permission. © 1996 Ibbotson Associates, Inc.; includes data from Standard & Poor's COMPUSTAT. All rights reserved. [Certain portions of this work were derived from copyrighted works of Roger G. Ibbotson and Rex Sinquefield.]

[a]Industry; [b]Large; [c]Small; [d]Year; [e]Discounted cash flow; [f]Not meaningful; [g]Capital asset pricing model; [h]Sharpe-Lintner; [i]Capitalization; [j]Fama-French; [k]Standard & Poors

Exhibit 22.28 Shannon's Bull Market Calculation of Present Value of Equity (Control Basis) ($000)

Calculation of Terminal Value (Using Gordon Growth Model)

$$\frac{\text{year 5 net cash flow to equity } X(1 + \text{long-term growth rate})}{\text{equity discount rate} - \text{long-term growth rate}} \qquad \frac{1,335X(1 + .07)}{.134 - .07}$$

Terminal value   22,320

Calculation of Present Value

$$\frac{NCF_1{}^a}{(1+k)} + \frac{NCF_2}{(1+k)^2} + \frac{NCF_3}{(1+k)^3} + \frac{NCF_4}{(1+k)^4} + \frac{NCF_5}{(1+k)^5} + \frac{\text{terminal value}}{(1+k)^5}$$

$$= \frac{767}{1.134} + \frac{898}{(1.134)^2} + \frac{1,036}{(1.134)^3} + \frac{1,180}{(1.134)^4} + \frac{1,335}{(1.134)^5} + \frac{22,320}{(1.134)^5}$$

$$= \frac{767}{1.134} + \frac{898}{1.268} + \frac{1,036}{1.458} + \frac{1,180}{1.654} + \frac{1,135}{1.875} + \frac{22,320}{1.875}$$

$$= \quad 676 \quad + \quad 698 \quad + \quad 711 \quad + \quad 713 \quad + \quad 712 \quad + \quad 11,904$$

$$= \quad 15,414$$

Alternately, set up in tabular format

	Amount *NCF*	Factor	Present Value[b]
Year 1	767	0.882	675
Year 2	898	0.778	698
Year 3	1,036	0.686	711
Year 4	1,180	0.605	713
Year 5	1,335	0.533	712
Terminal value	22,320	0.533	11,904
Total Present Value[b]			15,414

[a]*NCF*, net cash flow.
[b]Values vary slightly due to rounding.

Exhibit 22.29   Shannon's Bull Market Calculation of Present Value of Equity (Minority Basis) ($000)

Calculation of Terminal Value (Using Gordon Growth Model)

$$\frac{\text{year 5 net cash flow to equity } X(1 + \text{long-term growth rate})}{\text{equity discount rate} - \text{long-term growth rate}} \qquad \frac{874X(1 + .07)}{.134 - .07}$$

Terminal value   14,612

Calculation of Present Value

$$\frac{NCF_1{}^a}{(1+k)} + \frac{NCF_2}{(1+k)^2} + \frac{NCF_3}{(1+k)^3} + \frac{NCF_4}{(1+k)^4} + \frac{NCF_5}{(1+k)^5} + \frac{\text{terminal value}}{(1+k)^5}$$

$$= \frac{454}{1.134} + \frac{551}{(1.134)^2} + \frac{652}{(1.134)^3} + \frac{759}{(1.134)^4} + \frac{874}{(1.134)^5} + \frac{14{,}612}{(1.134)^5}$$

$$= \frac{454}{1.134} + \frac{551}{1.286} + \frac{652}{1.458} + \frac{759}{1.654} + \frac{874}{1.875} + \frac{14{,}612}{1.875}$$

$$= 400 + 428 + 447 + 459 + 466 + 7{,}793$$

$$= 9{,}993$$

Alternately, set up in tabular form

	Amount *NCF*	Factor	Present Value[b]
Year 1	454	0.882	400
Year 2	551	0.778	428
Year 3	652	0.686	447
Year 4	759	0.605	459
Year 5	874	0.533	466
Terminal value	14,612	0.533	7,793
Total Present Value[b]			9,993

[a] *NCF*, net cash flow.
[b] Values vary slightly due to rounding.

Exhibit 22.30   Shannon's Bull Market Calculation of Weighted Average Cost of Capital (WACC) December 31, 1996

Equity discount rate		0.134	
Cost of debt (pretax)	0.094		
$X(1 - .406)$	0.594		
Tax-affected cost of debt		0.056	
Debt/total capital (Book)		0.10	

Computation of *WACC*:

Capital Component	Capital Cost		Proportion	Weighted Cost
Equity	0.134	×	0.90	0.1206
Debt	0.056	×	0.10	0.0056
WACC				0.126 (rounded)

Exhibit 22.31   Shannon's Bull Market Calculation of Present Value of Invested Capital (Control Basis) ($000)

Calculation of Terminal Value (Using Gordon Growth Model)

$$\frac{\text{Year 5 net cash flow to invested capital } X(1 + \text{long-term growth rate})}{WACC^a - \text{long-term growth rate}} \qquad \frac{1,428 X (1 + 0.07)}{.126 - 0.07}$$

Terminal value   27,285

Calculation of Present Value

$$= \frac{NCF_1{}^a}{(1 + k)} + \frac{NCF_2}{(1 + k)^2} + \frac{NCF_3}{(1 + k)^3} + \frac{NCF_4}{(1 + k)^4} + \frac{NCF_5}{(1 + k)^5} + \frac{\text{terminal value}}{(1 + k)^5}$$

$$= \frac{860}{1.126} + \frac{991}{(1.126)^2} + \frac{1,129}{(1.126)^3} + \frac{1,273}{(1.126)^4} + \frac{1,428}{(1.126)^5} + \frac{27,285}{(1.126)^5}$$

$$= \frac{860}{1.126} + \frac{991}{1.268} + \frac{1,129}{1.428} + \frac{1,273}{1.608} + \frac{1,428}{1.810} + \frac{27,285}{1.810}$$

$$= 764 + 782 + 791 + 792 + 789 + 15,075$$

$$= 18,993$$

Alternately, set up in tabular form

	Amount *NCF*	Factor	Present Value
Year 1	860	0.888	764
Year 2	991	0.789	782
Year 3	1,129	0.700	791
Year 4	1,273	0.622	792
Year 5	1,428	0.552	789

Exhibit 22.31 (Continued)

	Amount *NCF*	Factor	Present Value
Terminal value	27,285	0.552	15,075
Total Present Value[c]			18,993

[a]*WACC*, weighted average cost of capital.
[b]*NCF*, net cash flow.
[c]Values vary slightly due to rounding.

Exhibit 22.32 Shannon's Bull Market Calculation of Present Value of Invested Capital (Minority Basis) ($000)

Calculation of Terminal Value (Using Gordon Growth Model)

$$\frac{\text{Year 5 net cash flow to invested capital } X(1 + \text{long-term growth rate})}{\text{WACC}^a - \text{long-term growth rate}} \qquad \frac{967X(1 + 0.07)}{.126 - 0.07}$$

Terminal value   18,477

Calculation of Present Value

$$\frac{NCF_1{}^a}{(1+k)} + \frac{NCF_2}{(1+k)^2} + \frac{NCF_3}{(1+k)^3} + \frac{NCF_4}{(1+k)^4} + \frac{NCF_5}{(1+k)^5} + \frac{\text{terminal value}}{(1+k)^5}$$

$$= \frac{547}{1.126} + \frac{644}{(1.126)^2} + \frac{745}{(1.126)^3} + \frac{852}{(1.126)^4} + \frac{967}{(1.126)^5} + \frac{18,477}{(1.126)^5}$$

$$= \frac{547}{1.126} + \frac{644}{1.268} + \frac{754}{1.428} + \frac{852}{1.608} + \frac{967}{1.810} + \frac{18,477}{1.810}$$

$$= 486 + 508 + 522 + 530 + 534 + 10,208$$

$$= 12,788$$

Alternately, set up in tabular form

	Amount *NCF*	Factor	Present Value
Year 1	547	0.888	486
Year 2	644	0.789	508
Year 3	745	0.700	528
Year 4	852	0.622	530
Year 5	967	0.552	534
Terminal value	18,477	0.552	10,208
Total Present Value[c]			12,788

[a]*WACC*, weighted average cost of capital.
[b]*NCF*, net cash flow.
[c]Values vary slightly due to rounding.

Exhibit 22.33 Computed Shannon's Bull Market Fundamentals

	Control Value	Source	Minority Value	Source
Net income	$1,077	Adjusted income statement	$795	Income statement as reported
Gross cash flow	$1,821	Adjusted income statement (net income + noncash charges)	$1,539	Income statement as reported (net income + noncash charges)
Earnings before taxes	$1,813	Adjusted income statement (net income + taxes)	$1,339	Income statement as reported (net income + taxes)
Net sales	$29,748	Historical income statement	$29,748	Income statement as reported
Net tangible asset value	$4,063	Historical balance sheet (Total equity—net intangible assets)	$4,063	Balance sheet (total equity—net intangible assets)
Earnings before interest, taxes, depreciation, and amortization	$2,795	Adjusted income statement (net income + interest expense + taxes + noncash charges)	$2,321	Income statement as reported (net income + interest expense + taxes + noncash charges)
Earnings before interest and taxes	$2,051	Adjusted income statement (net income + interest expense + taxes)	$1,577	Income statement as reported (net income + interest expense + taxes)
Debt in capital structure	$1,647	Balance sheet (long-term debt + current portion long-term debt)	$1,647	Balance sheet (long-term debt + current portion long-term debt)

Exhibit 22.34 Shannon's Bull Market Guideline Public Company Valuation Multiples

	Market Value of Equity/Book Equity	Market Value of Equity/Pretax Earnings	Market Value of Equity/Net Income	Market Value of Equity/Gross Cash Flow	Market Value of Equity/Sales	Market Value of Invested Capital/EBITDA[a]	Market Value of Invested Capital/EBIT[b]	Market Value of Invested Capital/Sales	Market Value of Invested Capital/Discretionary Earnings	Market Value of Invested Capital/Tangible Asset Value
Timber Lodge	1.24	9.79	12.57	6.47	0.60	5.65	9.79	0.60	4.10	0.90
Ark Restaurants	1.76	15.79	26.20	9.00	0.44	8.14	17.51	0.48	6.94	1.33
Max & Erma's	1.59	8.98	13.20	3.72	0.36	7.01	19.17	0.76	5.53	1.05
J Alexanders	1.12	3.94	6.26	4.44	0.50	4.24	5.34	0.67	3.76	0.91
Morton's Restaurants	5.16	12.42	20.69	9.97	0.56	8.13	12.22	0.71	N/A	0.71
Range	1.12–5.16	3.94–15.79	6.26–26.2	3.72–9.97	0.36–0.60	4.24–8.14	5.34–19.17	0.48–0.76	3.76–6.94	0.71–1.33
Mean	1.43	9.63	23.97	10.60	0.49	6.26	12.95	0.65	14.13	0.98
Median	1.59	9.39	13.20	6.47	0.50	6.33	13.65	0.67	5.53	0.91
Coefficient of variation[c]	0.18	0.33	0.44	0.44	0.15	0.21	0.42	0.14	0.64	0.14

[a] *EBITDA*, earnings before interest, taxes, depreciation, and amortization.
[b] *EBIT*, earnings before interest and taxes.
[c] Excluding Morton's.

Exhibit 22.35 Guideline Public Company Method Value Summary (Controlling Interest Basis) ($000)

Equity Multiples	Selected Multiple	×	Shannon's Bull Market Fundamental	=	Indicated Value	−	Debt	=	Indicated Equity Value	×	Weight	=	Weighted Value
MVE^c/net income	13.20	×	1,077	=	14,216	−	0	=	14,216	×	0.05	=	$711
MVE/gross cash flow	6.47	×	1,821	=	11,782	−	0	=	11,782	×	0.05	=	$589
MVE/earnings before taxes	9.39	×	1,813	=	17,024	−	0	=	17,024	×	0.05	=	$851
MVE/net sales	0.50	×	29,748	=	14,874	−	0	=	14,874	×	0.15	=	$2,231
MVE/book equity	1.59	×	4,063	=	6,460	−	0	=	6,460	×	0.10	=	$646
Invested Capital Multiples													
MVIC^d/EBITDA^a	6.33	×	2,795	=	17,692	−	1,647	=	16,045	×	0.10	=	$1,605
MVIC/EBIT^b	13.65	×	2,051	=	27,996	−	1,647	=	26,349	×	0.05	=	$1,317
MVIC/net sales	0.67	×	29,748	=	19,931	−	1,647	=	18,284	×	0.20	=	$3,657
MVIC/discretionary earnings	5.53	×	2,917	=	16,131	−	1,647	=	14,484	×	0.05	=	$724
MVIC/net tangible asset value	.91	×	4,063	=	3,697	−	1,647	=	2,050	×	0.20	=	$410
													$12,741

^{a}EBITDA, earnings before interest, taxes, depreciation, and amortization.

^{b}EBIT, earnings before interest and taxes.

^{c}MVE, market value of equity.

^{d}MVIC, market value of invested capital.

Exhibit 22.36 Guideline Public Company Method Value Summary (Minority Interest Basis) ($000)

Equity Multiples	Selected Multiple	×	Shannon's Bull Market Fundamental	=	Indicated Value	−	Debt	=	Indicated Equity Value	×	Weight	=	Weighted Value
MVE^c/net income	13.20	×	795	=	10,494	−	0	=	10,494	×	0.05	=	$525
MVE/gross cash flow	6.47	×	1,539	=	9,957	−	0	=	9,957	×	0.05	=	$498
MVE/earnings before taxes	9.39	×	1,339	=	12,573	−	0	=	12,573	×	0.05	=	$629
MVE/net sales	0.50	×	29,748	=	14,874	−	0	=	14,874	×	0.15	=	$2,231
MVE/book equity	1.59	×	4,063	=	6,460	−	0	=	6,460	×	0.10	=	$646
Invested Capital Multiples													
MVIC^d/EBITDA^a	6.33	×	2,321	=	14,692	−	1,647	=	13,045	×	0.10	=	$1,304
MVIC/EBIT^b	13.65	×	1,577	=	21,526	−	1,647	=	19,879	×	0.05	=	$994
MVIC/net sales	0.67	×	29,748	=	19,931	−	1,647	=	18,284	×	0.20	=	$3,657
MVIC/discretionary earnings	5.53	×	2,767	=	15,302	−	1,647	=	13,655	×	0.05	=	$683
MVIC/net tangible asset value	.91	×	4,063	=	3,697	−	1,647	=	2,050	×	0.20	=	410
													$11,577

^{a} EBITDA, earnings before interest, taxes, depreciation, and amortization.
^{b} EBIT, earnings before interest and taxes.
^{c} MVE, market value of equity.
^{d} MVIC, market value of invested capital.

with sources, replicate calculations, and check the accuracy of all material presented. We have omitted this information for the sake of brevity. Also for the sake of brevity, we have shown value multiples based only on the latest fiscal years' results. A more comprehensive analysis could include income value multiples based on any or all of the following time periods:

- Latest 12 months.
- Estimated next 12 months or next fiscal year (from publicly available analysts' estimates).
- Average of some historical period, such as three or five years.
- Weighted average of some historical period, such as three or five years.

Criteria for Selection of Guideline Public Companies

Using SIC Code 5812 for restaurants, we searched through Deloitte & Touche L.L.P.'s *Corporate Analytics,* concentrating on companies with sales of less than $300 million. Of that initial group, we selected companies that stressed high-quality food, service, and beverages and had a positive net income in 1996. We preferred companies that served American food entrees that centered on prime rib, steaks, and high-quality seafood but were open to chains serving high-quality ethnic food as long as alcoholic beverages were sold; part of the success of Shannon's Bull Market is believed to include the margins resulting from 28% of sales being for alcoholic beverages.

Descriptions of Selected Guideline Public Companies

Ark Restaurants Corp.: The company owns and operates 23 restaurants located in the Northeast United States. Liquor is sold, and the menu focuses on high-quality American beef. Sales were $104 million, and the quality menu and ambience closely resemble those of Shannon's Bull Market. The number of restaurants is slightly larger and growing more rapidly.

J Alexanders Corp.: Sales for 1996 were $90 million, with alcohol sales making up 15% of total sales. The company owns 14 high-quality mesquite grill restaurants that feature prime rib. High-quality food items are stressed, including using Häagen-Dazs ice cream for milkshakes. The company has been operating Wendy's restaurants but plans on ridding itself of the four remaining.

Max & Erma's: Sales were $80 million in 1996, with 39 operating restaurants. Although quality is emphasized, Max & Erma's has a larger menu that includes hamburgers and popular southwestern items such as fajitas. The quality of service deserves recognition: Servers are empowered to please customers without management approval to ensure that an item in question by the customer is taken care of immediately.

Morton's Restaurant Group: The largest of the comparables had $193 million in sales in 1996. The Chicago-based company's reputation is on very high quality beef. Unfortunately, the company experienced negative net income three out of five years, thus making many growth comparisons difficult against SBM and the other comparables. The reputation of the high-quality food, especially beef, is second to none for a restaurant chain.

Timber Lodge Steakhouses: With sales of $20 million in 1996, Timber Lodge is the only guideline company smaller than SBM. The company operates 12 restaurants, exactly the same number as SBM, in Minnesota, Wisconsin, and the Dakotas. It believes the focus of being a high-quality steakhouse will encourage repeat business. The company opened three steakhouses in 1996 and as of the valuation date planned to open five in 1997; it is thus growing much faster than SBM.

Selection of Guideline Company Multiples

We looked carefully at the comparative financial analysis between SBM and the public guideline companies. On the negative side, what stood out was a lower rate of growth for SBM relative to the public guideline companies. On the positive side, however, SBM demonstrated much more stability in its year-to-year results than any of the public companies, indicating a lower risk profile (also reflected in our negative specific-company adjustment to the discount rate in the income approach). In the final analysis, we judged that these factors balanced each other, and we selected the median public company value multiples.

Weights Assigned to Guideline Public Company Valuation Multiples

Heavier weight was given to the sale and net tangible asset values due to their low coefficients of variation. The remaining value multiples were given lower weight (5% except for the MVIC/EBITDA ratio, which was given 10%) due to their higher coefficients of variation.

GUIDELINE MERGER AND ACQUISITION METHOD

Guideline Merger and Acquisition Company Data Presentation

- Exhibit 22.37, guideline merger and acquisition company valuation multiples.
- Exhibit 22.38, guideline merger and acquisition method value summary (controlling interest basis).
- Exhibit 22.39, guideline merger and acquisition method value summary (minority interest basis).

Note: To the extent that data are available, the same comments as for the publicly traded guideline companies apply. However, unless the acquired company was public before the acquisition, less information is usually available. All three of the acquired companies used in this analysis were privately held.

Exhibit 22.37

Shannon's Bull Market Guideline Merger and Acquisition Company Valuation Multiples

Company	Equity Price/ Net Income	Equity Price/ Gross Cash Flow	Equity Price/ Earnings before Taxes	Equity Price/ Net Sales[a]	Equity Price/ Tangible Asset Value	Deal Price/ EBITDA[b]	Deal Price/ EBIT[c]	Deal Price/ Net Sales[a]	Deal Price/ Discretionary Earnings
1	32.48	20.83	19.81	0.81	179.66	12.42	14.9	1.04	12.42
2	17.85	15.52	17.85	1.12	4.11	16.39	19.01	1.12	10.87
3	29.01	13.09	29.01	0.74	6.32	13.41	19.29	1.37	7.28
Range	17.85–32.48	13.09–20.83	17.85–29.01	0.74–1.12	4.11–179.66	12.42–16.39	14.9–19.29	1.04–1.37	7.28–12.42
Mean	26.45	16.48	22.22	0.89	63.36	14.07	17.74	1.18	10.19
Median	29.01	15.52	19.81	0.81	6.32	13.41	19.01	1.12	12.42
Coefficient of variation	0.29	0.024	0.27	0.23	1.59	0.15	0.14	0.15	.43

[a] The sales for all the comparative companies were within a reasonably close time period. Therefore, we did not feel that any adjustments were necessary to adjust for time.

[b] EBITDA, earnings before interest, taxes, depreciation, and amortization.

[c] EBIT, earnings before interest and taxes.

Exhibit 22.38 Shannon's Bull Market Guideline Merger and Acquisition Method Value Summary (Controlling Interest Basis) ($000 for dollar amounts)

Equity Multiples	Selected Multiple	×	Shannon's Bull Market Fundamental	=	Indicated Value	−	Debt	=	Indicated Equity Value	×	Weight	=	Weighted Value
Equity price/net income	29.01	×	1,077	=	31,244	−	0	=	31,244	×	0.05	=	$1,562
Equity price/gross cash flow	15.52	×	1,821	=	28,262	−	0	=	28,262	×	0.10	=	$2,826
Equity price/earnings before taxes	19.81	×	1,813	=	35,916	−	0	=	35,916	×	0.10	=	$3,592
Equity price/net sales	0.81	×	29,748	=	24,096	−	0	=	24,096	×	0.10	=	$2,410
Equity price/net tangible asset value	6.32	×	4,063	=	25,678	−	0	=	25,678	×	0.05	=	$1,284
Invested Capital Multiples													
Deal price/EBITDA[a]	13.41	×	2,795	=	37,481	−	1,647	=	35,834	×	0.15	=	$5,375
Deal price/EBIT[b]	19.01	×	2,051	=	38,990	−	1,647	=	37,343	×	0.15	=	$5,601
Deal price/net sales	1.12	×	29,748	=	33,318	−	1,647	=	31,671	×	0.15	=	$4,751
Deal price/discretionary earnings	12.42	×	2,917	=	36,229	−	1,647	=	34,582	×	0.15	=	$5,187
													$32,588

[a] EBITDA, earnings before interest, taxes, depreciation, and amortization.

[b] EBIT, earnings before interest and taxes.

Exhibit 22.39 Shannon's Bull Market Guideline Merger and Acquisition Method Value Summary (Minority Interest Basis) ($000 for dollar amounts)

Equity Multiples	Selected Multiple	×	Shannon's Bull Market Fundamental	=	Indicated Value	−	Debt	=	Indicated Equity Value	×	Weight	=	Weighted Value
Equity price/net income	29.01	×	795	=	23,063	−	0	=	23,063	×	0.05	=	$1,153
Equity price/gross cash flow	15.52	×	1,539	=	23,885	−	0	=	23,885	×	0.10	=	$2,389
Equity price/earnings before taxes	19.81	×	1,339	=	26,526	−	0	=	26,526	×	0.10	=	$2,653
Equity price/net sales	0.81	×	29,748	=	24,096	−	0	=	24,096	×	0.10	=	$2,410
Equity price/net tangible asset value	6.32	×	4,063	=	25,678	−	0	=	25,678	×	0.05	=	$1,284
Invested Capital Multiples													
Deal price/EBITDA[a]	13.41	×	2,321	=	31,125	−	1,647	=	29,478	×	0.15	=	$4,462
Deal price/EBIT[b]	19.01	×	1,577	=	29,979	−	1,647	=	28,332	×	0.15	=	$4,250
Deal price/net sales	1.12	×	29,748	=	33,318	−	1,647	=	31,671	×	0.15	=	$4,751
Deal price/discretionary earnings	12.42	×	2,767	=	34,366	−	1,647	=	32,719	×	0.15	=	$4,908
													$28,260

[a] EBITDA, earnings before interest, taxes, depreciation, and amortization.
[b] EBIT, earnings before interest and taxes.

Criteria for Selection of Guideline Merged and Acquired Companies

The guideline merger and acquisition company information used for the merger and acquisition method was taken from the fourth-quarter 1997 edition of *Pratt's Stats™*, a private business transaction database. The companies used in the comparison were selected based on certain criteria. The transaction information used for comparison was within one year of the date of the valuation. The types of restaurants selected were comparable in style to SBM. Sales of the comparison companies were between $3 million and $100 million. Net cash flow had to be positive, and there had to be enough information to create the necessary value multiples.

Descriptions of Selected Guideline Merged and Acquired Companies

Company 1: This company is the most similar to SBM. The transaction occurred on February 2, 1997, so closely following the valuation date that we believe it provides valid evidence of value at the valuation date. The company is 25 years old and based mainly in the Northwest. It is composed of 16 restaurants. Dining capacities range from 139 to 290 customers. Sales of alcoholic beverages accounted for 30% of total sales. Sales for the last year were $65,680,000. Net income for the year came to $1,632,000.

Company 2: This company is located in Miami Beach, Florida. The transaction date was September 9, 1996. Sales for the last year totaled $4,255,552, and net income was $266,154.

Company 3: This company is located in Clearwater, Florida. The transaction date was February 2, 1997. The company consists of 19 restaurant-microbrewery locations. Alcoholic beverages accounted for 18% of sales. Here, dining capacities range from 160 to 240 customers. Sales and net income for the last year came to $42,330,000 and $1,086,000, respectively. The cost to develop and open one restaurant in 1996 was approximately $1,400,000, excluding land costs, and included approximately $160,000 worth of microbrewery equipment.

Selection of Merged and Acquired Company Multiples

On the basis of the limited data available (only the latest year for each of the three companies), we were not able to distinguish any significant differences in performance factors, especially risk and growth, between SBM and the acquired companies. Therefore, we used median valuation multiples to apply to SBM fundamental data.

Weights Assigned to Guideline Merger and Acquisition Valuation Multiples

The lowest coefficients of variation were in the invested capital multiples; therefore, they were assigned a weight of 15% each. The remaining 40% was spread among the equity multiples, giving the least weight (5% for price/net income) because it had one of the highest variances. The price/net tangible asset value was given a weight of 5% because this multiple is not usually significant for a business of this type.

RECONCILIATION OF VALUATION METHODS

Reconciliation of Controlling Interest Methods

- Not counting the merger and acquisition method, value indications range from $12,741,000 to $17,346,000, as shown in Exhibit 22.40.
- We have decided not to give any weight to the merger and acquisition method indicated value because it is so far away from the others, we had only three guideline companies, and we believe that SBM is more comparable, on average, to the public guideline companies.
- We have a high level of confidence in the SBM projections and believe that the discounted present value of cash flows to equity represent the most reliable of the indications of value.
- All factors considered, we would estimate the market value of SBM's equity at $15 million.

Discount for Lack of Marketability for Controlling Interest

- Our value estimate is slightly above the value indicated by the public guideline companies, calling into question whether the full amount could be realized in a public offering.
- Even if we could issue stock on the basis of a $15 million value, we could not sell all of our stock initially and would be left with restricted stock.
- To effect a sale of the entire company, we would need to incur audited statement and legal expenses, and there would a considerable time lapse and risk that the strong market for restaurant companies could weaken.

All things considered, we believe that a 10% discount for lack of marketability is appropriate for the controlling interest, resulting in a value of $13,500,000.

Reconciliation of Minority Interest Methods

- The indications of value range from $9,993,000 to $11,577,000 ($99.93 to $115.77 per share, based on 100,000 shares outstanding), summarized in Exhibit 22.41.

Exhibit 22.40   Shannon's Bull Market Reconciliation of Valuation Methods (Control Basis) ($000)

Discounted Cash Flow		
Value of equity computed directly		$15,414
Value of invested capital	$18,993	
Less long-term debt	1,647	$17,346
Market Approach		
Publicly traded guideline companies		$12,741
Merged and acquired companies		$32,588

Exhibit 22.41   Shannon's Bull Market Reconciliation of Valuation Method (Minority Basis) ($000)

Discounted Cash Flow		
Value of equity computed directly		$9,993
Value of invested capital	$12,788	
Less long-term debt	1,647	$11,141
Guideline Public Company Method		$11,577

- All of the difference between indicated control and minority values is due to SBM's excess compensation and rent, the overall effect of which is diminishing somewhat as the company grows.
- Because of the diminishing difference between minority and control cash flows over time, and the fact that this difference would diminish very quickly if the company decided to have a public offering (which is a realistic possibility), we lean toward the upper end of the range of indicated values.
- All things considered, we would estimate the value of minority stock (before discount for lack of marketability) at $110 per share.

Note: The above statement is actually too loose for a written report valuation estimate. Normally we would provide more detailed reasoning and would reiterate a description of property valued, the date, and the purpose

Discount for Lack of Marketability for Minority Interests

- Letter stock studies indicate average discounts for companies of about 35%, and pre-IPO studies indicate discounts of about 45%.
- Although the company is very strong and stable financially, it does not pay any dividends (which is generally true for most of the pre-IPO study stocks and many of the public companies with restricted stock transactions).

- All things considered, we believe that a 40% discount for lack of marketability is appropriate, resulting in a minority value of $66 per share.

EPILOGUE TO THE SAMPLE CASE

- In an actual case write-up, there would be far more text in many places, justifying the figures chosen:
  - More comparison discussion about subject relative to guideline companies leading to selection of multiples.
  - Several pages of extended discussion and empirical data presentation supporting chosen discounts for marketability.
- Multiples would be chosen much more carefully:
  - Not likely (although possible) at median levels.
  - Not necessarily the same level of multiple relative to the range for each variable (e.g., high return on equity might lead to high price/book multiple; low return on sales to low price/sales multiple).
- It is unlikely (although possible) that 9 or 10 different valuation multiples would be used and each accorded some mathematical weight; more often a few of the most relevant variables are used, along with explanations.
- The differences between a $135 ($13,500,000 ÷ 100,000) control share value and a $66 minority share value is not uncommon; however, most clients do not expect this difference.
- Shannon's five-year old grandson, Randall, was recently added to the payroll as chief engineer. He trains all new staff on running the G-scale railroad properly to deliver food and drinks to the patrons in the booths along the railroad lines. The IRS investigated Shannon for deducting Randall's salary as a tax fraud scheme but ultimately became convinced that Randall was more qualified as chief engineer than Shannon himself.

PART VII

Valuation for Specific Purposes

Chapter 23

Tax-Related Valuations

TYPICAL PURPOSES OF TAX-RELATED VALUATIONS

- Gift taxes
- Estate taxes
- Purchase price allocation
- Charitable contributions
- Buy-sell agreements (if object is to make value determinative for estate tax purposes)
- Inheritance taxes (levied by states on recipients rather than on estate; values accepted by Internal Revenue Service [IRS] for estate taxes usually but not always accepted by states)
- Ad valorem (property) taxes
- Employee stock ownership plans (ESOPs) (see Chapter 24 regarding special considerations for ESOPs)

STANDARD OF VALUE IS FAIR MARKET VALUE

• Fair market value is standard of value for most tax valuations.
• See Chapter 3 for definition and discussion of fair market value.

REVENUE RULING 59-60 (RR59-60) GIVES PRIMARY GUIDANCE

Eight Basic Factors to Consider

1. The nature of the business and the history of the enterprise from its inception.
2. The economic outlook in general and the condition and outlook of the specific industry in particular.
3. The book value of the stock and the financial condition of the business.
4. The earning capacity of the company.
5. The dividend-paying capacity of the company.
6. Whether the enterprise has goodwill or other intangible value.
7. Sales of the stock and the size of the block of stock to be valued.
8. The market prices of stock of corporations engaged in the same or a similar line of business having their stocks actively traded in a free and open market, either on an exchange or over the counter.

Some Highlight Quotes from RR59-60

• "A determination of fair market value, being a question of fact, will depend on the circumstances in each case. No formula can be devised that will be generally applicable to the multitude of different valuation issues arising in estate and gift tax cases."
• "The appraiser must exercise his judgment as to the degree of risk attaching to the business."
• "Valuation of securities is, in essence, a prophesy as to the future, and must be based on the facts available at the required date of appraisal."
• "Because valuations cannot be made on the basis of a prescribed formula, there is no means whereby the various applicable factors in a particular case can be assigned mathematical weights in deriving the fair market value. . . . Such a process excludes active consideration of other pertinent factors."

Note: When using mathematical weights, include the disclaimer noted in Chapter 17 on reconciliation and value conclusion *and* recap the pertinent factors to demonstrate that all were considered.

INTERNAL REVENUE CODE (IRC) CHAPTER 14 SPECIAL VALUATION GUIDELINES: SECTIONS 2701 TO 2704

Background of IRC Chapter 14

- Enacted in 1990.
- Has special valuation rules applicable to transfers of family-owned business interests.
- Has effect of making some special modifications to fair market value when applicable.
- Four main sections: 2701 to 2704.

Section 2701: Preferred Interests

When Section 2701 Is Applicable

Note: Consult a tax attorney. This discussion is provided for valuation guidance and does not purport to provide tax, accounting, or legal advice.

Section 2701 is applicable when a junior interest is transferred from one family member to another and the transferor retains a senior interest. The following characteristics trigger section 2701:

- The retained security must be of a class senior to the transferred junior security.
- The subject securities (both the retained senior preferred and transferred junior securities) must be nonpublicly traded.
- The transaction must result in a transfer (directly or indirectly) between members of the family.
- Immediately before the transfer, the transferor and applicable family members in the aggregate have 50% or more (by vote or value) control of the corporate stock, or of the capital or profit interests in a partnership or limited liability company; or the transferor and the applicable family members must own any general partnership interest in a limited partnership.
- The transfer is not a proportionate transfer of all senior and junior equity interests, and, as mentioned, the transferor must retain a senior equity interest.

Special Rules If Section 2701 Is Applicable

Section 2701 basically requires that all rights and features of the preferred senior security that have any optional features in terms of payment amounts or timing that potentially can be manipulated by the controlling family be ignored or valued in a manner that results in the lowest possible value for the preferred senior interest. As a result, all noncumulative distribution rights (e.g., dividends) are valued at zero. Similarly, any extraordinary payment right, such as a put, call, conversion, liquidation right, or option to acquire equity interests, is valued at zero, with certain exceptions described in the following.

The practical effect of these rules, from an appraisal standpoint, is that only a few features will provide a basis for attributing value to the applicable retained senior securities. These features include:

- *Cumulative dividends or distribution rights:* These rights can be either fixed in amount or variable if linked by a fixed ratio to a public market interest rate. They are called qualified distribution rights. The taxpayer may make a permanent election to treat any noncumulative distribution right as a cumulative, qualified distribution right. Therefore, the appraiser should check with the client or the client's tax advisors to see whether such an election has been made or will be made. If such qualified distributions are not actually made within four years of their scheduled payment date, then these unpaid distributions are treated as gifts and compounded forward for ultimate payment when the holder dies or transfers his or her interest.
- *Voting rights:* In valuing voting rights, however, any of the extraordinary payment rights discussed earlier are either assumed not to exist or exercised under the "lower-of" rule discussed later.
- *Mandatory redemption rights:* This category of redemption rights requires the retained preferred senior interest to receive a specific amount on a specific date. Optional extraordinary payment redemption rights that can be exercised voluntarily by either the holder or the company do not count.
- *Nonlapsing conversion rights:* Conversion rights that add value under section 2701 require that the senior interests be convertible into a stated number of shares or percentage of the same class as the transferred interest. Obviously, such conversion rights will tend to make the preferred interest increase in value with the underlying junior equity securities and thus will not accomplish a freeze of the senior preferred interest. The timing of conversion can be optional.

Section 2702: Retained Interests in Trusts

- Because section 2702 deals with retained life, annuity, and unitrust interests transferred via trusts for lifetime gift tax purposes, there are no special valuation rules included in this section that directly relate to closely held business interests.
- Closely held business interests often are placed into various grantor-retained annuity trusts (GRATs), grantor-retained unitrusts (GRUTs), charitable remainder annuity trusts (CRATs), or charitable lead trusts (CLTs). But the primary valuation issue in these cases is the application of the IRS annuity and life expectancy tables.

Section 2703: Buy-Sell Agreements or Options

- Four factors that determine whether the buy-sell agreement is conclusively binding for estate tax purposes:

1. The agreement must restrict the transfer of the securities to the buy-sell price during the owner's life as well as at death.
2. There must be a valid business purpose for establishing the agreement.
3. The value established in the agreement must have been an adequate and fair price at the time the agreement was executed.
4. The value must reflect those typical of arm's-length transactions in the subject company's industry.

- Thus, a properly drawn, "grandfathered" buy-sell agreement (i.e., one that pre-dates Chapter 14) with a fixed transfer price may, over time, have provided a way to freeze the value of family members' shares at a value perhaps less than fair market value as of a subsequent date of death. Since October 9, 1990, this technique is unworkable from an estate tax standpoint for newly created or substantially modified buy-sell agreements due to the passage of section 2703 of Chapter 14.

Section 2704: Lapsing Rights and Liquidation Restrictions

- The special valuation rules of this section require the analyst to include certain rights, even if they lapse in conjunction with a transfer by gift or death (e.g., voting rights that lapse if the original holder sells or transfers his or her shares).
- These special valuation rules also require the analyst to ignore certain "applicable restrictions" on the right of an interest holder to liquidate the entity (in whole or in part) when an interest is transferred for the benefit of a family member. These types of applicable restrictions are generally provisions that are more restrictive than those found under the basic state laws for the entity. Therefore, it is critical that the appraiser be familiar with the applicable state law governing transferability of partnership or LLC interests. Without such knowledge, the appraiser cannot possibly know whether the provisions are more restrictive or not.

Estate and Gift Taxation References

Guide Ch. 10 Sections 1407, 1408
Lawyer Ch. 18
VAB4 Ch. 27, 28
VSB3 pp. 56, 250, 472, 679–693, 815–816

CHARITABLE CONTRIBUTIONS

- RR66-49 applies to appraisals of noncash property for federal income tax purposes.
- The appraiser must be *qualified* and *independent.*
- *Qualified appraisers:* According to regulation section 1.17OA-13(c)(5), a qualified appraiser is an individual who

1. Holds himself out to the public as an appraiser or who regularly performs appraisals.
2. Is qualified to appraise property because of his qualifications.
3. Is aware of the appraiser penalties associated with the overvaluation of charitable contributions.

- *Qualified appraisals:* Pursuant to regulation section 1.170A-13(c)(3), a qualified appraisal is an appraisal document that:
   1. Relates to an appraisal that is made not earlier than 60 days before the date of contribution of the appraised property and that must be updated if made earlier.
   2. Is prepared, signed, and dated by a qualified appraiser.
   3. Does not involve a prohibited type of appraisal fee, such as that in which a part or all of the fee arrangement is based on a percentage (or set of percentages) of the appraised value of the property.
   4. Includes the following information:
       a. A description of the donated property.
       b. In the case of tangible property, the physical condition of the property.
       c. The date of contribution.
       d. The terms of any agreement entered into by the donor that relates to the use, sale, or other disposition of the contributed property.
       e. The name, address, and taxpayer identification number of the qualified appraiser and the appraiser's employer or partnership.
       f. The qualifications of the qualified appraiser.
       g. A statement that the appraisal was prepared for income tax purposes.
       h. The date on which the property was valued.
       i. The appraised fair market value of the property on the date of contribution.
       j. The method of valuation used.
       k. The specific basis for valuation, if any, such as any specific comparable sales transactions.
       l. A description of the fee arrangement between the donor and the appraiser.

- The appraisal summary, which is made on Form 8283 (Noncash Charitable Contributions), must be signed and dated by both the donee and the qualified appraiser, and it must be attached to the donor's return on which a deduction for the appraised property is first claimed or reported.

Charitable Contributions References

Lawyer pp. 301, 317
VAB4 pp. 644–649, 674–679
VSB3 pp. 56–57, 691–693

Chapter 24

Employee Stock Ownership Plans

BASIC FEATURES OF ESOPS

Employee Benefit Plans

- Qualified defined contribution employee benefit plan under the Employee Retirement Income Security Act (ERISA) of 1974.
- Designed to invest primarily in employer securities.
- Have a fiduciary to handle plan administration.

- Qualifications for eligibility and amounts of contributions similar to pension and profit-sharing plans, with some differences (e.g., some instances allow larger tax-deductible contributions).
- Qualifying contributions are a tax-deductible expense to the corporation.
- Contributions can be in either cash or employer stock.
- ESOPs can own anywhere from a tiny percentage to 100% of the company's stock.
- Starting in 1998, both S and C corporations can have ESOPs (it is still an open issue as to whether the S corporation earnings should be tax-affected for ESOP valuation purposes).
- As with other employee benefit plans, ESOPs are administered by plan fiduciaries.

Traditional Uses of ESOPs

- Provide liquidity and diversification for shareholders.
- Provide means of capital formation.
- Finance corporate acquisitions.
- Incentive to increase employee productivity and retain personnel.
- Provide a succession plan.

Unleveraged and Leveraged ESOPs

Unleveraged ESOPs

- The ESOP has no debt.
- ESOP obtains stock by either:
  - Contributions from the company in the form of stock.
  - Contributions from the company in the form of cash, with which the ESOP buys stock from the company and/or from one or more existing stockholders.

Leveraged ESOPs

- The ESOP incurs debt to purchase stock.
- The stock may be purchased from either existing stockholders or the company.
- The ESOP repays the debt from cash contributions and/or dividends from the company.
- Leverage guaranteed by the company is a risk factor that should be considered and that may impact the value of the sponsoring company.
- Leveraged ESOPs most often are valued on an invested capital basis.
- Companies that have guaranteed ESOP loans must show the full amount of the debt on their balance sheets, thus reducing retained earnings and the book value of stockholders' equity.

REQUIREMENTS FOR STOCK VALUATION

When to Value (If Not Publicly Traded)

• When ESOP first acquires stock.
• At least annually (per Tax Reform Act of 1986).
• Whenever there is a transaction with a controlling stockholder or member of a controlling group.
• If ESOP sells out its stock position (including merger with another company's ESOP).
• If company converts to S corporation status.

Appraiser Must Be Independent

• Not a party to the transaction.
• Not related or married to a party to the transaction.
• Not regularly engaged by any of the parties to the transaction.
  Note: The corporation *is* a party to most ESOP transactions.
• Fee not based on percentage of value.
• No specific written guidance on rules for independence; consult Internal Revenue (IRC) Code section 170 regarding charitable contributions.

Appraiser Must Be Qualified

• Holds self out to public as an appraiser or performs appraisals on a regular basis.
• Qualified to value ESOP stock by background, experience, education, and memberships, if any, in professional associations.

   Note: The appraiser is a financial advisor to the ESOP fiduciary, but the appraiser is *not* a fiduciary.

Identity of Client

• Not the plan sponsor.
• Not the company shareholders or officers.
• The client is the ESOP fiduciary.

Price Must Represent Adequate Consideration

• Department of Labor (DOL) proposed regulation relating to the definition of adequate consideration (53 Fed. Reg. 17632, 1988) was never finalized but is used as guidance.

- Adequate consideration met by (1) the assigned value reflecting fair market value and (2) the fiduciary acting in good faith.
- Regulation defines *fair market value* in the same way as Treasury regulations.
- Basic factors outlined are consistent with RR59-60.
- Regulation requires that the marketability, or lack thereof, be addressed as a relevant factor:
  - Enforceability of stock put rights.
  - Company's financial ability to meet put rights.
- If control premium is reflected in value, whether seller would be able to get a similar control premium from an unrelated third party, considering the following:
  - Actual control (in both form and substance) is passed to buyer in transaction or will be passed within a reasonable time under a binding agreement.
  - Control will not be dissipated within a short period of time.

Note: Control could be dissipated, for example, as a result of company repurchase of stock held by the ESOP for the benefit of retiring plan participants. Control or lack of it can be a significant issue as to the fairness of the transaction to the ESOP and must be carefully analyzed if a control premium is involved.

- The majority of ESOP valuations are done on a minority interest basis, including some in which the ESOP actually does have control.

SPECIAL FEATURES OF ESOPS

Put Option

- Since 1986 ESOPs have been required to give employees the option to sell (put) their ESOP stock *to the company* (not to the ESOP) following retirement, disability, or termination, at the ESOP stock's appraised value.
- Put option creates liquidity for ESOP stock:
  - Reduces or sometimes even eliminates discount for lack of marketability.
  - This factor must be analyzed in an ESOP valuation report.
- Put option creates repurchase liability for company:
  - Repurchase liability must be addressed.
  - Ability to meet repurchase liability is a potential risk factor.
  - Employers typically hire a professional firm.

Tax-Free Rollover

In some circumstances, under IRC section 1042, parties selling stock to an ESOP can get a one-time tax-free rollover (sometimes referred to as a "1042 rollover"):

- The ESOP must own 30% or more of the stock following the transaction.

- The seller's proceeds must be invested in other domestic securities within one year.
- The 1042 rollover does not apply to S corporations.

Treatment of Dividends

- *Tax deductibility:* Dividends paid to the ESOP are a tax-deductible expense if either of the following is true:
  - They are used to repay ESOP debt.
  - They are passed through to ESOP participants.
- *Tax free to participants:* Dividends received on ESOP stock by plan participants are tax-free to the recipient.
- Because of these dividend tax features, many companies establish a separate class of dividend-paying stock specifically for the ESOP; such securities also may have other preferences.

Special Features of ESOPs References

BV204 Module 7
FBVI Ch. 6
IBA2 Ch. 13
NACVA BV Ch. 1
VAB4 Ch. 32
VSB3 Ch. 39

ADVANTAGES AND DISADVANTAGES OF ESOPS

Advantages

- Section 1042 tax-free rollover.
- Deductibility of contributions:
  - In leveraged ESOPs, amounts to repay principal as well as interest are tax deductible.
  - Tax deductibility of dividends paid on ESOP stock (can be over and above maximum allowable plan contributions).
  - Contributions made in stock are deductible with no cash outlay.
- Potentially improve employee morale and productivity.
- Sometimes can be used to obtain wage and/or benefit concessions.

Disadvantages

- Costs to administer.
- Dilution of contributions made in stock (must be factored into valuation).

- Repurchase liability (potential valuation issue).
- Added risk if leveraged (also must be considered in valuation posttransaction).

RELEVANT COURT CASES

Donovan v. Cunningham, 541 F. Supp. 276 (S.D. Tex. 1982), *affirmed in part, reversed in part, vacated in part, and remanded*, 716 F.2d 1455 (5th Cir. 1983), *certiorari denied, Cunningham v. Donovan*, 467 U.S. 1251 (1984).

Las Vegas Dodge, Inc. v. United States, 1985 U.S. Dist. LEXIS 21577 (D. Nev. 1985).

Eyler v. Commissioner, T.C. Memo 1995-123, 69 T.C.M. (CCH) 2200 (U.S. Tax Ct. 1995), *affirmed*, 88 F.3d 445 (7th Cir. 1996).

SOURCES OF CHALLENGE TO ESOP VALUATIONS

Because an ESOP is an employee benefit plan subject to ERISA, and because ESOP contributions are tax-deductible expenses, ESOP valuations are subject to challenge from an unusually wide variety of sources, including (but not necessarily limited to):

- The Department of Labor.
- The Internal Revenue Service.
- Plan participants.
- Beneficiaries or spouses of plan participants.
- Any party to an ESOP transaction.

ESOP References

BV204 Module 7
FBVI Ch. 6
Lawyer Ch. 21
NACVA-BV Ch. 1
VAB4 Ch. 32, 33
VSB3 Ch. 39

The ASA offers a course specifically on ESOPs, BV206. In addition, the ESOP Association, through its Advisory Committee on Valuation, publishes *Valuing ESOP Shares* and *Report Valuing Leveraged ESOP Shares*.

Chapter 25

Shareholder Buyouts and Disputes

SQUEEZE-OUT MERGERS AND DISSENTING STOCKHOLDER ACTIONS

Background

- All states allow controlling stockholders to take actions such as mergers or reverse stock splits that cause minority stockholders to be bought out or to exchange their holdings for some other consideration, such as stock in another company.

- Some states require approval by only 50% plus one share to effect such actions; others require approval by some supermajority percentage, which varies from state to state.

- All states have statutes allowing minority stockholders to dissent from such major corporate actions, generally mergers or sale of all or most corporate assets.

- State laws grant the dissenters appraisal rights or the right to be paid in cash for the appraised value of their shares.

Fair Value Statutory Standard for Dissent

- Most states have statutes stating that dissenters will be paid *fair value.*
- Most state statutes add that fair value *excludes any appreciation in value as a result of the corporate action.*
- Some states add *unless that would be inequitable.*
- In most states, the effective date for valuation is the day before the corporate action takes place.
- Beyond the preceding provisions, statutes provide little guidance for defining *fair value,* and the interpretation of *fair value* must be found in the case law precedents, which vary greatly from state to state.

Case Law Interpretation of Fair Value

- More than half of the states have precedential cases on interpretation of fair value.
- In cases of first impression (the first decision under a particular statute), courts tend to look at precedential case law in other states, especially those with identical or similar statutory law wording.
- Many precedential case law decisions have allowed discounts *neither* for minority interest *nor* for lack of marketability (buyer was willing, seller was not).
- However, some states value as if on a freely tradeable basis, which some argue inherently reflects a minority discount.
- Some state case precedents indicate that minority and/or marketability discounts are applicable, but the trend is away from this.
- Some state case precedents require that the questions of minority and/or marketability discounts be decided on a case-by-case basis, depending on the facts and circumstances of each case.

Delaware Fair Value Case Law

Impact of Delaware Case Law

- Delaware has by far the most dissenting stockholder case law.
- Other states tend to look at Delaware case precedents in cases of first impression.

Delaware Block Rule

- Until 1983 most Delaware dissent cases were decided by applying a percentage weight to the value indicated by each of three factors:
  1. Market value.
  2. Asset value.

3. Earnings or investment value (value by the income approach, *not* investment value to a particular buyer or seller).

• 1983 case: *Weinberger v. UOP, Inc.,* was remanded because projections that existed for selling company (discounted cash flow method) were not considered; *Weinberger* said *all* relevant factors must be considered.

Current Delaware Posture

• Still considers all relevant factors.
• Discounted cash flow increasingly the valuation method of choice.
• Typically, no minority or marketability discounts.

Dissenting Stockholder Suit References

BV204 Module 6
Guide Ch. 15
Lawyer Ch. 20
VAB4 pp. 352–353, 790–794, Ch. 36
VSB3 pp. 45–46, 60, 250, 432, 716–717, 811–814, 848

MINORITY OPPRESSION DISSOLUTION ACTIONS

Background

• Some states have statutes allowing minority stockholders to sue to dissolve the corporation or partnership if certain actions constituting minority oppression can be shown.
• Percentage holding required for such actions varies from state to state (e.g., California $33\frac{1}{3}\%$; some states less).
• Statutes allow control stockholders to avoid dissolution by cashing out the minority stockholders at the appraised value.

Fair Value Statutory Standard for Oppression Dissolution Actions

• Most states with minority oppression statutes specify *fair value* as the standard for appraisal.
• As for dissenter actions, *fair value* is not defined in statutes but interpreted in case law.
• Case interpretation of fair value for oppression cases is not always the same as for dissent cases.

Minority Oppression References

BV204 Module 6
FBVI Ch. 1 p. 18
Guide Ch. 15
Lawyer Ch. 20
VAB4 pp. 794–796, Ch. 36
VSB3 pp. 60–61, 714

BANKRUPTCY

- Standard of value in most bankruptcy reorganizations or liquidations is *fair market value* or *market value.*
- Whether premise of value should be *going concern* or *liquidation* is often a major issue and can greatly affect value and thus a trustee's or court's acceptance or rejection of a proposed plan of reorganization.
- The three traditional appraisal approaches (income, market, and asset based) are all recognized by the bankruptcy courts.

Bankruptcy References

VAB4 p. 860
VSB3 pp. 717–718, 816–817

BUY-SELL AGREEMENTS

- Standard of value and procedures for valuation under buy-sell agreements can be anything to which the parties willingly commit.
- Failure to explicitly define *value* is often a serious flaw in buy-sell agreements (as well as arbitration agreements), leading to costly and protracted litigation.
- *Fair market value* often is used without minority owners realizing that fair market value may invoke minority and marketability discounts rather than value as a pro rata portion of the overall company value.

Buy-Sell Agreement References

FBVI Ch. 4 p. 40
FBVII Ch. 2 p. 11
Guide 803.27, 1002.67–1002.68, 1002.71, 1002.83, 1103.25, 1105.15, 1106.16
VAB4 Ch. 29
VSB3 pp. 27, 58, 446, 560–561, 673–679, 814–815

Chapter 26

Marital Dissolutions

OVERVIEW OF MARITAL DISSOLUTION

- One of the leading reasons for valuing businesses and professional practices.
- Governed by state law:
  - *Community property states:* All assets acquired during a marriage assumed part of the marital estate (owned jointly by the "community") and generally divided equally.
  - *Equitable distribution/separate property states:* May or may not divide property equally; may make adjustments based on court's view of the facts and circumstances.
- Statutes are very general, courts have a high degree of discretion, and fundamental valuation issues are more nebulous than decisions in other areas of valuation practice.

STANDARD OF VALUE

- State statutes do *not* specify standard of value for marital dissolutions.
- Should study and consider case law in relevant jurisdiction but still likely to find inconsistencies.
- Terminology used in case decisions is inconsistent; even if a case says *fair market value,* the valuation methods and/or assumed ownership characteristics ac-

cepted often are not consistent with the normal fair market value definition and often incorporate elements of investment value (e.g., relationship to other owners, value specifically to the operating spouse).

- Some states follow the fair market value standard reasonably consistently, whereas others do not follow it at all.

VALUATION DATE

- Values as of any or all of the following may be required:
  - Date of marriage. (Often the marital property is the *appreciation* in value during marriage.)
  - Date of separation.
  - Date of filing.
  - Date of trial.
  - Date of gift/inheritance.
- Most states allow courts wide discretion in setting the valuation date.
- Sometimes it is possible to get the court to specify the valuation date so that the appraiser does not have to prepare valuations for several different dates.

VALUATION METHODS

- Family law courts generally recognize each of the three basic approaches to value:
  1. Income approach (both capitalization and, increasingly, discounted cash flow [DCF]).
  2. Market approach.
  3. Asset-based approach (including the excess earnings method).
- Some states insist that no value should be included that depends on either the future efforts of the spouse or restrictions on the spouse's activities (e.g., value of a noncompete covenant); case law should be studied carefully; it is often necessary to make clear that future income expected in the income approach is based on normal entity operations and not on future spousal efforts.

GOODWILL

States vary on their posture toward the goodwill of a business or practice as a marital asset, generally falling into one of three categories:

1. Goodwill is never a distributable marital asset (unusual).
2. Entity or practice goodwill *only* (as distinguished from personal goodwill) is a distributable marital asset.

3. All intangible value in the nature of goodwill (both personal and practice goodwill) related to the small business or professional practice is distributable.

However, many states have no precedential cases on this issue, and others are inconsistent.

BUY-SELL AGREEMENTS

Before you undertake a divorce valuation engagement, be sure you understand what precedent has been set in your state, and be sure that the attorney understands it as well! In some states, buy-sell agreements take precedent, in others they are ignored, and in still others there are cases going both ways.

COVENANTS NOT TO COMPETE

It is very important that the appraiser consider the issue of covenants not to compete in arriving at the value conclusion. Covenants not to compete are not marital property in many states. If a considerable part of your value is predicated or would be allocated to a covenant not to compete with the spouse retaining the business, you need to be aware that part of the value may not be part of the marital estate.

ADJUSTMENTS TO FINANCIAL STATEMENTS

As in any valuation, there are often a number of adjustments that need to be made to the financial statements. The most obvious adjustment is for owner salary, when the owner has taken out too much or too little, compared with what a hypothetical buyer would pay for a comparable employee. In some states the issue of the value of the business and the rest of the divorce settlement can become entangled, and there is a risk of "double counting" the owner's excess salary by capturing it both in the value of the business and in the calculation of alimony. Be very clear on the judicial precedent in your state, as well as with the attorney on how you are handling this.

Another common and difficult adjustment to financial statements is the case in which the nonparticipating spouse tells you that the family business really produced more money than what was reported on the company tax returns. Here a difficult conundrum is raised: if you don't include the underreported income, you undervalue the company; if you do include it, the spouse (who no doubt signed the tax return) risks retribution from the IRS. This is obviously an issue you should discuss with counsel and carefully consider whether and how to include this in your value determination.

CAPITAL GAINS TAXES

Family law courts have been reluctant to allow a deduction for the trapped-in capital gains tax liability on appreciated property retained by the operating spouse unless:

• The tax liability is imminent.
• The tax will be triggered as a result of the court's property distribution.

VALUATION DISCOUNTS AND PREMIUMS

Family law courts are inconsistent in applying discounts for both lack of control and lack of marketability.

DISCOVERY

• The appraiser retained by the nonoperating spouse often has difficulty with the necessary discovery (documents, site visits, and interviews) normal to the valuation process.
• The analyst should prepare a complete (but reasonable) documents request list.
• If possible, reach an understanding that a follow-up list may be necessary because some questions might be raised in the course of analyzing the basic documents.
• Case law broadly supports the proposition that the nonoperating spouse has a financial interest in the property and that the spouse and his or her appraiser are entitled to all of the information available to the operating spouse; sometimes it is difficult to convince attorneys to enforce this right.

Marital Dissolutions References

FBVI Ch. 6 p. 25
Guide Ch. 12
IBA1 A.6
Lawyer Ch. 19
NACVA Sect. Z
VAB4 Ch. 37, 38
VSB3 pp. 248–249, 336, 591–594, Ch. 41, 46, 48

APPENDIXES

Bibliography of
Reference Sources

IRS Authority
 IRS Valuation Training for Appeals Officers Coursebook
 Revenue Rulings, Revenue Procedures, Technical Advice Memorandums,
  Private Letter Rulings, and Field Service Advice Memorandums
 IRS Business Valuation Guidelines
Professional Association Publications
 American Institute of Certified Public Accountants
 American Society of Appraisers
 Institute of Business Appraisers
 The Appraisal Foundation
Books
Video Courses
Periodicals
 General Business Valuation Periodicals
 Periodicals Oriented to Marital Dissolution

This bibliography is limited to major sources, mostly those referenced in this book. Most of the sources listed herein contain their own bibliographies cataloging literally thousands of books, periodicals, databases, articles, audio- and videotapes, and other materials relevant to various types of business and intangible property valuations.

IRS AUTHORITY

IRS Valuation Training for Appeals Officers Coursebook

The book is available in electronic form (may be downloaded from *BVLibrary* *.com*ˢᵐ) and in print from Commerce, Clearing House, 4025 W Peterson Avenue, Chicago, IL 60646; (800) 324-3248.

Revenue Rulings, Revenue Procedures, Technical Advice Memorandums, Private Letter Rulings, and Field Service Advice Memorandums

- These references are widely distributed, and many are reprinted in various publications listed in other parts of this bibliography.
- Two sources containing all revenue rulings, revenue procedures, Technical Advice Memorandums, Private Letter Rulings, and Field Service Advice Memorandums referenced in this book are the following:
  - *BVLibrary.com*^{sm}.
  - Kleinrock Tax Library, Kleinrock Publishing, 11300 Rockville Pike, Rockville, MD 20852; (800) 678-2315.

IRS Business Valuation Guidelines

Available on the Free Downloads page of *BVResources.com.*

PROFESSIONAL ASSOCIATION PUBLICATIONS

American Institute of Certified Public Accountants

Understanding Business Valuation: A Practical Guide to Valuing Small to Medium-Sized Businesses, Second Edition, 2002, by Gary R. Trugman; American Institute of Certified Public Accountants, 1211 Avenue of the Americas, New York, NY 10036; (212) 596-6200; *www.aicpa.org.*

American Society of Appraisers

- *Principles of Appraisal Practice and Code of Ethics.*
- *Business Valuation Standards.*

American Society of Appraisers, 555 Herndon Parkway, Suite 125, Herndon, VA 20170; (800) ASA-VALU; *www.appraisers.org.*

Institute of Business Appraisers

- *Business Appraisal Standards.*
- *Code of Ethics.*
- *Technical studies of the IBA Database.*

Institute of Business Appraisers, P.O. Box 17410, Plantation, FL 33318; (954) 584-1144; *www.instbusapp.org.*

The Appraisal Foundation

Uniform Standards of Professional Appraisal Practice is published annually in November by The Appraisal Foundation, 1029 Vermont Avenue, NW, Suite 900, Washington, DC 20005; (202) 347-7722.

BOOKS

- *Basic Business Appraisal* by Raymond Miles (John Wiley & Sons, 1984), available from IBA, P.O. Box 17410, Plantation, FL 33318; (954) 584-1144.
- *Business Appraisal Reports Library,* available from IBA, P.O. Box 17410, Plantation, FL 33318; (954) 584-1144.
- *Business Valuation Discounts & Premiums,* by Shannon Pratt, 2001, John Wiley & Sons, 111 River Street, Hoboken, NJ 07030; (800) 225-5945; also available from Business Valuation Resources; (888) BUS-VALU; *www.BVResources.com.*
- *Cost of Capital: Estimation and Applications,* 2d ed., by Shannon Pratt, 2002, John Wiley & Sons, 111 River Street, Hoboken, NJ 07030; (800) 225-5945; also available from Business Valuation Resources; (888) BUS-VALU; *www .BVResources.com.*
- *Financial Valuations: Applications and Models,* by Ronald L. Seigneur and James Hitchner, expected first quarter 2003, John Wiley & Sons, 111 River Street, Hoboken, NJ 07030; (800) 225-5945.
- *Guide to Business Valuations,* by Jay Fishman, Shannon Pratt, Clifford Griffith, and Keith Wilson, updated annually in May. Practitioners Publishing Company, 1320 South University Drive, University Centre II, Suite 500, Fort Worth, TX 76107; (800) 323-8724. Companion software templates are also available, as well as several of the databases discussed herein.
- *The Lawyer's Business Valuation Handbook,* by Shannon Pratt, 2000, American Bar Association, 750 North Lake Shore Drive, Chicago, IL 60611; (312) 988-5000; also available from Business Valuation Resources; (888) BUS-VALU; *www.BVResources.com.*
- *The Market Approach to Valuing Businesses,* by Shannon Pratt, 2001, John Wiley & Sons, 111 River Street, Hoboken, NJ 07030; (800) 225-5945; also available from Business Valuation Resources; (888) BUS-VALU; *www.BVResources.com.*
- *Quantifying Marketability Discounts: Developing and Supporting Marketability Discounts in the Appraisal of Closely Held Business Interests,* 2d ed., by Christopher Mercer, 2002, Peabody Publishing, 5860 Ridgeway Center Parkway, Suite 410, Memphis, TN 38120; (800) 769-0967.
- *Valuing a Business: The Analysis and Appraisal of Closely Held Companies,* 4th ed., by Shannon Pratt, Robert Reilly, and Robert Schweihs, 2000, McGraw-Hill, 11 West 19th Street, New York, NY 10021; (800) 722-4726; also available from Business Valuation Resources; (888) BUS-VALU; *www.BVResources.com.*

- *Valuing Small Businesses and Professional Practices,* 3d ed., by Shannon Pratt, Robert Reilly, and Robert Schweihs, 1998, McGraw-Hill, 11 West 19th Street, New York, NY 10021; (800) 722-4726; also available from Business Valuation Resources, (888) BUS-VALU; *www.BVResources.com.*

VIDEO COURSES

- *Business Valuation Videocourse,* 1993 (accompanying handbook updated in 1997), moderated by Shannon P. Pratt, with Robert F. Reilly, Robert P. Schweihs, and Jay E. Fishman. Available from Business Valuation Resources, *www .BVResources.com.*
- *Valuation of Closely Held Businesses* (accompanying handbook updated in 1998), by James R. Alerding. Research Institute of America, 117 East Stevens Avenue, Valhalla, NY 10595; (800) 431-9025 ext. 4.

PERIODICALS

General Business Valuation Periodicals

- *Business Appraisal Practice,* published three times per year by the Institute of Business Appraisers, 7420 N.W. 5th Street, Suite 103, P.O. Box 17410, Plantation, FL 33318; (954)-584-1144; *www.go-iba.org.*
- *Business Valuation Review,* quarterly journal published by the Business Valuation Committee of the American Society of Appraisers, 2777 S. Colorado Boulevard, Suite 200, Denver, CO 80222; (303) 758-6148; *www.bvappraisers.org.*
- *CPA Expert,* quarterly journal published by the American Society of Certified Public Accountants, 1211 Avenue of the Americas, New York, NY 10036; (800) 862-4272.
- *Shannon Pratt's Business Valuation Update®,* monthly newsletter that includes abstracts of all important federal and state appellate court cases dealing with business valuation issues, any legal or regulatory changes, abstracts of new and updated business valuation books, data sources, articles, audio- and videotapes, online and Internet sources, coverage of business valuation professional conferences, calendar of upcoming meetings, cost of capital update, special reports, guest articles and interviews, editor's column, reader/editor exchange, and professional association and business valuation appraisal company news update. Annual subscription includes six supplements. Business Valuation Resources, 7412 S.W. Beaverton-Hillsdale Hwy, Suite 106, Portland, OR 97225; (888) BUS-VALU; *www.BVLibrary.com.*
- *The Valuation Examiner,* bimonthly magazine published by NACVA, 1245 East Brickyard Road, Suite 110, Salt Lake City, UT 84106; (801) 486-0600.

- *Valuation Strategies,* bimonthly multidisciplinary journal on valuation issues, with emphasis on business and intangible asset valuations. Warren Gorham & Lamont, RIA Group, 117 East Stevens Avenue, Valhalla, NY 10595; (800) 431-9025.

Periodical Oriented to Marital Dissolution

- *Family Advocate,* quarterly journal. Published by the Section of Family Law, American Bar Association, 750 N. Lakeshore Drive, Chicago, IL 60611; (312) 988-6113.

Federal Rule of Civil Procedure 26: General Provisions Governing Discovery; Duty of Disclosure

(a) REQUIRED DISCLOSURES; METHODS TO DISCOVER ADDITIONAL MATTER.

(1) *Initial Disclosures.* Except in categories of proceedings specified in Rule 26(a)(1)(E), or to the extent otherwise stipulated or directed by order, a party must, without awaiting a discovery request, provide to other parties:

(A) The name and, if known, the address and telephone number of each individual likely to have discoverable information that the disclosing party may use to support its claims or defenses, unless solely for impeachment, identifying the subjects of the information;

(B) A copy of, or a description by category and location of, all documents, data compilations, and tangible things that are in the possession, custody, or control of the party and that the disclosing party may use to support its claims or defenses, unless solely for impeachment;

(C) A computation of any category of damages claimed by the disclosing party, making available for inspection and copying as under Rule 34 the documents or other evidentiary material, not privileged or protected from disclosure, on which such computation is based, including materials bearing on the nature and extent of injuries suffered; and

(D) For inspection and copying as under Rule 34 any insurance agreement under which any person carrying on an insurance business may be liable to satisfy part or all of a judgment which may be entered in the action or to indemnify or reimburse for payments made to satisfy the judgment.

(E) The following categories of proceedings are exempt from initial disclosure under Rule 26(a)(1) :

(i)   An action for review on an administrative record;

(ii)   A petition for habeas corpus or other proceeding to challenge a criminal conviction or sentence;

(iii)   An action brought without counsel by a person in custody of the United States, a state, or a state subdivision;

(iv)   An action to enforce or quash an administrative summons or subpoena;

(v)   An action by the United States to recover benefit payments;

(vi)   An action by the United States to collect on a student loan guaranteed by the United States;

(vii)   A proceeding ancillary to proceedings in other courts; and

(viii)   An action to enforce an arbitration award.

These disclosures must be made at or within 14 days after the Rule 26(f) conference unless a different time is set by stipulation or court order, or unless a party objects during the conference that initial disclosures are not appropriate in the circumstances of the action and states the objection in the Rule 26(f) discovery plan. In ruling on the objection, the court must determine what disclosures—if any—are to be made, and set the time for disclosure. Any party first served or otherwise joined after the Rule 26(f) conference must make these disclosures within 30 days after being served or joined unless a different time is set by stipulation or court order. A party must make its initial disclosures based on the information then reasonably available to it and is not excused from making its disclosures because it has not fully completed its investigation of the case or because it challenges the sufficiency of another party's disclosures or because another party has not made its disclosures.

(2) *Disclosure of Expert Testimony.*

(A) In addition to the disclosures required by paragraph (1), a party shall disclose to other parties the identity of any person who may be used at trial to present evidence under Rules 702, 703, or 705 of the Federal Rules of Evidence.

(B) Except as otherwise stipulated or directed by the court, this disclosure shall, with respect to a witness who is retained or specially employed to provide expert testimony in the case or whose duties as an employee of the party regularly involve giving expert testimony, be accompanied by a written report prepared and signed by the witness. The report shall contain a complete statement of all opinions to be expressed and the basis and reasons therefor; the data or other information considered by the witness in forming the opinions; any exhibits to be used as a summary of or support for the opinions; the qualifications of the witness, including a list of all publications authored by the witness within the preceding ten years; the compensation to be paid for the study and testimony; and a listing of any other cases in which the witness has testified as an expert at trial or by deposition within the preceding four years.

(C) These disclosures shall be made at the times and in the sequence directed by the court. In the absence of other directions from the court or stipulation by the parties, the disclosures shall be made at least 90 days before the trial date or the date the case is to be ready for trial or, if the evidence is intended solely to contradict or rebut evidence on the same subject matter identified by another party under paragraph (2)(B), within 30 days after the disclosure made by the other party. The parties shall supplement these disclosures when required under subdivision (e)(1).

(3) *Pretrial Disclosures.* In addition to the disclosures required by Rule 26(a)(1) and (2) , a party must provide to other parties and promptly file with the court the following information regarding the evidence that it may present at trial other than solely for impeachment:

(A) The name and, if not previously provided, the address and telephone number of each witness, separately identifying those whom the party expects to present and those whom the party may call if the need arises;

(B) The designation of those witnesses whose testimony is expected to be presented by means of a deposition and, if not taken stenographically, a transcript of the pertinent portions of the deposition testimony; and

(C) An appropriate identification of each document or other exhibit, including summaries of other evidence, separately identifying those which the party expects to offer and those which the party may offer if the need arises.

Unless otherwise directed by the court, these disclosures must be made at least 30 days before trial. Within 14 days thereafter, unless a different time is specified by the court, a party may serve and promptly file a list disclosing (i) any objections to the use under Rule 32(a) of a deposition designated by another party under Rule 26(a)(3)(B), and (ii) any objection, together with the grounds therefor, that may be made to the admissibility of materials identified under Rule 26(a)(3)(C). Objections not so disclosed, other than objections under Rules 402 and 403 of the Federal Rules of Evidence, are waived unless excused by the court for good cause.

(4) *Form of Disclosures.* Unless the court orders otherwise, all disclosures under Rules 26(a)(1) through (3) must be made in writing, signed, and served.

(5) *Methods to Discover Additional Matter.* Parties may obtain discovery by one or more of the following methods: depositions upon oral examination or written questions; written interrogatories; production of documents or things

or permission to enter upon land or other property under Rule 34 or 45(a)(1)(C), for inspection and other purposes; physical and mental examinations; and requests for admission.

(b) DISCOVERY SCOPE AND LIMITS. Unless otherwise limited by order of the court in accordance with these rules, the scope of discovery is as follows:

(1) *In General.* Parties may obtain discovery regarding any matter, not privileged, that is relevant to the claim or defense of any party, including the existence, description, nature, custody, condition, and location of any books, documents, or other tangible things and the identity and location of persons having knowledge of any discoverable matter. For good cause, the court may order discovery of any matter relevant to the subject matter involved in the action. Relevant information need not be admissible at the trial if the discovery appears reasonably calculated to lead to the discovery of admissible evidence. All discovery is subject to the limitations imposed by Rule 26(b)(2)(i), (ii), and (iii).

(2) *Limitations.* By order, the court may alter the limits in these rules on the number of depositions and interrogatories or the length of depositions under Rule 30. By order or local rule, the court may also limit the number of requests under Rule 36. The frequency or extent of use of the discovery methods otherwise permitted under these rules and by any local rule shall be limited by the court if it determines that: (i) the discovery sought is unreasonably cumulative or duplicative, or is obtainable from some other source that is more convenient, less burdensome, or less expensive; (ii) the party seeking discovery has had ample opportunity by discovery in the action to obtain the information sought; or (iii) the burden or expense of the proposed discovery outweighs its likely benefit, taking into account the needs of the case, the amount in controversy, the parties' resources, the importance of the issues at stake in the litigation, and the importance of the proposed discovery in resolving the issues. The court may act upon its own initiative after reasonable notice or pursuant to a motion under Rule 26(c).

(3) *Trial Preparation: Materials.* Subject to the provisions of subdivision (b)(4) of this rule, a party may obtain discovery of documents and tangible things otherwise discoverable under subdivision (b)(1) of this rule and prepared in anticipation of litigation or for trial by or for another party or by or for that other party's representative (including the other party's attorney, consultant, surety, indemnitor, insurer, or agent) only upon a showing that the party seeking discovery has substantial need of the materials in the preparation of the party's case and that the party is unable without undue hardship to obtain the substantial equivalent of the materials by other means. In ordering discovery of such materials when the required showing has been made, the court shall protect against disclosure of the mental impressions, conclusions, opinions, or legal theories of an attorney or other representative of a party concerning the litigation.

A party may obtain without the required showing a statement concerning the action or its subject matter previously made by that party. Upon request, a person not a party may obtain without the required showing a statement concerning the action or its subject matter previously made by that person. If the request is refused, the person may move for a court order. The provisions of Rule 37(a)(4) apply to the award of expenses incurred in relation to the motion. For purposes of this paragraph, a statement previously made is (A) a written statement signed or otherwise adopted or approved by the person making it, or (B) a stenographic, mechanical, electrical, or other recording, or a transcription thereof, which is a substantially verbatim recital of an oral statement by the person making it and contemporaneously recorded.

(4) *Trial Preparation: Experts.*

(A) A party may depose any person who has been identified as an expert whose opinions may be presented at trial. If a report from the expert is required under subdivision (a)(2)(B), the deposition shall not be conducted until after the report is provided.

(B) A party may, through interrogatories or by deposition, discover facts known or opinions held by an expert who has been retained or specially employed by another party in anticipation of litigation or preparation for trial and who is not expected to be called as a witness at trial, only as provided in Rule 35(b) or upon a showing of exceptional circumstances under which it is impracticable for the party seeking discovery to obtain facts or opinions on the same subject by other means.

(C) Unless manifest injustice would result, (i) the court shall require that the party seeking discovery pay the expert a reasonable fee for time spent in responding to discovery under this subdivision; and (ii) with respect to discovery obtained under subdivision (b)(4)(B) of this rule the court shall require the party seeking discovery to pay the other party a fair portion of the fees and expenses reasonably incurred by the latter party in obtaining facts and opinions from the expert.

(5) *Claims of Privilege or Protection of Trial Preparation Materials.* When a party withholds information otherwise discoverable under these rules by claiming that it is privileged or subject to protection as trial preparation material, the party shall make the claim expressly and shall describe the nature of the documents, communications, or things not produced or disclosed in a manner that, without revealing information itself privileged or protected, will enable other parties to assess the applicability of the privilege or protection.

(c) PROTECTIVE ORDERS. Upon motion by a party or by the person from whom discovery is sought, accompanied by a certification that the movant has in good faith conferred or attempted to confer with other affected parties in an effort to resolve the dispute without court action, and for good cause shown, the court in which the action is pending or alternatively, on matters relating to a deposition, the court in the district where the deposition is to be taken may make any order which justice requires to protect a party or person from annoyance, embarrassment, oppression, or undue burden or expense, including one or more of the following:

(1) that the disclosure or discovery not be had;

(2) that the disclosure or discovery may be had only on specified terms and conditions, including a designation of the time or place;

(3) that the discovery may be had only by a method of discovery other than that selected by the party seeking discovery;

(4) that certain matters not be inquired into, or that the scope of the disclosure or discovery be limited to certain matters;

(5) that discovery be conducted with no one present except persons designated by the court;

(6) that a deposition, after being sealed, be opened only by order of the court;

(7) that a trade secret or other confidential research, development, or commercial information not be revealed or be revealed only in a designated way; and

(8) that the parties simultaneously file specified documents or information enclosed in sealed envelopes to be opened as directed by the court.

If the motion for a protective order is denied in whole or in part, the court may, on such terms and conditions as are just, order that any party or other person provide or permit discovery. The provisions of Rule 37(a)(4) apply to the award of expenses incurred in relation to the motion.

(d) TIMING AND SEQUENCE OF DISCOVERY. Except in categories of proceedings exempted from initial disclosure under Rule 26(a)(1)(E), or when authorized under these rules or by order or agreement of the parties, a party may not seek discovery from any source before the parties have conferred as required by Rule 26(f) . Unless the court upon motion, for the convenience of parties and witnesses and in the interests of justice, orders otherwise, methods of discovery may be used in any sequence, and the fact that a party is conducting discovery, whether by deposition or otherwise, does not operate to delay any other party's discovery.

(e) SUPPLEMENTATION OF DISCLOSURES AND RESPONSES. A party who has made a disclosure under subdivision (a) or responded to a request for discovery with a disclosure or response is under a duty to supplement or correct the disclosure or response to include information thereafter acquired if ordered by the court or in the following circumstances:

(1) party is under a duty to supplement at appropriate intervals its disclosures under subdivision (a) if the party learns that in some material respect the information disclosed is incomplete or incorrect and if the additional or corrective information has not otherwise been made known to the other parties during the discovery process or in writing. With respect to testimony of an expert from whom a report is required under subdivision (a)(2)(B) the duty

extends both to information contained in the report and to information provided through a deposition of the expert, and any additions or other changes to this information shall be disclosed by the time the party's disclosures under Rule 26(a)(3) are due.

(2) A party is under a duty seasonably to amend a prior response to an interrogatory, request for production, or request for admission if the party learns that the response is in some material respect incomplete or incorrect and if the additional or corrective information has not otherwise been made known to the other parties during the discovery process or in writing.

(f) CONFERENCE OF PARTIES; PLANNING FOR DISCOVERY. Except in categories of proceedings exempted from initial disclosure under Rule 26(a)(1)(E) or when otherwise ordered, the parties must, as soon as practicable and in any event at least 21 days before a scheduling conference is held or a scheduling order is due under Rule 16(b), confer to consider the nature and basis of their claims and defenses and the possibilities for a prompt settlement or resolution of the case, to make or arrange for the disclosures required by Rule 26(a)(1), and to develop a proposed discovery plan that indicates the parties' views and proposals concerning:

(1) what changes should be made in the timing, form, or requirement for disclosures under Rule 26(a), including a statement as to when disclosures under Rule 26(a)(1) were made or will be made;

(2) the subjects on which discovery may be needed, when discovery should be completed, and whether discovery should be conducted in phases or be limited to or focused upon particular issues;

(3) what changes should be made in the limitations on discovery imposed under these rules or by local rule, and what other limitations should be imposed; and

(4) any other orders that should be entered by the court under Rule 26(c) or under Rule 16(b) and (c).

The attorneys of record and all unrepresented parties that have appeared in the case are jointly responsible for arranging the conference, for attempting in good faith to agree on the proposed discovery plan, and for submitting to the court within 14 days after the conference a written report outlining the plan. A court may order that the parties or attorneys attend the conference in person. If necessary to comply with its expedited schedule for Rule 16(b) conferences, a court may by local rule (i) require that the conference between the parties occur fewer than 21 days before the scheduling conference is held or a scheduling order is due under Rule 16(b), and (ii) require that the written report outlining the discovery plan be filed fewer than 14 days after the conference between the parties, or excuse the parties from submitting a written report and permit them to report orally on their discovery plan at the Rule 16(b) conference.

(g) SIGNING OF DISCLOSURES, DISCOVERY REQUESTS, RESPONSES, AND OBJECTIONS.

(1) Every disclosure made pursuant to subdivision (a)(1) or subdivision (a)(3) shall be signed by at least one attorney of record in the attorney's individual name, whose address shall be stated. An unrepresented party shall sign the disclosure and state the party's address. The signature of the attorney or party constitutes a certification that to the best of the signer's knowledge, information, and belief, formed after a reasonable inquiry, the disclosure is complete and correct as of the time it is made.

(2) Every discovery request, response, or objection made by a party represented by an attorney shall be signed by at least one attorney of record in the attorney's individual name, whose address shall be stated. An unrepresented party shall sign the request, response, or objection and state the party's address. The signature of the attorney or party constitutes a certification that to the best of the signer's knowledge, information, and belief, formed after a reasonable inquiry, the request, response, or objection is:

(A) consistent with these rules and warranted by existing law or a good faith argument for the extension, modification, or reversal of existing law;

(B) not interposed for any improper purpose, such as to harass or to cause unnecessary delay or needless increase in the cost of litigation; and

(C) not unreasonable or unduly burdensome or expensive, given the needs of the case, the discovery already had in the case, the amount in controversy, and the importance of the issues at stake in the litigation.

If a request, response, or objection is not signed, it shall be stricken unless it is signed promptly after the omission is called to the attention of the party making the request, response, or objection, and a party shall not be obligated to take any action with respect to it until it is signed.

(3) If without substantial justification a certification is made in violation of the rule, the court, upon motion or upon its own initiative, shall impose upon the person who made the certification, the party on whose behalf the disclosure, request, response, or objection is made, or both, an appropriate sanction, which may include an order to pay the amount of the reasonable expenses incurred because of the violation, including a reasonable attorney's fee.

Self-Study
CPE Examination

ABOUT THE SELF-STUDY CPE EXAMINATION

Prerequisites:	*None*
Recommended CPE credits:	*8 Hours*
Knowledge level:	*Basic*
Area of study:	*Management/Consulting Services*

The credit hours recommended are in accordance with the AICPA Standards for CPE programs. Since CPE requirements are set by each state, you need to check with your State Board of Accountancy concerning required CPE hours and fields of study.

If you decide to take this CPE examination, follow the directions below. This examination fee is $59.00. Means of payment are shown on the answer form.

The CPE examination is graded no later than 2 weeks after receipt. The passing score is at least 70%. John Wiley & Sons, Inc. will issue a certificate of completion to successful participants to recognize their achievement.[*]

Photocopy one copy of the answer for each additional participant who wishes to take the CPE examination. Each participant should complete the answer form and return it with the $59 fee.

The enclosed CPE examination will expire on January 31, 2006. Completed exams must be postmarked by that date.

---

[*] Registered with the National Association of State Boards of Accountancy as a sponsor of continuing professional education on the National Registry of CPE Sponsors. State boards of accountancy have final authority on the acceptance of individual courses. Complaints regarding registered sponsors may be addressed to NASBA, 150 Fourth Avenue North, Suite 700, Nashville, TN 37219-2417; (615) 880-4200; fax (615) 880-4292.

Directions for the CPE Course:

Complete the examination after reading all chapters in *Business Valuation Body of Knowledge: Exam Review and Professional Reference*, Second Edition. Record your answers by writing a letter (a–e), true, or false on the line for that question on the answer form. Upon completion of the examination, cut out the answer sheet, enclose it in a stamped envelope, and mail to the following address:

CPE Program Director
John Wiley& Sons, Inc.
7222 Commerce Center Drive
Suite 240
Colorado Springs, CO 80919

Business Valuation: Exam Review and Professional Reference, Second Edition

CPE Examination

Record your CPE answers on the answer form provided below and return this page for grading.

Mail to:

CPE Director

John Wiley & Sons, 7222 Commerce Center Drive, Suite 240, Colorado Springs, CO 80919

Name _____

PAYMENT OPTIONS

☐ Payment enclosed ($59.00)

Firm Name _____

(Make checks payable to John Wiley & Sons, Inc.)

Please add appropriate sales tax.

Address _____

Be sure to sign your order below.

Charge my:

☐ American Express   ☐ Master Card   ☐ Visa

Phone ( ) _____

Account number _____

Expiration date _____

CPA State License # _____

Please sign below for all credit card orders.

Signature _____

SEE THE OTHER SIDE OF THIS PAGE FOR THE CPE FEEDBACK FORM

CPE ANSWERS

1. ___	2. ___	3. ___	4. ___	5. ___	6. ___	7. ___	8. ___	9. ___	10. ___
11. ___	12. ___	13. ___	14. ___	15. ___	16. ___	17. ___	18. ___	19. ___	20. ___
21. ___	22. ___	23. ___	24. ___	25. ___	26. ___	27. ___	28. ___	29. ___	30. ___
31. ___	32. ___	33. ___	34. ___	35. ___	36. ___	37. ___	38. ___	39. ___	40. ___

CPE Exam ISBN: 0-471-454346

347

Business Valuation: Exam Review and Professional Reference
CPE Feedback

1. Do you agree with the publisher's determination of CPE Credit hours? Yes ____ No ____

2. Was the content relevant? Yes ____ No ____

3. Was the content displayed clearly? Yes ____ No ____

4. Did the content enhance your professional competence? Yes ____ No ____

5. Was the content timely and effective? Yes ____ No ____

How can we make the examination/content better? If you have any suggestions please summarize them in the space below. We will consider them in developing future examinations.

_____

_____

_____

_____

Copyright © 2002 John Wiley & Sons, Inc.
All rights reserved

348

CONTINUING PROFESSIONAL EDUCATION: EXAMINATION

Multiple Choice:

1. Which of the following is the most correct statement about the composition of The Appraisal Foundation?
   a. Its members are professional real estate appraisal organizations.
   b. Its members are a group of professional appraisal organizations involved in real estate, personal property, and businesses.
   c. Its members are professional business appraisal organizations.
   d. Its members are individual business appraisers.

2. Which of the following types of fee arrangements are NOT allowed by *Uniform Standards of Professional Appraisal Practice* (USPAP)?
   a. Hourly
   b. Fixed fee
   c. Combination of fixed fee and hours worked
   d. Percentage of value

3. Which type of value is akin to a security analyst's value and not frequently referred to as a legal standard of value?
   a. Transaction value
   b. Fair value
   c. Investment value
   d. Intrinsic value

4. Which one of the following valuation methods is most likely to produce a minority (versus control) value?
   a. Guideline merger and acquisition method
   b. Guideline publicly traded company method
   c. Asset accumulation method
   d. Excess earnings method

5. The following are all different types of market approach methods for valuing a business EXCEPT:
   a. Publicly traded guideline company method
   b. Prior transactions, offers, and buy-sell agreements
   c. Asset accumulation method
   d. Guideline merger and acquisition method

6. Which of the following is defined as "the value to a *particular* buyer or seller"?
   a. Transaction value
   b. Fair value
   c. Investment value
   d. Intrinsic value

7. Which of the following is a correct statement about cost of capital?
   a. It is based on historical returns relative to book value.
   b. It is based on historical returns relative to market prices.
   c. It is based on expected returns relative to book value.
   d. It is based on expected returns relative to market prices.
8. Which of the following models *specifically* recognizes systematic risk?
   a. Build-up model
   b. Capital Asset Pricing Model (CAPM)
   c. Discounted cash flow (DCF) model
   d. Arbitrage pricing model (APM)
9. The uncertainty of future returns due to the sensitivity of the return on the subject investment to the movements in the return for the investment market as a whole is called:
   a. Systematic risk
   b. Coefficient of variation
   c. Unsystematic risk
   d. Equity risk premium
10. Which of the following is a correct statement about the relationship of the midyear discounting convention and the year-end discounting convention (assuming that there are no negative numbers in the forecasts)?
    a. The midyear convention always produces a lower value.
    b. The midyear convention produces the same value as the year-end convention, all other things being equal.
    c. The midyear convention always produces a higher value.
    d. The midyear convention produces the same value as the year-end convention only in the unique circumstance in which every year's forecast is identical.
11. Which of the following is a correct statement about the relationship between the capitalization rate and the discount rate?
    a. The capitalization rate is the discount rate minus the long-term growth rate.
    b. The capitalization rate is the discount rate plus the long-term growth rate.
    c. The capitalization rate is the reciprocal of the discount rate.
    d. The capitalization rate is the same as the discount rate.
12. Which of the following is NOT true about cost of capital?
    a. The cost of capital is the expected rate of return that the market requires in order to attract funds to a particular investment.
    b. The cost of capital is based on book value, not on market value.
    c. Actual past returns are relevant to an estimate of cost of capital only to the extent that there is reason to believe that they are representative of future expectations.
    d. Cost of capital for a given investment such as an acquisition may be at, above, or below a company's overall cost of capital, depending on relative riskiness.

13. Which of the following is NOT used as an invested capital multiple in the market approach to valuation?

    a. MVIC/sales

    b. MVIC/EBIT

    c. MVIC/net income

    d. MVIC/EBITDA

14. All of the following are databases of transactions involving controlling interests in private companies EXCEPT:

    a. *Pratt's Stats*™

    b. *BIZCOMPS®*

    c. *Mergerstat/Shannon Pratt's Control Premium Study*™

    d. *The IBA Market Database*

15. All of the following databases of merged and acquired company transactions can be searched simultaneously online EXCEPT:

    a. *Pratt's Stats*™

    b. *BIZCOMPS®*

    c. *Mergerstat/Shannon Pratt's Control Premium Study*™

    d. *The IBA Market Database*

16. From an estimate of value by the adjusted net asset method (asset accumulation method), which of the following discounts, if any, should be applied when valuing a minority interest in most cases?

    a. Discount for lack of control but not a discount for lack of marketability

    b. Discount for lack of marketability but not a discount for lack of control

    c. Both a discount for lack of control and a discount for lack of marketability

    d. Neither a discount for lack of control nor a discount for lack of marketability

17. In what year was the method we now know as the excess earnings method first introduced?

    a. 1920

    b. 1934

    c. 1963

    d. 1968

18. In the excess earnings method, for which of the following categories on the balance sheet must capitalization rates be estimated?

    a. Both debt and equity

    b. Equity but not debt

    c. Both tangible assets and intangible assets (goodwill)

    d. Intangible assets but not tangible assets

19. Of the public companies acquired from 1998 to 2001, what percentage were acquired at *less than* their public market trading prices before the acquisition?

    a. Less than 5%

    b. 5 to 10%

    c. 10 to 15%

    d. Over 15%

20. Which of the following is a correct statement about discounts for lack of control and lack of marketability?

    a. Lack of control and lack of marketability are generally combined as one discount.

    b. Lack of control and lack of marketability are always differentiated as separate discounts.

    c. Lack of control and lack of marketability are sometimes combined as one discount, but the trend is to separate them.

    d. The trend is toward combining lack of control and lack of marketability into one discount.

21. All of the following are pre-IPO studies EXCEPT:

    a. FMV Opinions study

    b. Willamette Management Associates studies

    c. John Emory (formerly Baird & Co.) studies

    d. Valuation Advisors studies

22. From the following, select which are legally binding:

    I. Statutes in the relevant jurisdiction

    II. IRS Revenue Rulings

    III. Appellate case law in the relevant jurisdiction

    IV. Appellate case law in other jurisdictions

    a. I, II, and III

    b. I and III

    c. I, II, and IV

    d. I and II

23. All of the following performance ratios can be obtained *from the income statement alone* EXCEPT:

    a. Gross profit as a percentage of sales

    b. Operating profit (EBIT) as a percentage of sales

    c. Pretax income as a percentage of sales

    d. Return on investment ratios

24. When is it generally best to conduct the site visit and interviews?

    a. It should be the first step after being retained.

    b. After at least a preliminary financial statement analysis, comparative industry analysis, and study of the industry outlook.

    c. After the report is issued but prior to deposition.

    d. After deposition but prior to trial.

25. All of the following are pre-IPO (transactions preceding a public offering) databases used to estimate the discount for lack of marketability EXCEPT:

a. SEC Institutional Investor Study

b. Willamette Management Associates studies

c. John Emory (formerly Baird & Co.) studies

d. Valuation Advisors studies

26. For the purpose of appraising charitable contributions (according to regulations section 1.170A-135(c)(5)), a "qualified appraiser" is one who is required to meet all of the following EXCEPT:

a. Holds himself or herself out to the public as an appraiser who regularly performs appraisals

b. Is qualified to appraise property because of his or her qualifications

c. Is aware of the appraiser penalties associated with overvaluation of charitable contributions

d. Is a certified member of a recognized professional appraisal association

27. Each of the following is one of the eight basic factors listed in Revenue Ruling 59-60 EXCEPT:

a. The dividend-paying capacity of the company

b. Whether the enterprise has goodwill or other intangible value

c. Whether the enterprise has a buy-sell agreement and, if so, its terms

d. Sales of stock in the company and the size of the block to be valued

28. What percentage of the stock of an ESOP company must the ESOP own after the transaction for the seller to qualify for a section 1042 tax-free rollover?

a. 5%

b. 15%

c. 30%

d. 50.1%

29. Which of the following is the correct statement about the statutory standard of value for dissenting stockholder actions and dissolution actions under minority oppression statutes?

a. In most states with both dissenting stockholder and minority oppression statutes, the standard of value is *fair value*, which courts always interpret the same way under both sets of statutes.

b. In most states with both dissenting stockholder and minority oppression statutes, the standard of value is *fair value* under dissent statutes and *fair market value* under oppression statutes.

c. In most states with both dissenting stockholder and minority oppression statutes, the standard of value is *fair value*, but courts sometimes interpret it differently in dissent cases than in oppression cases.

d. In most states with both dissenting stockholder and minority oppression statutes, the standard of value is *fair market value* under dissent statutes and *fair value* under oppression statutes.

30. Which of the following is a correct statement about the statutory standard of value for marital dissolution?

   a. In most states it is fair market value.

   b. In most states it is fair value.

   c. In most states it is investment value.

   d. In most states there is no statutory standard of value for marital dissolutions.

True/False

True/False 31. The value of a share of stock is the same regardless of the premise of value or the purpose for which it is being valued.

True/False 32. For a past transaction or an offer to buy or a buy-sell agreement to be determinative value for gift and estate tax purposes, one of the criteria it must meet is evidence of negotiation on an arm's-length basis in coming to the agreement.

True/False 33. The effective date of valuation for a marital dissolution is always the date of filing for divorce.

True/False 34. A capitalization factor is any multiple or divisor used to convert income to value.

True/False 35. Since RR68-609 provides detailed guidance on issues such as the definition of tangible assets and capitalization rates, the excess earnings method results in consistent implementation and is often the only method of valuation used by a practitioner.

True/False 36. Fair market value considers the facts and circumstances of a particular buyer or seller in arriving at a value conclusion.

True/False 37. A greater dividend or withdrawal amount usually results in a greater discount for lack of marketability.

True/False 38. Multistage discounted cash flow models are generally much less reliable than single-stage models.

True/False 39. Compliance with *Uniform Standards of Professional Appraisal Practice* is legally mandatory for all federally related real estate transactions.

True/False 40. Private letter rulings have the force of law.

Index